In the Ruins
of the Church

In the Ruins of the Church

Sustaining Faith in an Age of Diminished Christianity

R. R. Reno

Brazos Press
A Division of Baker Book House Co
Grand Rapids, Michigan 49516

© 2002 by R. R. Reno

Published by Brazos Press
a division of Baker Book House Company
P.O. Box 6287, Grand Rapids, MI 49516-6287

Printed in the United States of America

Library of Congress Cataloging-in-Publication Data

Reno, Russell R., 1959–
    In the ruins of the church : sustaining faith in an age of diminished Christianity / R.R. Reno.
        p.   cm.
    Includes bibliographical references.
    ISBN 1-58743-033-9 (pbk.)
    1. Church. I. Title.
    BV600.3 .R46 2002
    262′.001′7—dc21   2002005445

For current information about all releases from Brazos Press, visit our web site:
http://www.brazospress.com

To George Lindbeck

What can I say for you, to what compare you,
　　O daughter of Jerusalem?
What can I liken to you, that I may comfort you,
　　O virgin daughter of Zion?
For vast is the sea of your ruin;
　　who can restore you?

Lamentations 2:13 RSV

They shall build up the ancient ruins,
　　they shall raise up the former devastations;
they shall repair the ruined cities,
　　the devastations of many generations.

Isaiah 61:4 RSV

Contents

Acknowledgments

Some books grow step by step from an intensive focus on an idea or problem. Others stem from a seemingly diffuse array of concerns and projects that, in a moment of recognition, come together as a whole. This book is of the latter sort, and as a consequence, my debts to friends and colleagues are as many as were the book's origins.

For financial and institutional support, I wish to thank Wallace Alston and the Center of Theological Inquiry in Princeton, New Jersey. A great deal of the thinking and writing that make up these chapters was done while I was a resident fellow at the Center working on another project of the intensive sort. The same thanks must go to Carl Braaten and the Center for Catholic and Evangelical Theology. The ecumenical ecclesiology consultation launched by the Center, the opportunity to write for the Center's journal, *Pro Ecclesia*, as well as the opportunity to lecture at one of the Center's conferences, have provided invaluable stimuli. Thanks as well to a peculiar society of churchly theologians, Scholarly Engagement with Anglican Doctrine (SEAD), and especially its patron, C. FitzSimons Allison, as well as David Scott and Chris Seitz, presidents past and present. SEAD has helped me find an articulate theological loyalty to the church

As I have struggled to understand the vocation of the theologian in the ruins of the church, many friends have provided aid and comfort. George Sumner, Bruce Marshall, and David Yeago have been constant companions, with words of advice and guidance. Stanley Hauerwas has offered great encouragement, both with his example of honest, forceful theology for the church and with kind words. He urged me to gather my thoughts into this imperfect whole. I can think of many others who offered advice and encouragment. Richard John Neuhaus and his staff at *First Things* have disciplined me to write well about what matters. John O'Keefe has puzzled with me over right reading of Scripture. David Dawson has listened to me with bemused sympathy. Rodney Clapp, the estimable editor of Brazos Press, offered helpful comments for the improvement of this book, and copyeditor Ruth Goring saved me from innumerable errors.

Before turning to a proper acknowledgement of the original invitations and publications that serve as the basis for this book, there are two incalculable debts I must recognize. The first is to Ephraim Radner. In the struggle to understand how to serve a ruined church in faithfulness he has gone before me, and I have gratefully followed. I feel as though I have written little more than a commentary upon his pnuematology of modern Christianity, *The End of the Church*. I hope that what I feel is the case. The second great debt is to a teacher both Radner and I share in common. Unlike Radner's influence, materially I can trace no particular thought in this book to George Lindbeck. Yet, when I ask myself why I should find myself so alienated from the standard assumptions of modern theology, indeed, from the spiritual strategies of modernity, I must answer that Lindbeck has played a key role. I now I see that he beckoned me into the ruins of the church all along. In gratitude, I dedicate this book to him.

Sources:

Chapter two: This chapter was originally presented as a lecture, "The Moral Challenges of Evangelism," at the Reevangelizing in the Postmodern World Conference, sponsored by the Center for Catholic and Evangelical Theology conference, September 2000. A revised form was published under the title "American Satyricon" in *First Things*, no. 116 (October 2001): 32–41. Some of this material was given as a lecture, "Heroism and the Noonday Devil," at the Symposium on Heroism and the Christian Life: Disclosures of Human Excellence, sponsored by Providence College, April 2001.

Chapter three: An earlier version of this chapter was delivered as a lecture at the annual SEAD conference in Charleston, South Carolina, January 1997. It was then published with conference proceedings in *The Rule of Faith: Scripture, Canon, and Creed in a Critical Age*, ed. George Sumner and Ephraim Radner (Harrisburg, Penn.: Morehouse, 1998), pp. 63–76.

Chapter four: This chapter is a revised form of an essay published in *First Things*, no. 100 (February 2000): 37–44, under the title "The Radical Orthodoxy Project." That essay is based upon material developed in an extended review of John Milbank's *Word Made Strange*, published in *Pro Ecclesia* 8, no. 2 (spring 1999): 231–238.

Chapter five: An earlier draft of this chapter was prepared for the February 2000 meeting of the Ecumenical Ecclesiology Consultation, sponsored by the Center for Catholic and Evangelical Theology.

Chapter six: This chapter is based on a short essay that appeared in *The Harvest* 10, no. 1 (Incarnation 2000): 3–10.

Chapter seven: This chapter is an expansion of an opinion essay, "Good Restaurants in Gomorrah," *First Things*, no. 80 (February 1998): 14–16.

Chapter eight: The material in this chapter was first developed as a lecture given at the annual SEAD conference in Charleston, South Carolina, January 2000.

Chapter nine: This meditation on the Daily Office was first drafted as part of a planned SEAD commentary on the *Book of Common Prayer*.

Chapter ten: This chapter is a modestly revised version of a paper delivered at the Symposium on the Theological Interpretation of Scripture, sponsored by the North Park Theological Seminary, Chicago, September 2000. A version of it was published in *Touchstone* 15, no. 6 (July / August 2002): 40–48.

Chapter eleven: The exegesis first appeared as "The Marks of the Nails: Theological Exegesis of the First Letter of John for Easter," *Pro Ecclesia* 6, no. 1 (winter 1997): 43–54.

1

Introduction

"I will rise now and go about the city,
     in the streets and in the squares;
I will seek him whom my soul loves."
     I sought him, but found him not.
The watchmen found me,
as they went about in the city.
     "Have you seen him whom my soul loves?"
Scarcely had I passed them,
     when I found him whom my soul loves
I held him, and would not let him go.

Song of Solomon 3:2–4

This book tries to provide spiritual guidance to Christians seeking faithfulness within increasingly dysfunctional churches. I am neither a priest nor a pastor, so I can claim no expertise or experience in the cure of souls. Moreover, I am an academic more given to severe conceptual analysis than to effective homiletical meditation. Nonetheless, I am not blind to my own situation. I worry about my own faithfulness, both to the gospel of Jesus Christ and to the church that has brought me to him. I am trying to find the way toward discipleship in a world that treats obedience and discipline as scandalous impositions. I wish to draw

nearer to the apostolic tradition in a church that is moving in the opposite direction. Both the culture and the church make faith difficult.

I do not think my situation, my worries, my efforts are singular. Many
of us seek the embrace of divine love in what can only be called the
chaotic atmosphere of Western Christianity. But what we share in common concern we may not necessarily share in common judgments about
the proper form of faithfulness. Thus this book seeks to guide by arguing for a narrow path of discipleship that requires a redoubled loyalty
to the church. As Reinhard Hütter has so powerfully argued, the future
of theology depends upon a reaffirmation of this narrow path.[1] We must
nurture a recovered commitment to suffer divine things. However
chaotic and dysfunctional the institutional and doctrinal life of the
church, we must endure that which the Lord has given us. However
inauspicious and maddening, we must allow the realities of the body of
Christ to shape us so that our voice and vision might be sanctified by
his power. In so doing, we need to properly anticipate the cruciform
pattern of this shaping. For to suffer divine things will entail enduring
the way of the cross.

Let me state more clearly the two propositions that express this truth
and guide my own reflections in these chapters. (1) As a believer in the
now late (or post) modern West, I suffer the diminishment and debilitation of Christianity. The church, as the title of this book broadcasts
so brashly, is in ruins. If you, the reader, have faith, then you suffer this
ruination as well. It is the great and inescapable fact about modern Christianity. To be in the church is to endure a broken form of life. (2) You
and I need to avoid recoiling from that suffering as if it were evil. We
need to draw ever nearer to the reality of Christian faith and witness in
our time, however burdensome, however heavy with failure, limitation,
and disappointment. The reason is simple. Our Lord Jesus Christ comes
to us in the flesh. We can draw near to him only in his body, the church.
Loyalty to him requires us to dwell within the ruins of the church.

I have written these chapters in the hope of convincing you of the
truth of both propositions. I want you to see the failures of the churches.
I focus on my church, the Episcopal Church, because I know it well. But
I doubt that the Episcopal Church is unique. It may, in fact, be transparently typical. Of course, I cannot prejudge the personal satisfaction
any reader might feel within his church or denomination. In fact, I am
consistently buoyed by the shining moments of integrity of worship and
faith in my own church. However, the gifts and comforts that the Lord
gives us in this and every age should not blind us to the reality we face.
Throughout I will try to bring you to see the fundamental and debilitating difficulties that I see running throughout modern Christianity. I
will insist that, however winsome might be individual stones, the walls

of the church have been thrown down and the gates of its sanctuaries are fallen. If you will but open your eyes, you cannot help but see the ruins.

To see the church in ruins has not led me to despair, and it certainly has not led me to curse God for failing to provide me with a triumphant and splendid church in which to dwell. These reflections, then, seek to bring you to see the spiritual imperative of redemptive suffering that is, I think, the only proper response to the ruination of the church. I want to tempt you toward the second proposition, the imperative that we draw near to that Christian reality that we must endure. There is no hope in detachment or separation, whether in the form of critical judgment, hesitant loyalty, individualistic faith, theological abstraction, or self-protective spiritual illusions. Throughout this book I war against the many paths that lead us away from that which the Lord has given us to suffer. I reject our desire for a liberating distance. Our vocation is to dwell within the ruins of the church. We must bear the reality of the church and wear the fetters that our age has given us to wear: an increasingly inarticulate theological tradition, a capitulating and culturally captive church, a disintegrating spiritual discipline. How can we do otherwise? For it is written that we are to endure everything for the sake of the elect (2 Tim. 2:9–10).

Running from the Ruins

The image of ruins is not my own. It is, of course, scriptural, and it is applied to the city of Jerusalem, ruined by foreign invaders but also by infidelity and injustice. This image of ruins was taken up by one of the modern era's most interesting and visionary thinkers, John Nelson Darby. He is not well known to many contemporary readers, but his remarkable biblical vision made him an important figure in modern fundamentalism. Ordained priest in the Church of Ireland in the early 1800s, Darby despaired of the integrity of the established church. He left the priesthood and affiliated with the Plymouth Brethren. Eventually his pursuit of the perfect community of the saints would lead him to dissociate himself from the Brethren. His final isolation, however, did not impair his remarkable influence. He traveled to the United States, and by the end of the nineteenth century his dispensational interpretation of biblical history had come to define the apocalyptic imagination of a great deal of American fundamentalism. From the Moody Bible Institute to Dallas Theological Seminary, Darby's theology was taught to generations of students throughout the twentieth century. The Scofield Reference Bible is the product of one of Darby's followers. The bumper sticker that says, "In the event of rapture, this car will be unoccupied," reflects Darby's distinctive account of the sequence of events that will usher in the millennial reign of Christ.

However, by my reading Darby's importance is not to be found in his idiosyncratic dispensational scheme, influential though it has been. He is important because his exegetical and theological program exemplifies the broad modern spiritual consensus. Darby sought spiritual power and purity. The more he grasped the gravity and consequence of the gospel promise, the more he recoiled from the failures of the church. "Whilst men slept," wrote Darby with his usual astringent directness, "the enemy has sown tares. The church is in a state of ruin, immersed and buried in the world—invisible, if you will have it so; whilst it ought to be held forth, as a candlestick, the light of God."[2] Darby saw how denominational fragmentation, complacent establishment, the mediocrity and unbelief of church leaders, and the flying buttresses of scholastic argument designed to hold up increasingly feeble and failing ecclesiastical structures and disciplines all debilitated the church. Moreover, Darby lacked retrospective nostalgia. He harbored no medieval romanticism. He understood the ways in which the modern state, as well as the intellectual elite, had taken a decisive secular turn. Still further, Darby made no reassuring distinctions between the "visible" and "invisible" church in order to deflect his eyes from the ruined condition of modern Christianity. After all, an invisible church is a failed church. In all this Darby was a man of his age, cruelly casting an empirical gaze onto the church, uncovering her nakedness.

I admire Darby's theological courage, and I share his assessment. It is very difficult to believe that the church is the light of the world, ordained by God as the champion of his holy Word, and at the same time to face the fact that it is in ruins. To deny the former entails a massive repudiation of the plain sense of Scripture. To deny the latter requires an equally massive act of self-deception. This Darby grasps. He will not falsify or palliate the experience of the church in the modern era—its compromises, its smug but increasingly irrelevant establishment, its faithless leadership, and most of all its fragmentation and division.[3] He will not traffic in myths and mystifications. He reads the Scriptures and draws this conclusion: "The gathering together of all the children of God in one body is plainly according to the mind of God in the world."[4] This is not a spiritual interpretation of Scripture. It is not an interpretation that depends upon strained exegesis or doctrinal assumptions. It is not the result of a "fundamentalist" mentality. Any number of modern historical critics have drawn the same conclusion.

Yet just as "factual" is the evident disunity of the churches. Unlike most church members, Darby did not simply discount those outside the walls of the church in which he was first ordained. With vision purified by a modern respect for the facts, he could see that other Christians were baptized and celebrated the holy feast. He refused to theologize these observations with distinctions between valid and invalid Eucharists, between rites of true and false churches, between orthodox and heterodox doctrines. Thus just as Darby did not spiritualize the scriptural call to unity, he did not abstract himself from the evident contemporary realities of disunity. The same holds true for his analyses of other failures of modern Christianity. Thus under Darby's guidance we cannot avoid ruins of the church with incantations. We must face the facts.

For Darby, the ruination of the church forces us to consider our vocations anew. Instead of assuming all is well, we must open the Scriptures, "searching for what the word and the Spirit have declared concerning our present condition."[5] What does the Lord will that we might do within the ruined walls of the church? Darby's answer is as unpersuasive as his posing of the question is clear. Searching the Scriptures, Darby discerned a dispensational scheme of decay and destruction, out of which the elect are separated and held aloof. The details of the scheme are not decisive. What is important is the spiritual stance Darby endorsed. For him, a proper reading of Scripture guides us away from the ruined church. "Let us not," he wrote, "like foolish children who have broken a precious vase, attempt to join together its broken fragments."[6] For Darby, faith separates us from the ruins of the church, for faith distances us from the old dispensation, now presently working toward destruction, and prepares us for the new. We should not step forward into an ever deeper loyalty to the ruined church. We should step back and away instead.

Thus not only is Darby relentlessly modern in his determined empiricism, in his insistence on literal meaning and the "facts," but more important, the spiritual response he identifies, the strategy of separation, typifies the modern project. Consider the basic logic of his thought. A new and disturbing reality—the ruination of the church—forces him to rethink the deepest spiritual imperatives of the Christian life. In this way Darby endorses the modern presumption that we have in some decisive sense "turned the corner" in history, and "old ways" must be set aside so that "new ways" might emerge to serve the "new situation." Specifically, the old ways of "being church" are no longer viable (an assumption Darby shares with the modern theological tradition as a whole); therefore we need to prepare ourselves for new ways of "being church." We must distance ourselves from a dying past in order to receive the redemptive future.

Whatever the assumptions or goals, whether seemingly "liberal" or "conservative," the very essence of modernity is this embrace of liberating distance, this will to separation for the sake of the "not yet." For the modern the past is a burden, and the task of spiritual life is to throw off its debilitating weight. Separation, then, is the discipline of freedom. Only when we shake off the shackles of a decaying present order can we be free to participate in the new and future order.[7] In Darby's case, separation serves to prepare us for the rapturing power of the Spirit, and the scriptural content of that hope seems quite "traditional." But this is to confuse form with content. The basic spiritual move of separation joins Darby to those who seek liberating distance from the apostolic tradition as a whole, not just its institutional manifestations. In all cases we are modern insofar as we will not suffer that which we have received. We must step back in order to unburden ourselves, to lighten our lives so that we can be raptured away from the hindering, limited, ruined forms that the past has imposed upon the present. This is the spiritual pattern that makes modernity modern, and Darby embraces it. All that distinguishes him from the most extreme modernist is his inability to see how Scripture itself is a hindering, limited, and ruined artifact of a now dead past.

I can hear the reader objecting. "Do not be obtuse. Darby endorsed a hopeless scriptural literalism, and his dispensationalism characterizes the most retrogressive forms of fundamentalism." My response is to reiterate. Beware confusing terms such as *liberal* and *conservative* with *modern* and "that which came before." Consider that the most ardent and polemical historical critics of the Bible are "recovering fundamentalists." Trained in Darby's clarity about the ruination of the church and his path of purity through separation, these scholars recapitulate the pattern even as they attack their original piety. These biblical scholars exhibit horror over the redactional ruination of the Scriptures. The debilitations of oral transmission, the diminishments of communal purpose, the ideological distortions of faith itself—all these and more corrupt the accuracy of the text. Just like Darby, these critics counsel separation. We must use historical context, critical analysis, and other distancing techniques to free ourselves from the commanding authority of the canonical text. Only then can we be free to receive the proper spiritual power of the historical Jesus. Thus the Darbyite may resent the impieties of the Jesus Seminar, but their underlying spiritual strategy is the same, and equally modern. The dispensationalist may cling to Scripture as somehow exempt from corruption, but both flee from the body of received tradition. Both endorse separation in order to avoid suffering the ruined forms of Christian witness.

The odd alliance of Darby's dispensational endorsement of separation and modern historical-critical study of the Bible is but one instance. More famously, in his *Discourse on the Method of Rightly Conducting* the *Reason and Seeking the Truth in the Sciences* (1637), René Descartes advocates sweeping away the many prejudices and influences that we must suffer in education and society. While traveling, he reports, "The setting in of winter arrested me in a locality where, as I found no society to interest me, and was besides fortunately undisturbed by any cares or passions, I remained the whole day in seclusion, with full opportunity to occupy my attention with my own thoughts."[8] The separation, initially enforced, is soon sought for its own sake. It becomes the pattern of Descartes's method.

The image of a disordered city serves as a metaphor for the mind that needs the purifying ministrations of an isolating distance. Descartes observes that the sedimented layers of a medieval city, its crooked and irregular streets, its confusing and inefficient layout, can be made open, spacious, and regular only if the magistrate has the strength and vision to order some houses pulled down. A city planner with Cartesian ambitions must have the courage to do some demolition, the courage to break with the past, in order to make progress. Ruins command no loyalty; they should be swept away to make room for a new beginning. The same holds for inherited knowledge. For Descartes, we need to "pull down the house of knowledge that, upon closer inspection, is structurally unsound and at the point of collapse." We need to enter into isolation, separating ourselves from the claims of past theories and principles. Just this will-to-separation leads Descartes to claim "that I could not do better than resolve at once to sweep [inherited knowledge] wholly away."[9] Only then can we rebuild our knowledge in an orderly and open fashion, unhindered by the limitations of the past.

For Descartes, skeptical doubt was the instrument of distance. Doubt, he famously demonstrated, will sweep away all but the indubitable proposition *cogito ergo sum*. However, the crucial point is not Descartes's skepticism. What is decisive is the conviction that separation yields a purifying preparation of the soul. "I firmly believed," confesses Descartes of his decision to pull down the house of knowledge, "that in this way I should better succeed in the conduct of my life, than if I built only upon old foundations, and leant upon principles which, in my youth, I had taken upon trust."[10] The imperative is clear. We must distance ourselves from ruined structures—Descartes's metaphor of foundations was to become extraordinarily influential—and we must do so in order to build without the hindering legacy of a disordered and failed inheritance. Thus as different as Descartes may be from Darby on any number of substantive matters, they had a common spiritual project. Darby's dispensationalism mandated the same strategy of separation for the same reason—to flee a ruined inheritance—and for the same purpose—to free the soul for the rapturing power of an untethered and unburdened truth.

But we do not need a seminar in the history of philosophy. You and I have been to college, and we have been taught to champion the virtues of "critical thinking." And what are those virtues but the many different names for liberating distance? Here are some obvious truisms. "We should step back from the corrupting immediacy of prejudice and presupposition, for they often deceive. Common sense says that the sun rises and sets, and prevailing opinion condemns homosexuality, but common sense lies, and prevailing opinion perverts conscience. We must separate ourselves from mere custom and convention, for they often veil injustice and oppression. We should break the magical spell of taboo so that we can rationally assess social practices and moral expectations." These truisms seek to create a distance and detachment within ourselves. In the void a new future may be born.

Notice, again, the way in which Darby follows the same pattern. Darby's dispensational scheme omits retrospection. Indeed it actively prohibits return to the past. We are being carried away from the apostolic age and toward something new. Is it not odd that revisionist theologians in my own church, theologians who have drunk deeply at the well of critique, can speak in similar ways about the need for us to be "open" to the "new things" that the "Spirit" is giving us? Of the future Darby writes, "As soon as the 'things that are' (that is, the seven churches [of Revelation]) are brought to a close, the prophet is carried to heaven, and all that follows has to do, not with anything acknowledged as a church, but with God's providence in the world."[11] The disjunction is complete. The ruined church is part of the dead past, and as God prepares to rapture the faithful, the new future is entirely worldly. Could any liberationist or feminist theologian have put the matter more clearly? Surely we must jettison the dead weight of a clerical, patriarchal past in order to have a theological vision that seeks to transform the world according to God's inclusive love rather than trying to protect the boundaries of desiccated orthodoxy and the prerogatives of a merely institutional church. Is it not remarkable how the same imperative predominates? Suffer not that which has been received! Cast away that which constrains the spirit! Embrace the new future!

My point is not to tar Darby with a revisionist brush. I only wish to bring you, the reader, to see how pervasive and tempting is the modern strategy of separation. We deceive ourselves if we think revisionists separate themselves from apostolic authority out of pride or will to power. They do so for the same reason Darby wished to separate himself from the ruins of the church. He writes, "It is clearly the duty of the believer to separate himself from every act that he sees to be not according to the word, . . . even though his faithfulness should cause him to stand alone."[12] We should stand alone so that we are fully free and ready to hearken to the new dispensations of the Spirit. Distance is the first commandment; separation is the proper state of spiritual readiness.

The revisionist thinks in exactly the same way. We have a duty to separate ourselves from inherited liturgies that perpetuate oppressive images of God. We have a duty to war against church authorities and structures that exclude and marginalize. Even though faithfulness should cause them to stand alone, the prophets of "New Being" will distance themselves from all they see as archaic and ridiculous in the Christian tradition. After all, how can the Holy Spirit be free if fettered by finite forms of ancient doctrine and practice? True freedom, the revisionist sees, is the freedom of distance. It will suffer no limitations, not even the limits of the scriptural word that Darby thought transcended the ecclesiastical ruination that characterizes this age. Thus does the revisionist outdo Darby at his own dispensationalist project.

As I have said, however much I might admire Darby's clear assessment of the present age and the seriousness with which he searches the Scriptures, I am opposed to his strategy of separation. Darby is more clear-minded than many revisionists, whose ideological mystifications of the past and present are contemptible, but his desire to shed the past for the sake of the future is as destructive of Christian faith as any revisionist project. To try to escape from the ruins of the church, as did Darby and his followers, with a highly speculative theory of the end times, parallels the revisionist desire to do an end run around the apostolic inheritance by appealing to abstract ideals such as inclusion or justice or New Being.

Of course the Darbyite and the revisionist are often bitterly opposed on moral and doctrinal questions. The Darbyite regards the impieties of the revisionists as yet another piece of evidence that the present age has descended into hopeless corruption. The revisionist rails against "fundamentalist" interpretations of Scripture, denouncing them as signal instances of the authoritarian structure of traditional views of apostolic authority. Yet the same spiritual pattern obtains. Make no mistake. A radical revisionist sees a church ruined by traditions of patriarchy and homophobia, exclusion and repression. Like Darby, that revisionist invests his loyalty in the weightless future, not the burdensome past. The house must be demolished in order to make way for a new structure.

Darby differs from the revisionist only in remaining an Augustinian rather than Pelagian. According to Darby, we should step back and from a safe distance watch the Lord destroy the church. According to the revisionist, we need to do God's work and actively tear down the apostolic inheritance ourselves. But we kid ourselves if we think that this difference makes a difference. Neither will suffer the ruins of the church, and for just this reason both adopt the modern stance.[13]

This refusal to dwell within that which has been received strikes me as the greatest failure of modern Christianity, a failure that is now pervasive, not only in the church but in what we now call postmodern culture. The strategy of separation is a failure because it is utterly at odds with the scriptural pattern. Consider the book of Nehemiah. There we find a pattern that urges us forward toward an embrace of the ruined church.

> In the month of Chislev, in the twentieth year, while I was in Susa the capital, one of my brothers, Hanani, came with certain men from Judah; and I asked them about the Jews that survived, those who had escaped the captivity, and about Jerusalem. They replied, "The survivors there in the province who escaped captivity are in great trouble and shame; the wall of Jerusalem is broken down, and its gates have been destroyed by fire."
>
> When I heard these words I sat down and wept, and mourned for days, fasting and praying before the God of heaven (Neh. 1:1–4).

Nehemiah's situation seems strikingly similar to the situation that Darby recognized and that I will insist upon in these essays. The holy city of God is in ruins. But Nehemiah's response contradicts the modern strategy of separation, whether inspired by the Darbyite Scofield Reference Bible or the latest in French literary theory. A desire for distance has no role to play in the story of Nehemiah. He reports that he was a "cupbearer to the king" (1:11), and when he heard of Jerusalem's ruin, his distance from its suffering afflicted him with sadness. He asked the king, "Send me to Judah, to the city of my ancestors' graves, so that I may rebuild it" (2:5).

Nehemiah seeks that which Darby and his revisionist allies think impossible, even sinful. Nehemiah wishes to return to the city of graves. He will not embrace the distance that separates him from Jerusalem's failure and defeats. He turns back toward the past with repentant tears. Whatever the future God might bring, it will be in and through the people and city he has chosen. The king grants Nehemiah his wish, and to ruined Jerusalem he travels.

If we are to follow the scriptural pattern rather than the modern pattern, then we must turn as did Nehemiah and travel back, as he did, to the city of graves, to the monuments kept living by the passion of memory even as they lie wrecked. For this city is hallowed by the presence of the Lord, and to return to its sanctuaries, however ruined, is to return to the instruments of redemption that God has graciously provided. We must suffer its ruins if we are to rebuild its walls.

The Debilitation of Christianity

Nehemiah can seem irrelevant, and he did so seem to me. I teach theology at a university. I attend a very pleasant Episcopal parish. I know clergy whom I respect. I have friends with a deep and lively faith. I can honestly say that for many years I hectored revisionists and decried the compromises with culture that I imagined the church was making. Yet I did not see the ruins of the church, and I could not recognize my own strategies of separation. An appreciative reader of Karl Barth, I thought that I had a place to stand, a place of articulate and sophisticated scriptural vision from which to correct errors and speak truths. As an Episcopalian with Anglo-Catholic leanings, I felt the liturgical life of the church to be a stable rock amidst admittedly troubled ecclesiastical waters. So, for reasons that often make Anglicans seem hopelessly conceited, I imagined myself standing against the spirit of the age, drawing on the clarity of the Protestant confessional tradition and the stability of the Catholic sacramental system. Here I could safely stand at an appropriately critical yet faithful distance from the failures of Christian witness in the modern age.

Then I read drafts of the shattering chapters of Ephraim Radner's groundbreaking study of post-Reformation Christianity, *The End of the Church*.[14] I could feel the ground shift under my feet, throwing me off balance. Radner shows how the tribulations of modernity are not external to the life of the church, not an alien infection that one might treat with my personal mixture of neo-Barthian Anglo-Catholicism. These tribulations are not an extrinsic invasion that one can fight with a theological redeployment of the tradition or a punctilious sacramental piety. Quite the contrary, modernity is a cultural extrusion of the hot magma of ecclesiastical affairs. It is a deeply theological and spiritual reality that emerges from the fact that post-Reformation churches anticipated Darby and modern revisionists by making distance and separation the very instruments of faithfulness.

After the Reformation, whether Roman Catholic or Protestant, one either faced the ruinous fact of division or retreated into communities in which separation purified the church of debilitating error. Few acknowledged the ruinous fact. Most endorsed some version of the strategy of separation. In that sense, however eccentric Darby's dispensationalism might have been, his turn away from the corrupted church was entirely conventional. Yet as Radner shows in painful detail, the "step back" from ruin has produced a deeper and more fundamental debilitation of Christianity in the West. Refusing to suffer the failure of the apostolic witness to bind us together in love, indeed making that refusal an actual sign of virtue (doctrinal purity! apostolic succession! *sola scriptura!* Petrine primacy! the Great Tradition!—all appeals to the great strength that one has and the other does not), Western Christianity has trained us to turn away from particular forms of the apostolic witness as soon as we perceive spiritual impotence and weakness.

But this is too cryptic. Let me try to explain with two examples.

First, consider Scripture. The Word of God endures, even amidst the undoubted failure of the church and its leaders. Nonetheless, in our day scriptural glory is agonistic and veiled. Notice how the very ubiquity of Scripture leads to its eclipse. All sides of the Reformation debate appealed to Scripture, and as a result it became an increasingly mute site of contest and struggle rather than the illuminative center of (undoubtedly unwieldy and contested) unity. Scripture, in other words, was part of the problem. One side cited verses against the other. As a result, Scripture was drawn into the debilitating lifelessness of the space between Protestant and Roman Catholic, and all too soon between Protestant and Protestant.

Given this, was Descartes anything but clear-minded when he rejected the house of knowledge he inherited? He saw, just as Darby would, that the probative and illuminate force of doctrinal argument was ruined, for not even Christians could agree on the most basic questions of what we are taught by the Word of God.

Is our time any different? Either we quote Scripture against each other, or we search for something that supersedes the exegetical and doctrinal debates. We look for something greater, something higher, something universal, and we look always with the goal of overcoming the ruined harmony and universality of Christian forms of argument and investigation. The "facts" of Christianity (Scripture, liturgy, polity) become recondite ciphers over which the churches bicker.

Under the circumstances, I am not surprised that modernity began journeying away from this apostolic immediacy and toward something, anything, that promises to do what mere Christianity cannot—establish a consensus among intelligent and well-meaning minds. I would be surprised had it not, for only a remarkable spiritual discipline could have sustained hope. And this is by no means simply a "secular" phenomenon. Modern theology has sought a philosophical idiom, a mediating concept, a controlling motif that will shed light on the language of Scripture that brings only darkening dispute and a confusion of tongues. Historical study of the Bible has attempted to recover, by critical methods, the original context, to discern a supra-theological perspective that is sanctified by an objectivity of judgment that might convict intellects if not consciences. Theological exegesis has withered because it has yielded the bitter fruit of enmity, and the distancing and palliating techniques of modern historical inquiry have taken its place.

Can we then fall back upon the sacraments? Surely God's promises are not in vain, and the Eucharist brings us into the real presence of our Lord. Here as well Radner has spoken to me as did Nehemiah's brethren. For how has the Western church responded to the simple facts that Darby refused to deny or distort? The eucharistic meal is the very sign of unity in Christ, and yet, of all the sacraments, it has remained the most visible instrument of separation. The upshot is an extraordinary contradiction within the central mystery of the faith. We are united in the sharing of the body of our Lord—yet we are not.[15]

Thus we swing wildly from one pole to another. A "conservative" insists that Scripture or the sacraments (or both) are authoritative and powerful. Should you or I point out that they do not seem powerful enough to join Roman Catholics and Baptists in fraternal fellowship around a common altar, various subterfuges emerge, all of which involve the strategy of separation. First, the "conservative" can insist (explicitly or implicitly) that the Eucharist, or right reading of Scripture, does indeed unify all *true* Christians. Heresy must be kept at a distance! Or the "conservative" can invoke a distinction between the visible church (admittedly divided) and invisible church (unified in common faith). Or the "conservative" can appeal to eschatology (which Darby does with exemplary consistency). This was, in fact, the most popular twentieth-century device for separating God's power from what we actually experience here and now. A promissory "Not Yet" allows us to avert our eyes from the ruined "Already."

But now we no longer sound like a "conservative" at all. Instead, under the bewitchment of "invisible" and "eschatological" realities, we easily fall under the spells of passing fashions. A "liberal" sets out to modify and adjust received forms (which, after all, are merely visible and part of the *chronos* of the church, not the *kairos*). Just open a theological journal and read something along these lines: "We need to rethink the Eucharist as the sacrament of our common humanity and as a sign of the unity of all peoples. To do so we need to renounce the exclusionary practice of requiring baptism before communion." The same pattern holds for revisionary biblical interpretation and even "corrective" translation. This turn away from the apostolic tradition would be comical, had it not been so tragically foreshadowed by the many strategies of separation that have dominated theology and Christian practice for the last five hundred years.

So, after reading Radner, I have come to see that the errors, difficulties, failures, and diminishments of Christianity in our time are central to the Christian experience in the West. We have all adopted Darby's strategy of separation. We have all stepped back from the horrifying thought that our denominational "system" is no system at all; it is a disordered vacuum of absent love. And for just this reason, no matter how ecumenical and sensitive, no matter how "open" and "inclusive," each church actively seeks a purifying distance from all others—or it accepts its own aphasia and ruination.

Thus does modernity experience Christianity as ruined. What Radner calls the "separative logic" of Western Christianity so contradicts the unitive momentum of love that a spiritually sensitive observer is repulsed by the poverty of the churches. As we have all heard thousands of times: "I am very religious, but I just don't like organized religion." Indeed, if I am right about Darby and modern revisionism, if Radner is right about the basic logic of Western Christianity since the Reformation, then at the heart of modern Christianity is a dislike of "organized religion," a distancing habit that keeps at bay the demands of a suffering intimacy with the concrete and particular forms of the apostolic witness.

Clearly, then, we face a difficult vocation. For we must suffer divine things even as they are ruined with a darkening heaviness, and we must suffer them in an age that counsels distance and separation from all that is not aglow with a radiant and weightless perfection.

Intimacy and Embrace

In view of the difficulty of our vocation, the structure of this book is simple. Part one attempts to outline some of the ways in which *distance* and *separation* have become watchwords for our age. In chapter two I try to show how protective isolation characterizes the contemporary spiritual project, and I conclude by arguing that the moral demand of chastity has an immediacy that overcomes our defenses of "critical distance" and irony. But an obvious question emerges. Why are we so standoffish when shelves groan with books proclaiming the rapturous joys of intimacy and our moral duty to embrace "the other"? Chapter three explores the subcurrents of anxiety that drive our will-to-distance. We adopt strategies of separation not because we are confident in our own powers but because we have a cautious temper. We recognize that spiritual submission often leads to destruction and dissolution, and we begin to think that no redemptive promises are trustworthy. Then, in chapter four, I analyze a bold contemporary attempt to overcome the separative violence of modernity and postmodernity. John Milbank and others have undertaken a radical revision of our metaphysical assumptions in order to build reciprocity and participation into the very order of things. While I have great sympathy for this project, appropriately named by its proponents "Radical Orthodoxy," I continue to see evidence that separation and distance exert their influence. The spiritual pattern that makes modern theology modern recurs, regardless of the new metaphysical program. Against the disjunction that makes Radical Orthodoxy radical, I urge the path of Nehemiah: we must dwell as closely as possible to the ruined forms of modern Christianity.

The urge to separate is altogether understandable. A spiritually destitute and prostituted church seems unable to motivate a desire for intimacy. Part two is devoted to evoking the impoverished condition of the Episcopal Church. I want to bring you to see these ruins in theological practice (chapter five, "The Theological Vocation in the Episcopal Church"), in liturgy and worship (chapter six, "The Drive Toward Change"), and in moral discipline (chapter seven, "Sex in the Episcopal Church"). In view of what I say, I am quite sure that no reader will think me Pollyannaish. But I also want to insist that I am not despairing and pessimistic. My goal is to see as clearly as did Darby in his own day. We must acknowledge reality if we are to be faithful rather than fantastical. Moreover, we need to see that in Christ we are not called to love strength and power and beauty. Ruins are not unfit for Christian habitation.

Part three is my attempt to articulate the way of Nehemiah in our situation. This will require renouncing Darby's—and modernity's—pattern of separation. Chapter eight presents a case for redoubled intimacy. We are to turn toward the *concreta Christiana,* the stones of Jerusalem, however fallen and disordered. I try to give content to this path back to Jerusalem in chapter nine. The absorptive practice of a fixed and repetitive daily round of prayer is one of the forces that direct us toward apostolic intimacy. Within that absorptive practice Scripture plays a foundational role. Therefore the book concludes with two chapters that address what may be the deepest and most defining distance of modernity: our alienation from the canonical authority and divine power of Scripture. Chapter ten treats the problem and solution broadly. Chapter eleven offers an exegetical performance to support my programmatic statements on behalf of a theologically robust interpretation of Scripture.

With this synopsis in mind, I want to make a closing plea. While I have found these chapters helpful to write, they may fail to stir assent. I may fail to convince you that the strategy of separation is the dominant feature of our once modern and now postmodern culture. I may do little to bring you to acknowledge that the church is in ruins. After all, my engagement with Darby suggests a mind laboring in marginal characters best left forgotten, and this may signal an eccentric and unstable approach to other issues. Maybe you think Radner a romantic who loves the lost cause or an Anglo-Catholic who needs a despairing nostalgia in order to avoid the "real options" of confident evangelicalism or magisterial Roman Catholicism. Still further, you may be amused by my all too convincing descriptions of the diminished Episcopal Church, happy that you have either left or no longer take seriously the "old line" or "sideline" Protestant churches. Is not the very title of this book, *In the Ruins of the Church*, exactly the kind of negativity and self-doubt that stands in the way of church growth? I can hear you saying right now, "I don't want to be infected with that debilitating pessimism." There are indeed many reasons to withhold assent, both from part one of this book and, even more, from part two.

I will argue my case as best I can, but in the end I will accept all these criticisms and reservations if you will but agree with the positive program outlined in part three. Follow the path of Nehemiah, and I will happily debate the cultural criticism and ecclesial diagnosis. Imagine Jerusalem splendid with the beauty of holiness. Have its walls neat and trim. See its gates grand and secure. If you will not weep for the ruined church, you may at least do as Christians have always done: weep for your ruined soul and turn toward that which you have received from the apostles as the power of salvation. See that you need to draw close to the power of a God who has a city, a people, and a Son. See that the "step back," the cherished distances of critique and therapy, the serene detachment of impartiality—could I name all the strategies of separation without telling the whole history of modernity?—these cannot mark the path of those who would suffer that which the Lord has wrought with his people. See that these many strategies of separation certainly cannot be the way of those who wish to follow the Son, who drew us so closely to his breast that he suffered even the ruin of our sin.

Thus it is my hope that these reflections will convince you of the one thing needful, in this time as in Nehemiah's. Our journey must be toward an ever deeper loyalty to our ancestors' graves in Jerusalem. We must draw near to the memory of the apostles, made sensuous and available in the words of Scripture, in the ancient liturgies, in the dogmatic and disciplinary traditions of the church. These things, the *concreta Christiana*, are the *media divina*, and as Nehemiah knew, faith must draw us back toward them. Reject, then, every diagnostic claim and observation, but affirm at least this: we need a redoubled intimacy if we are to suffer divine things in an age that urges us to flee.

The Temptations of Distance

2

Postmodern Irony and Petronian Humanism

Being unable to cure death, wretchedness and ignorance, men have decided, in order to be happy, not to think about such things.

Blaise Pascal, *Pensées*

We live in what we like to think of as a very sophisticated society. International commerce keeps the economy humming day and night. Silicon chips grease the wheels of calculation and communication. Medical centers are engaged in perpetual expansion as research facilities grow at a furious pace. Life gets more and more complicated. We can buy and sell Eurobonds on our cell phones while watching Monday night football at a Mexican-theme sports bar owned by a partnership of German orthodontists. We can kill time after yet another flight cancellation by sipping lattes and reading about treks from Lhasa to the Rongbuk Buddhist monastery at the base of Mount Everest. Yes, our postmodern world is quite remarkable. There can be no doubt about it, the tectonic plates of culture are shifting.

If we care about evangelism, then surely we need to get our bearings in this strange postmodern world. If we wish to preach and teach effectively, then we must be clear about where the sharp and double-edged sword of the gospel cuts into the spirit of the age. This is especially important because our own churches are awash with disorienting analysis. Some are eager to convince us that our sophisticated scientific culture just cannot accept the simplistic mythological worldview of traditional Christianity. Others are certain that the new world of global communication makes us so aware of cultural and religious diversity that the traditional exclusivist claims of Christianity are untenable. Still others drink deeply at the well of literary theory and in an intoxicated reverie announce that old ideas of meaning and truth have been transcended. The essence of Scripture is not the person of Jesus Christ but its openness to "difference." Most, however, offer a straightforward assessment: our postmodern world is so very, very complex that the traditional forms of Christian preaching and teaching must be updated and revised. I can hear the sound bite: "We need a message that speaks to the Internet Age."

These approaches to the no-doubt new challenges of evangelism are wrongheaded. Each interprets the difficulties we face as the result of new facts. Somehow scientific discovery or the global village of instant communication makes Christianity less plausible, as if the invention of the Internet posed sudden spiritual difficulties for Christian teaching. Somehow new theoretical and philosophical fashions alter the landscape of consciousness, as if our minds were so much flotsam and jetsam pressed forward by the surging flood of cultural change. Somehow the mere fact of social and technological complexity overwhelms the presumptive simplicity of old-fashioned Christianity, as if human beings were ruminating animals without a care in the world before the advent of cellular phones and cable TV.

These approaches will not do. Instead I propose another approach. The challenges facing Christian evangelism are not scientific; they are not technological; they are not philosophical or cultural in any theoretical or abstract sense. Our challenges are moral and religious. The spirit of the age is, after all, *spiritual*. My goal, then, is to analyze these moral and spiritual challenges, for they, and not the remarkable changes on the surface of our society, shape the real task of evangelism. My thesis shall be that the confident humanism of modernity has given way to an anxious desire to escape moral demand and the pressure it puts on us to change.

Promethian Humanism

To a great degree, we are told a story about modernity that emphasizes Promethean ambition. The high labors of freedom, the noble quest for equality, the rigors of critical thought are all championed as great achievements of the human spirit. In many cases this story is accurate. Seminal modern figures were extraordinarily ambitious. For Jean-Jacques Rousseau the human desire to integrate duty and sensibility was unquenchable, and for Immanuel Kant the light of conscience burned ever bright. Though unsentimental and often ruthless, both Friedrich Hegel and Karl Marx believed in the benevolent march of history toward a crowning humanism. John Stuart Mill and Bertrand Russell never underestimated the depths of human ignorance and irrationality, but both retained confidence in the integrity of reason and the triumphant power of argument. They differed from each other in many ways, but they held in common a confident hope: our humanity, however understood, provides the sufficient basis for the highest good.

This confidence in human potency and potential defines modern humanism, and it creates a field of moral concerns that is shaped by two centers of gravity. The first is preoccupied with the creative potential of human agency. We have the spark of justice within, and the proper spiritual labor assigned to us is liberation. We must break down the constraining barriers that limit individuality and self-expression. Here modernity is given over to the redemptive project of freedom. The other center of gravity is more cautious, but it is equally influential. This moral sensibility seeks to weigh evidence and avoid error. Quiet and uncoerced debate yields reliable truths, and our job is to resist the temptations of passionate excess and restrain foolhardy illusion. More skeptical and less speculative, this cautious humanism counsels moderation. We must be careful to tether our lives to secure and reliable anchors. We must build upon a firm and stable foundation.

The great American prophet Ralph Waldo Emerson penned epigrams that capture the ambition of the first aspect of modern humanism, its redemptive project, and his ambition certainly challenges Christian proclamation. Against the obedient discipline of *imitatio Christi*, Emerson claimed that "imitation is suicide." Against the self-condemning introspection of St. Augustine's repentant autobiography, Emerson substituted the affirmative principle "Trust thyself." Against the hierarchy of creature and Creator, Emerson insisted, "Nothing is sacred but the integrity of your own mind." Against the penitential imperative, Emerson interjected, "I do not wish to expiate, but to live." Against reliance on a faith once delivered, Emerson stated, "The centuries are conspirators against the sanity and authority of the soul."[1] At every turn Emerson is a brilliant strategist of the Promethean ambition of modernity. We must throw off the chains that bind, especially our psychic bondage to social and moral expectation, and then, in freedom, we can live according to the pure dictates of personal conscience.

Empiricists such as John Locke support the other side of modern humanism, its more cautious approach. For Locke mental life is riven with prejudice and instability. The project of philosophy is to identify simple ideas that promise to remain stable, and on this basis to rebuild intellectual life. In this effort, however, the true philosopher recognizes limits. As Locke writes, "It becomes the Modesty of Philosophy, not to pronounce Magisterially where we want that Evidence that can produce Knowledge."[2] Here a skeptical temper moderates dogmatic tendencies. We should withhold assent to propositions unsupported by evidence. The goal, however, is not to propagate doubt for its own sake. Instead, for Locke and subsequent generations of empiricists, the purpose of the critical temper is to create social and psychic space for the incremental progress of scientific inquiry. Only if we release some of the pressure of traditional faith, only if we step back from the highly charged atmosphere of speculation and dogma, can we engage in the dispassionate and free exchange of ideas that leads to genuine and reliable intellectual results.[3]

Together, a zeal for freedom and a cool empiricism have nourished the modern spirit, and in both cases our humanity must take pride of place. For redemptive humanists such as Emerson, once liberated from the dead hand of dogma, our humanity is the creative and bountiful source of moral insight. For cautious humanists such as Locke, if we use critical doubt to reduce the demands of prejudice and social convention, then we can undertake the painstaking and slow process of empirical inquiry. In both cases, human power displaces divine power as the source of hope. Emerson's hot passion and Locke's sweet reason guide us toward fulfillment. We are to break from traditional authority in order to release ourselves from hindering fetters, and in so doing we accelerate the natural human push toward freedom and truth.

Not surprisingly, then, modern Christianity has fenced with modern humanism. After all, God comes first, not us. We must serve him in order to attain freedom. His truth shall judge the minds of humankind, and his Word leads to all truth. Far from a hindering fetter, the authority of the gospel is the engine that drives us toward fulfillment.

In spite of this obvious conflict, modern Christianity has not always opposed modern humanism, and for good reason. The antitheses are sufficiently pointed to suggest important common interests. The modern defense of individuality echoes the Christian confidence that God calls each of us by name. The new birth promised in baptism is not at all alien to Emerson's hope that we might disentangle ourselves from the cruel weight of the past. Justification by faith also turns us away from expiation and toward "life." Furthermore, like the close reasoning and rigorous argument endorsed by Locke, Christianity teaches doctrines as claims of truth and not as nuggets of meaning. They possess public solidity and personal force. Against willfulness and inveterate human self-delusion, faith involves disciplining the mind to conform to the God-given facts. Like the empiricist, the theologian must serve that which is given.[4]

In both cases, whether ambitious or cautious, modern humanism shares with Christianity an interest in transformative power. Both are champions of change. For Emerson, freedom impels, for the restless divine spark of individuality always seeks full expression. He hopes for a time when the radiance of individuality will illuminate the cosmos. For Locke, facts have force; our minds receive the impress of their reality, and we should discipline ourselves to believe accordingly. Christianity preaches neither Emersonian freedom nor Lockean empiricism, but the gospel also has potency to convert minds and change lives. The power of the cross transforms sinner into saint.

For this reason, modern humanism and Christianity share a love of power and a hope for change, and given this common love and common hope, many have sought to reevangelize modern Western culture by reinterpreting modern humanism and redirecting its account of the power of life toward the properly Christian goal of putting God first. For apologists, the dynamics of freedom and force of facts properly orbit around the power of the cross, and Emerson and Locke, properly understood, advance the cause of the gospel.

Maybe this attempt to conscript modern humanism to the task of evangelism has been helpful. Maybe it has been a mistake. I have my own views on the history of modern theology and its relationship to modern humanism.[5] But I do not want to try to retrace the dialectical gymnastics of someone like Paul Tillich, who thought that the redemptive promise of the gospel could be translated into Emersonian phrases such as "Be all you can be." Such an exercise will not help us orient ourselves in this postmodern context. Tillich and modern theologians like him who tried to ride the tiger of humanism are no longer apt to the present. They no longer speak to the challenges of preaching the gospel. The patrons of the Eternal Now seem to have faded into the Already Past.

Why is someone like Tillich, the great patron of relevance, no longer relevant? I think the answer is simple. The tenor of our age, however humanistic in spirit, lacks the Promethean elements that modern theology long thought eternal. The Agent Orange of cultural critique has deforested our cultural imaginations, and we no longer imagine ourselves to be heralds of freedom and truth. Voices of evangelical condemnation and calls to repentance no longer challenge our confident humanism. After Freud, conscience cannot stand against social authority, for the two are intertwined. Individuality remains a cherished ideal, but the multicultural agenda places that ideal in the quicksand of race, class, and gender. For all our humanistic faith, we are not great believers in the intrinsic goodness and integrity of human nature. We shrink from the harsh disciplines that might shape our souls, even the humanistic disciplines of authenticity and rational inquiry. We need years of therapy in order to overcome self-doubt, and even then any consequent self-trust is fragile. Still further, we worry about ideology and wring our hands over the inevitable cultural limitations that undermine our quest for knowledge. The bogeyman of patriarchy is everywhere; everything depends upon one's perspective. In all this, the effect is not Emersonian ambition or Lockean confidence in reason. Pronouns are changed, symbols are manipulated, critiques are undertaken, but almost always in the spirit of a new conformity that fears imprisonment without cherishing freedom, flees from error without pursuing truth.

In these and many other ways the outlook of modernity has shifted from ambition and confidence to fear and anxiety. The spirit of the age is no longer self-expressive; it is self-protective. Whether one is a Derridian, a disciple of Foucault, or a student of Heidegger, the very potencies and powers that give human life dynamism and drive are laden with danger.

Allow me to list a few postmodern truisms. Language is a vessel of power that seeks dominion. Truth claims are tinged with imperial ambition. Technology alienates us from life. Economic dynamism produces rapacious inequality.

As a consequence, the slogans of modernity may well endure; liberty, equality, and fraternity may continue to be championed, but they are so against a background of menace and not promise. Postmodern culture continues to put humanity first, but it does so in an atmosphere haunted by fear.

Because postmodern culture is essentially defensive, the challenges of evangelism have changed, and the many modern theological strategies of mediation are altogether beside the point. One need not meet the rigorous demands of modern intellectual life when the present age is running in the opposite direction. One need not tailor the gospel to fit the ambitions of freedom if the postmodern soul endeavors to shrink to a point where it will no longer be noticed. But the demise of old challenges give rise to new challenges. Postmodern humanism may not be Promethean, but it most certainly is not Christian. In order to understand this new humanism, we need to examine its defensive posture. Two features are very much in evidence: a fear of authority and flight from truth. Both are integral to the strange way in which postmodern culture seeks to serve humanity by saving it from any and all power, by protecting us from the ambitions and demands that lead to change.[6]

Protective Distance

The contemporary allergy to authority and flight from truth are certainly familiar to anyone who has sampled the air of American culture. Consider the slogan "Celebrate diversity!" This platitude is so ubiquitous that it now seems self-evident. Some people are tall, others are short. It would be absurd to require all people to be the same height. Just as people are of different heights, we reason, so also do people have different spiritual sensibilities and needs. It would be absurd, then, to require them to hold the same beliefs or conform to the same moral rules. After all, only a violent attack on individual bodies would produce a world of people the same height. So also, we infer, enforced uniformity of belief and practice requires violent assaults upon conscience, intellect, and will. Therefore we must reject all authoritative claims as acts of violence.

Of course, Christianity is inevitably caught up in the postmodern flight from authority. As the most powerful force shaping Western culture, Christianity becomes the very essence of the authority against which we must protect ourselves. If we are afflicted with enduring divisions of race and class, then surely Christianity must have a hand in causing this evil. If Western societies subordinate women and deny them public roles, then, again, Christianity is at the root of the problem. The list of particulars is endless, varying in focus according to the interests of critics, but the basic logic is always the same. The authority of tradition must be overthrown, the sacred bonds of loyalty to what has been passed on must be broken, so that we can be released from the oppressive burdens of present power.

Anxieties about the closed circuit of dogma, the exhausting weight of tradition, and the crushing force of institutional authority lead our postmodern culture to the extreme of denying the authority of truth itself. Our efforts to shield ourselves from coercive demand and its violence against individuality make us fear that some proposition, some insight, some conclusion to a syllogism might gain control over our intellects and our souls. If any of us really believe that some proposition is true, then the diversity of our minds will fall victim to the uniformity of what is the case. Indeed I am convinced that if the Vatican were to promulgate a document advising Catholic theologians that $2 + 2 = 4$ and that theologians are not to say otherwise if they wish to speak the truth, then journalists would have no difficulty finding any number of sources who would denounce the authoritarian tone of such a directive.[7]

Such hyperbole can seem silly. Perhaps, but we should not underestimate the intensity of the postmodern horror of obedience, a horror that makes the power of truth itself a threat. "Sharing" now smothers debate. God forbid that anyone should formulate a reasoned argument; it might contradict or "marginalize" the experience of others. All sentences must begin with a compulsive ritual preface: "From my point of view . . ." The truth and falsity of all claims depend on one's "perspective." Everyone must be affirmed; the views of all must be validated.

Many of my colleagues in philosophy are convinced that this all-views-are-equally-valid approach stems from a widespread belief in relativism. We are all, these professors imagine, in the grips of a bad theory of truth, and they spend a great deal of time trying to disabuse their students of this bad theory.

The problem, however, is that this does not work. I can point out to my students that the truth that $2 + 2 = 4$ does not in fact depend on anyone's point of view. I can expand upon the objectivity of the natural sciences. I can lecture about the distinction between truth and justification. I can exhort all to recognize that the possibilities of error and prejudice do not make them inevitable.

My efforts are in vain because my students have a primitive and unreflective commitment to the proposition that all truth is relative. They hold such a view as dogma, not as theory. It is a presupposition, not a conclusion. To be sure, sometimes they use the techniques of cultural critique. Truth claims, they say, are relative to their cultural contexts. If I press the issue and ask them to explain how such a view is consistent with the fact that modern science is practiced in India, Japan, Russia, and the United States, and that scientists go to international conferences and seem to agree with each other about all sorts of things regardless of cultural context, they look at me and shrug. At other times they deploy sophistic tricks. A student insists that one cannot make non-mathematical claims about mathematics, and this demonstrates that all systems of thought are closed and self-referential. Therefore truth claims reduce to empty tautology. When I ask him in what sense the proposition that engineers find mathematics useful is a mathematical claim about mathematics, he just looks at me and repeats his conviction. His belief is more certain to him than anything I might say. It is a matter of faith, not evidence or inference.

These experiences in the classroom have convinced me that relativism is not a philosophical theory. It is a spiritual truth, a protective dogma designed to fend off any power that might claim our loyalty. It is a habit of mind that insulates postmodern life from the sober potency of arguments and the force of evidence, from the rightful claims of reason and the wisdom of the past. My students can look me in the eye and insist that one should never impose one's beliefs on others *and* that all truth claims—including, I presume, the moral rigors of never, never imposing on others—are relative. Here our contemporary horror of obedience joins hands with solipsism in order to protect the soul from all demands, rational or otherwise. Here we are face to face with the spirit of our age.

A comparison of this outlook with the approach of modern humanism illustrates the striking shift from outward ambition to inward self-protection. For Kant, the traditional authority of Christian dogma must be rejected because it is indefensible. In its place we must put the proper and humanizing authority of the moral law, the truth of which is clear to practical reason and the consequence of which is a restructuring of human society so as to respect and promote human dignity. In this way the criticisms of Christian claims serve an aggressive project. Unjust and wrongful authority must give way to a just and proper authority that will usher in a new age. The false and debilitating authority of dogma must be renounced so that human beings can undertake the revolutions of genuine freedom based on reason.

My students lack this rebellious spirit. Like so much of postmodern culture, their dispositions are submissive. They respect my authority as a teacher. They do not bridle against what they are told. They accept the fact that they must jump through educational hoops in order to get the professional certification they desire. They do not resent the harsh demands of the marketplace. They accept as a nonnegotiable fact the right of governments to punish, imprison, and make war to protect national interests. In this sense their attitude is not Promethean, but it is also not traditional. My students submit to the many demands of postmodern life, but with the knowing wink and sigh of a child raised on a steady diet of critique. They accept limitations, but they keep everything at a distance.

This distance, and the many spiritual disciplines of postmodern life that deflect and demystify the powers that would penetrate into our lives, is the most fundamental form of postmodern humanism. It is a protective distance. In a society socialized to be nonjudgmental, supported by the conviction that all truth is relative, the walls of defense against authority are strong indeed. We can safely navigate the danger of life, detached from the true and everlasting dangers of obedience and commitment, for nothing has the right to make a claim on our souls. Such is postmodern freedom.

Postmodern Irony

Many cultural observers have noticed this spiritual detachment. Usually it is described as the postmodern stance of irony. There are now classical instances of such irony in the postmodern literature. Jacques Derrida's address to the Société Française de Philosophie, "Différance," is a particularly witty performance.[8] What Derrida says about what is written but cannot be heard launches a spiraling series of meditations that culminate in observations about the role of *différance* as the "ground of being." (I must use quotation marks, for in his essay Derrida uses all metaphysical terms ironically.) I will not retrace the dialectical reductions but will simply report Derrida's conclusions. For Derrida, the power that produces meaning and claims of truth "governs nothing, and nowhere exercises authority. . . . Not only is there no kingdom of *différance*, but *différance* instigates the subversion of every kingdom." Roughly translated, Derrida is saying that our world is set in motion by power. Of that there is no doubt. But such power is originless and pointless. The order of things is a "bottomless chessboard on which Being is put into play." There is no beginning or end; there is no purpose or principle by which to regulate or judge the play.

What is so important about Derrida is not the detail of his various literary performances. To imagine that deconstruction offers theoretical insight is to fall victim to just that which Derrida mocks.[9] Instead the most telling aspect of Derrida's work is his spiritual advice. He does not rage against a meaningless cosmos. He does not adopt the young Sartre's existential determination in the face of a godless world, and he certainly does not adopt the older Sartre's strategy of Marxist dogmatism. Instead Derrida advises us to adopt lightheartedness. We should affirm the bottomless chessboard, he says, with "a certain laughter and a certain step of dance."[10] In short, we should recognize that deconstruction, whatever that finally means in terms of theoretical commitments and interpretive performances, yields spiritual freedom. Nothing can sustain the burden of ultimate meaning or final truth, and therefore nothing can rightfully put demands upon our soul.

In the hands of moralistic American critics, Derrida's work can take on ponderous significance. "Logocentrism" oppresses, and somehow "difference" liberates. The old humanism mixes with the new, and messianic theorists imagine that the critical sophistication of postmodernism more effectively clears the ground for the proper demands of freedom and justice. However, Derrida's spiritual advice is far more widely followed than either the preaching of his moralistic disciples or the theoretical twists and turns of his semiological method. To be sure, few break out in laughter and dance. The stress and strain of postmodern life leave little time for such indulgences. Nonetheless, the postmodern world cherishes the spiritual freedom that Derrida rightly identifies as the fruit of deconstruction. Ironic detachment, the smirk of critical tropes, the serene complacency made possible by the dogmatic belief that all truth is relative—these and other habits of mind keep our souls free from the disturbing need for inner personal change.

We should forswear conspiracy theories. Whatever we might imagine that Derrida represents—cynical French intellectual life, decadent academic self-indulgence, ruthless Nietzschean will to power—none of these things have caused or even influenced the world in which I live and work. My students certainly lack any knowledge of Derrida, and they could not begin to recapitulate the analysis of postmodern literary theory. Yet they are surprisingly close to his conclusions. Their relativism is painfully unsophisticated, but it serves the same purpose as Derrida's elaborate theoretical machinery. Their dogmatic conviction that truth is not really possible serves to promote spiritual freedom. Of course we must live according to countless rules; yet guided by the therapy of critique and buttressed by a dogmatic relativism, we know the chessboard is bottomless. We believe that we can simply float in the currents of outer cultural change, confident that there are no depths, no undertow of ultimate consequence. In such a world, delicious irony keeps us afloat.

Our New Patron Saint

If I am correct in reading the signs of the times, then the spirit of our postmodern age is Petronian, not Promethean, and this makes a great difference when we undertake to preach the gospel. Petronius was an enigmatic Roman who lived during the time of Nero. His notorious observations of Roman life come down to us in the *Satyricon,* a rambling narrative that is part soap opera, part *National Enquirer* article, and part serenely detached social description. In the *Satyricon* Petronius is a participant who stands at one remove. He is an observer who can mock and satirize. He can describe veniality without judgment; he can narrate vice without protest.

In these ways Petronius exemplifies the spiritual ideal that now dominates postmodern Western culture. He creates a pervasive atmosphere of superficiality that drains all spiritual significance from events. His characters are realistic, yet they are spectral, soulless creatures who utterly lack gravity. Never moralistic, never interjecting the voice of some loftier vision, Petronius can describe sexual violence with the same serene objectivity as a gluttonous dinner party. He is able to entertain us with an account of a tryst that founders on a failed erection. The scenes of deception and exploitation entertain; they neither edify nor entice. For this reason, as both writer and participant Petronius is in the world but not of the world. Yet his freedom has nothing to do with the ascetical disciplines that detach the Christian from the world. Instead Petronious enjoys a spiritual freedom similar to the dance and laugh advocated by Derrida. It is the freedom that comes from the confidence that there is no Lord of life, from the wry certainty that the world is carried forward on currents of instinct, veniality, and conceit.

Postmodern culture achieves the same effect with its many and diverse moral disciplines. The upshot is a Petronian humanism. We cultivate a cynicism that does not despair, because it serves to destroy the charms of truth and beauty that might corrupt our inner peace. We enjoy an irony that does not seek resolution, because it supports our desire to be invulnerable observers rather than participants at risk. We are spectators of our own lives, free from the strain of drama and the uncertainty of a story in which our souls are at stake. We conform because nothing finally matters except the superiority of knowing it to be so.

As I suggested earlier, modern humanism and its ambitions on behalf of freedom and reason often tempted theologians into various alliances with the Promethean spirit. Ill-advised or not, these alliances depended on a shared ambition, a shared joy in the promise of changes that would shape the soul. Emerson wished to clear away false dependency on external authority so that the voice of conscience could govern and transform. Locke hoped to set us on the sure path of clear thinking. Any Christian preacher worth his salt, whether borrowing from this humanist tradition or not, preaches repentance, wishing to turn those who listen away from sin and toward righteousness. Change is at the heart of the gospel.

At this strange juncture in human history, we need to realize that old debates about which way to turn for the power that might effect change—toward inner human potencies or toward the power of God in Christ—are now moot. Instead the present age wishes to insulate itself against *any call to turn*, either for or against; postmodern culture, for all its love of "difference," keeps demands for personal change at a distance. Postmodern humanism does not want to shoulder the gospel out of the center of life so that human potencies might burst forth from the chrysalis of ancient dogma or traditional morality. Quite the contrary, this Petronian humanism wishes to neuter all power and potency, human or otherwise. "Difference" is a flux and "swerve" that plays upon the surfaces of life. For this reason, no dynamism is allowed to penetrate the defenses of irony, satire, and critical sophistication. The soul must remain unaltered, unaffected.

The Need for Spiritual Ambition

The modern theological tradition is keyed to the challenges of Promethean ambition, not Petronian apathy. We are the inheritors of that tradition, and as a consequence we can respond to the postmodern age mistakenly. Cynicism can seem like a gain for the gospel. After all, the New Testament counsels Christians to take a jaundiced view of worldly wisdom. Furthermore, irony can appear to be an ally, for the postmodern reluctance to adopt the old humanistic projects with whole-hearted vigor, whether Emersonian or Lockean, suggests a newfound humility. Finally, the willing conformity that characterizes so much postmodern life can give the evangelist hope that the prideful self-sufficiency of modernity has finally exhausted itself. These are, however, deceptions made possible by a fixation on pride as the primary barrier to faith. Sloth and cowardice in reality are just as deadly. Both slink away from the urgency of conviction. Both fear the sharp edge of demand and expectation. Both have a vested interest in cynicism, irony, and outward conformity. These vices, not pride, now dominate our culture.

What do the vices of sloth and cowardice mean for evangelism in the postmodern context? How does this Petronian humanism and its commitment to spiritual freedom shape the challenges of preaching and teaching the gospel in our age? I am a university professor who observes his students and tries to orient himself in the increasingly strange landscape of this third millennium. I am not engaged in pastoral work, at least not in the primary sense of ordering the community of the faithful in worship. Nonetheless, in my own pedagogy I am constantly trying to penetrate the defenses of irony; I am always attempting to bridge the seemingly depthless chasms of critique. Furthermore, I am more a child of this age then I would like to admit. Petronius is closer kin than Prometheus, and to the extent that I know my own resistances to the gospel, I have some small insights into the pastoral challenges. Therefore I will venture a brief observation.

No moderation of the demands of the gospel will satisfy the postmodern spirit. To a great extent the modern project of apologetics involved trying to accentuate the humanistic dimension of the gospel. As I have suggested already, the redemptive promise of Christianity parallels the modern concern for freedom. Moreover, the strong claims of dogma are not dissimilar to modern science's insistence on obedience to evidence and argument. For this reason evangelism could undertake to redirect the passions of modernity toward the proper end of faith in Christ. The deepest hopes of modernity may find their fulfillment in the gospel. Yet if I am correct in my analysis, postmodern culture does not nurture hope in the human heart. Quite the contrary, it promises quiescent freedom from the disturbances of expectations and demands. For this reason the gospel of redemption will be an offense, no matter how carefully modulated, no matter how cleverly dressed up in the finery of modern ideals of freedom and rational responsibility. Therefore evangelism has no reason to hide the hard demands of the gospel.

John Paul II is a signal example in our own time. *Veritatis Splendor*, the encyclical concerning moral theology, warns against the dangers of moral relativism and subjectivism. What is striking about *Veritatis Splendor*, however, is not its polemic against moral relativism. As I have said, my philosophy colleagues do as much in their classes. Instead what is extraordinary is the view of freedom it advances, a view utterly at odds with the spiritual freedom so cherished by our age. The encyclical ends with a mediation on the Virgin Mary. She is commended as the exemplar of Christian freedom, and that freedom has the following form. Called to serve the Lord with body and soul, she gave herself in obedience to a demand whose scope and import she did not understand.

The upshot is more than the leverage that moral right and wrong give us against our bondage to worldly powers. For John Paul II, the Virgin Mary is the model of Christian moral obedience because she has the courage to accept disciplines and sacrifices that do not just yield freedom from sin but freedom for supernatural life. Only by taking the severe and dangerous risks of obedience to something beyond our comprehension can we have the freedom to participate in divine glory. For this reason Christian freedom requires a spiritual ambition that is very much at odds with the postmodern age. Such ambition does not throw up protective walls to block the demands of the gospel. Instead spiritual ambition forsakes prerogatives, renounces the rights and privileges of intellect and will. All defenses against the transforming power of grace are removed, even those that emerge out of the rightful worries we all have about dominion and deception. Only in this way, says John Paul II, can we draw near to the power of life. After all, Christian ambition is supernatural precisely because it seeks to become more than that which human power can produce.

The moral challenge of evangelism is, then, to nurture an ambition that has the courage of obedience, the courage to draw as near as possible to redemptive power by tearing down the walls of defense. Without doubt, this can be done in any number of ways, but I wish to end with a final word. It is hard truth that pastors know but do not wish to hear: Unless you preach chastity, and not the easy chastity of sex governed by commitment and love but the hard chastity taught by St. Paul, you will fail to meet the moral challenge of evangelism in this postmodern age. This is not because sex is the most important dimension of the Christian life; it is because sexual freedom is the most cherished, most morally sanctified, and most Petronian moral commitment of the postmodern age.

Sexual freedom is crucial because it has two aspects. It encourages the agitation of our passions, always distracting us from ourselves, and at the same time this postmodern sexual freedom insists that we should do absolutely nothing to alter the immediate demands of our lust. In this way our age runs from chastity for the same reason that St. Augustine, in his *Confessions,* reports that he always ended his prayer for chastity with the plea, "But not yet!"[11] As Augustine knew, if we can change this altogether fundamental part of our lives, a part woven into the fabric of instinct, then the defenses against redemptive change are down. If the perfectly normal and natural needs of the body can be directed toward God, then surely the higher faculties of will and intellect can as well. If something so "impossible" is indeed possible, then who knows what might happen next?

On this point, as on so many, St. Augustine is surely right. It is not an accident that those who have the least immediate and instinctual interest in resisting the classical Christian teaching on sexual morality—aged clerics—often offer the most ardent defenses of the rights and prerogatives of the libido. They love their freedom as much as my twenty-year-old students, indeed more so because the love has become both more habitual and more spiritual. What begins as a defense of the prerogatives of the body (my needs must not be stymied, my impulses not denied!) ends with a complacent self-assertion (God forbid that I should have to bring my reason to the authority of God's Word!).

Again, we need to see that this self-assertion is protective, not aggressive. We adopt critical cliches and habits of distance because we do not want to risk being ravished by a transforming truth. We do not want to submit the raw material of our lives to God so that we might be melted down and reformed into something very different. Thus, we defend ourselves against chastity not because we are prideful and self-confident hedonists, not because we find great joy in the confusing labyrinths of sexual desire and satisfaction, but because we are fearful that once the invasion of grace begins it will not relent until the capitol falls. We embrace sexual freedom because it is a crucial line of defense against spiritual and transformative demands.

My students may not know Derrida, but they are not fools. They well know that the imperative of Christian chastity is a direct assault on what is forbidden by the Petronian humanism of our postmodern age: allowing ideals to enter our soul in order to reshape our identity. It is a direct assault upon our spiritual freedom, but not because it involves restraint and limitation. I must reiterate. My students know and accept the many restraints the society imposes on them. The surfaces of their lives bear all the marks of hygienic and economic discipline. They embrace dieting and reject smoking. They line up to take required courses necessary for professional certification. No, it is not outward discipline that they fear; it is inner spiritual demand that would involve personal change that they cannot endure. Chastity is an assault from which they recoil in horror because, to the twenty-year-old mind, it is so insanely ambitious, so hopelessly impossible, so ruthlessly physical *and* personal. It is so ruthlessly about *you* and *me*.

At this point my students may understand next to nothing about the Christian ascetical tradition, its goals and methods, as well as the relation between self-denial and God's intentions for our salvation. These are matters I am not sure that I understand. But of this I *am* sure. In their recoil from chastity, they have difficulty maintaining Petronian equilibrium. It is difficult to contemplate chastity with "a laugh and a step of dance," for none of us can discipline lust at a distance from ourselves. We cannot cool the boiling caldron with the wink and nod of irony. The horrifying "No!" of sexual prohibition is intimate. This is why sexual freedom is the functional center of postmodern politics, morality, and culture. Without spiritual distance here, we become vulnerable to any number of calmer, cooler, and more reasonable changes that will reshape our identity. For this reason, at this flashpoint of dispersive fantasy and desire, the increasingly strange and ambitious teaching of Christianity must cut like a sharp and two-edged sword, or it cuts not at all.

3

Pro Nobis

Words We Do Not Want to Hear

In their perverted way all humanity imitates you. Yet they put themselves at a distance from you . . .

St. Augustine, *Confessions*

In the last chapter I sought to identify our postmodern condition. We resist the gospel because we fear all powers that effect change *in us*, even as we live in a society that constantly champions progress and development. The spiritual atmosphere in which we live is Petronian, because in such a world we can float free from the binding tethers of commitment and the wrenching forces of discipline. Change can occur across the surfaces of life, but it is carefully limited by irony. In this way ideas, decisions, and passions are never really our own; they are objects of critical inquiry and therapy. As a result, something like the ancient ideal of *apathia* or *ataraxia*—freedom from suffering and change—now predominates, and it wars against the classical Christian ideal of discipleship as following Christ in his suffering. Petronian humanism opens up a protective distance between us and anything that would transform our lives, and this makes repentant change difficult to imagine.

This Petronian humanism is neither superficial nor accidental. It reflects a pervasive caution in the face of powerful forces, and the power of Christianity most of all. This caution and the felt need for protective distance are, I think, familiar. Though I teach at an institution run by Catholic priests, even there the threat my colleagues in other departments feel is a constant reminder of how uncomfortably Christianity fits into the modern university, if at all. The biologists and physicists and sociologists and psychologists and philosophers and literary critics seem unable to suppress their fear that as a theologian I represent the inquisitors, the credulous fools, the haters of reason who are enemies of the life of the mind. The torque of faith, they worry, twists us into deformed shapes.

This same fear holds sway within our church and within our hearts. We are often dismayed when we read early Christian accounts of martyrdom ("fanatical!") or disciplinary manuals for medieval monks ("repressive!") or seventeenth-century Calvinist tracts ("irrelevant!"). "Christianity cannot possibly teach *that*," we insist to ourselves, and bookstores are jammed with modern theologies dedicated to reassuring us that our revulsion is entirely justified. Or we may read the Scriptures, balking at exhortations to sell our possession, to hate our mother and father, to excise lustful thoughts, to resist not evil, to believe that Jesus is the Son of God and that his death saves. So much is so indigestible. Of course we can go back to the bookstores and find endless volumes of modern scholarly study that try to put our worries to rest by explaining the alien force of the biblical text as purely a matter of cultural differences and historical distance.

Whether or not we rush to the latest in theological scholarship for reassurance, I think we all experience Christianity as a threatening thing. The gospel is not easy. The language of life and death is immediate and dangerous. Yet however much we may experience Christianity as a challenge and threat, we are not always clear about just how and why we flee from that which claims to be "good news."

My argument in this chapter will be simple. We need to realize that the real problems of our Christian vocation in the contemporary world do not stem from the supposed archaic irrelevance of the prescientific religious worldview of the Bible or the naive prescientific supernaturalism of the Christian system of belief. Quite the contrary, our difficulties, personal, pastoral, and theological, stem from the fact that Christian proclamation bites very deeply into our anxieties about our own lives. The gospel is about what concerns us most, ourselves, both in our dignity as persons and in our fragility, but far from reassuring and affirming us, the gospel threatens to judge and change us. Therefore we are both offended and frightened.

The voice of offense is familiar: "Why should I have to change? Am I not good enough, at least in part? Surely a loving God would recognize that I need to grow and develop—realize my potential—not *change*." The voice of fear is often hidden but even more powerful. "Change is too wrenching, too destabilizing. I am but mortal flesh; I cannot endure severe renunciations and disciplines. Surely a loving God would not put dangerously extreme demands upon my fragile soul."

Precisely because the voices of offense and fear dominate our responses to the gospel, we need to shed illusions. To put the matter bluntly, the problem with traditional Christianity does not rest in the fact that the so-called modern mind is too sophisticated, too scientific, too worldlywise to believe. Rather, the problem is that we do not want to believe. We want a "gospel" that affirms our increasingly fragile self-images. We want a "gospel" that helps us remain stable and unchanging in a world full of threatening forces that might sweep us away. We do not want repentance. We do not want transformation. In short, we do not want what Christianity teaches.

The Standard Story

We can easily fail to see and understand our real resistance to the gospel because of the standard story we were taught. This story sets out to explain why traditional Christian teaching seems so controversial, why my vocation as a theologian is presently regarded as irrelevant, if not actively hostile, to the university culture, which is, ironically, the very child of theology. I call this story Enlightenment Premillennialism in which Reason has arrived to establish her reign. It goes something like this.

Once, a long time ago, a small sect of Jews began teaching strange things about an itinerant sage and miracle worker, Jesus of Nazareth. It would have petered out on its own, but because the mythologies of Roman and Greek culture were at that time losing plausibility in the increasingly complex and cosmopolitan world of late antiquity, the nascent Christian mythic structure filled a need and flourished. The eventual alliance of Christianity and political power, beginning with Constantine, ensured the dominance of the Christian worldview for over a thousand years in the West. However, first in the Renaissance and then with the rise of modern science, this dominance was challenged. Science demanded evidence and reasoned argument, and this soon eclipsed the dogmatic structure of Christianity. The Age of Faith gave way to the Age of Reason. So now one should not expect well-educated modern people to believe traditional Christian claims about God, creation, salvation, and eternal life.

Whether one sets out to debunk or defend Christianity, this standard Enlightenment story has dominated attempts to interpret the modern religious experience. Everything turns on the supposed intellectual barriers to faith.

Consider, for example, the way Rudolf Bultmann describes the problem of biblical interpretation in his influential lectures *Jesus Christ and Mythology*. According to Bultmann, the worldview of the New Testament is mythological. A world of riddles and puzzles is given structure and meaning in a three-storied universe of heaven, earth, and hell; strange events are explained by appeal to the miraculous intervention of supernatural powers. This mythological consciousness is inconsistent with the cause-and-effect nexus of modern science. Supernatural explanations are incompatible with the methods of modern rational inquiry. In view of this conflict between science and mythology, for Bultmann, the modern person simply cannot accept traditional biblical claims. For example, the creedal demand of belief in the preexistent Son of God who became man for our sake and took upon himself suffering and death for our redemption is untenable. Such a notion, claims Bultmann, would require us to sacrifice our intellectual integrity. Of course Bultmann assumes that the modern person neither will nor should renounce the intellectual obligations of modern historical and experimental science. Thus the interpretive agenda is set. Either we deem the biblical text culturally irrelevant and rationally obnoxious, or we engage in the subtle task of demythologizing the text in order to titrate out the kerygmatic essence. Bultmann casts his lot with the latter, and in so doing thinks of himself as a defender of the faith.

If we accept the story of Enlightenment premillennialism, then surely Bultmann is right. He is not necessarily right in the particulars of his exegetical method or in his existentialist assumptions, and we need not worry about terms such as *demythologize* or *kerygma*. We need only assume that the concerns of the so-called modern person run on different rails from traditional Christian teaching and that the problem of faith is one of relevance. Then good theology, good preaching, and good pastoral practice are necessarily based on good translation. What is written in Scripture, the particular words, images, and narratives, is the problem. They are a dead letter that needs to be brought to life in a language and worldview that speak to our time.

Whether we undertake this project of translation in a "conservative" or "revisionary" manner is, finally, insignificant. If we have left behind the Age of Faith, then we must reinterpret Christianity so that it might be a living force in the Age of Reason, and the only real argument is how many of the archaic thought forms of the past need to be changed. And in this argument the impulse toward revision has a natural advantage.

After all, if the problem we face has to do with relevance, with speaking to our time, then surely one can never be *too* in touch with the Age of Reason.

We tend to cast our lot with Bultmann more often than we think. We tend to worry about science and religion, reason and revelation, faith and understanding, assuming that the wound of modernity is primarily a matter of what counts as reasonable. Consider these often repeated platitudes: "The notion of divine intervention cannot fit into the scientific world of cause and effect." "The modern person demands evidence and cannot accept the authority of revelation." The same assumptions hold true for biblical study. We distinguish between "theological exegesis" and "historical criticism," between "exegesis for the church" and "understanding the original meaning of early Christian documents." We assume exactly the gap that Bultmann sought to bridge.

This is all quite familiar. But notice the impersonal origin of the distances that separate us from the gospel. It is, somehow, a consequence of "history." It is our strange fate to follow the arrow of time away from that which we claim to love. Historical study, we imagine, stands in the way of traditional biblical piety. Or we might say that the developments of science prevent us from believing, or that our critical culture impedes belief. The particular formulations are not decisive. What matters is the fact that we suffer a distance we think beyond our ken; it is not a distance we create in ourselves. Therefore even as we seek to overcome these distances with all sorts of historical aids and spiritual techniques, nothing about *us* is at stake.

In Christian apologetics a similar pattern occurs. Here are more platitudes, again opening up gaps that keep Christian teaching at a distance: "Faithfulness is a special, existential, and subjective way of knowing in contrast to objective knowledge." "What counts as a fact in theology is different from that of science." "Principles of evidence do not apply to the heart as they do to the head." "Theology investigates meaning, while science is concerned with truth." These are just a few typical patterns for understanding our experience of disintegration in the modern period. I shall not waste time pursuing them.[1] The important point is that these patterns insert the difficulty of Christian teaching into the standard Enlightenment story. Whether our emphasis falls upon the apparent demands of scientific method or the constraints of modern historical consciousness, the wedge of difficulty is the same. Faith, we assume, spins in a different orbit from the real concerns and commitments of modernity. The teachings of the gospel stand at a distance, a distance that is the fault of a historical development beyond our control. The distance, we imagine, stems from the maturation of Western culture as a whole. Again, it is not a distance we create within ourselves.

I am increasingly convinced that this is a misdiagnosis, and not an innocent one, for we would rather not consider our real resistances to the gospel. Consider, for example, a passage from the epistle to the Romans in which St. Paul explains the faith that will be reckoned to us as righteousness. This faith is in "Jesus our Lord, . . . who was handed over to death for our trespasses and was raised for our justification" (Rom. 4:24–25). The vast amount of ink spilled over the question of belief in Jesus' resurrection misses the point. Is the difficulty of Christian faith a generic problem of believing the miraculous, the improbable, the extraordinary, or even the impossible? The standard Enlightenment story seems to force us to say that this is indeed the difficulty.

But is that really so? After all, we live in a stunningly credulous and uncritical age. Some people believe that the stock market will go up forever. Others hang on the every word of Hollywood celebrities when they preach about our moral obligations to animals. Not a few folks fervently believe that only a lack of sufficient funding prevents the success of welfare programs. Others believe that the market can solve all social problems. And such credulity is by no means a monopoly of the uneducated. The modern university is full of Ph.D.'s who believe in the sufficiency of naturalistic explanation. Still other professors enjoy an overwhelming moral certitude, and their accounts of history and current events easily parse as a battle of light against darkness, "genocidal cultures" against "liberative communities," "hegemonic practices" against "holistic worldviews."

In contrast, Christian salvation history seems the paragon of subtle attention to evidence. The more I have looked up from my books, so many of which take their cues from the standard Enlightenment story, and have paid attention to the strange world in which we live, the more I have come to see that believing the incredible hardly seems a difficulty in our day. However the role of faith has changed in contemporary culture—and surely it has—it does not seem to have been displaced by hard logic and reason.

What, then, *is* the difficulty of faith? Even if scholars are mistaken to think that the miraculous quality of the resurrection is the crux of the modern difficulty with faith, surely they are not wrong in assuming that Christian teaching has come under great pressure in recent centuries. So, assuming that the standard Enlightenment story is incorrect, what story should we tell? What is the appropriate context for thinking about the problem of belief in our age? If the problem is not relevance, then what is it?

Søren Kierkegaard makes a very pointed observation that suggests a way forward:

People try to persuade us that objections against Christianity spring from doubt. The objections against Christianity spring from insubordination, the dislike of obedience, rebellion against all authority. As a result, people have hitherto been beating the air in their struggle against objections, because they have fought intellectually with doubt instead of fighting morally with rebellion.[2]

Let us consider this observation for a moment. Kierkegaard was such a singular voice in the nineteenth century not just because he was a literary genius but also because he had a profound sense of how difficult Christianity is. His most famous book, *Fear and Trembling*, meditates on the collision of Abraham, the father of faith, with our normal sense of sane, responsible life. And this collision has nothing to do with evidence or argument. The collision is between Abraham's obedience and every other way in which we might conceive of living our lives. Abraham's scandal is moral—How could he ever set out to Mount Moriah to sacrifice his son in the first place?—not intellectual. We rebel against the specific form of Abraham's obedience. And, I might add, Kierkegaard suggests in *Fear and Trembling*, but never says, that the scene of obedience and sacrifice on Golgotha collides even more violently with our sensibilities than the story of Abraham and Isaac. For in the death of Jesus, the Father really *does* sacrifice the Son.

To the extent that Kierkegaard's meditation on Abraham ignores the Enlightenment way of posing the problem, he is inserting us into a very different interpretation of the difficulty of faith. For Kierkegaard, we do not turn away because of methodological, historical, or evidential doubts. The distance that makes faith seem remote and alien is not the result of an impersonal problem of cultural or intellectual relevance. Ours is a story of moral rebellion, of our recoil in horror, of our offended sensibilities. The distance is something we will for ourselves, and we do so in order to protect ourselves. Here Kierkegaard interprets the problem of faith in a way that should be called Augustinian. What we now think of as the standard story, the Enlightenment story of Western culture's awakening from faith to reason, replaced the Augustinian story. I want us to reconsider this replacement, because the Augustinian story casts a much more helpful light on the difficulties of faithfulness in our time.

A More Persuasive Analysis

St. Augustine's story is one of rebellion, self-wrought destruction, and divine deliverance. He tells it in his massive account of world history, the *City of God,* and of his own soul in the *Confessions.* I want to focus on the latter. There he illustrates how the transition from something so bad and self-destructive as sin to something so good and fulfilling as grace can be fraught with tension and travail.[3] The upshot is a strikingly clear and persuasive account of the intense resistance we put up against participation in that basic plot. He, more than any other early Christian writer, analyzes our rebellion against grace, our rejection of what is "for us." This rebellion and rejection has two crucial elements: a horror of dependence and a fear of difference. Both are defining features of our Petronian age.

Prideful self-sufficiency—or better, the prideful aspiration to self-sufficiency and the many fantasies that sustain that aspiration—is a major theme in St. Augustine's *Confessions.* He remembers as a child being intensely angry with adults "for not acting," as he says, "as though they were my slaves" (1.6). Of course we all quickly learn that angry tears do not make the world revolve around us, but as Augustine recounts, the educational system encourages grasping ambition, not only for riches but also for "a reputation among men" (1.9). If we cannot make people our slaves, at least we can make them our admirers. So Augustine goes off to make the world his admirer. First in North Africa and then in Italy, his ambition lashes him forward. Even his spiritual and intellectual life is driven by ambition, not so much for reputation as for the very possession of truth. And here he made God his slave. "Being subject to change myself," he confesses, "I preferred to think that you also were subject to change rather than I was not what you are" (4.15). Surely God is accessible and familiar. If not, then how we be fulfilled? Surely a saving truth must give us what we want. But what of Christian teaching? How can we be at the center of truth that is given rather than discerned? How can we find fulfillment under a condition of dependence to a God quite other than us?

These questions come to an excruciating point as Augustine's intellectual objections to Christianity begin to crumble. We can see how the horror of dependence is not based on Promethean ambition, not on a love of truth or loyalty to reason, but on an all too pinched and mean need for self-affirmation. After all, Augustine comes to see that Christian teaching is far more likely to be true than any of the alternatives in his world. And yet his vanity persists. He is willing to affirm the profound superiority of Jesus "as a man of the very highest wisdom" (7.18). In the shadow of such greatness, Augustine is willing to make Jesus his teacher. The most febrile dreams of world mastery are now in the past. Yet Augustine cannot submit to Jesus as his Savior, and the reason is concentrated in exactly what the gospel says is "for us." He cannot bring himself to lay hold of grace. "I was not humble enough," he writes, "to possess Jesus in his humility as my God, nor did I know what lesson was taught by his weakness" (7.19). And what is that lesson? We must put on his weakness; we must cast ourselves down in utter submission to the concrete form of God's divinity in the suffering and dying Jesus, so that we might rise with him (7.20). We must surrender ourselves in dependence upon the crucified Christ.

Here we cross over to the second of Augustine's difficulties, the one that is more fundamental, more controlling: the fear of difference. For all his well-known analysis of pride, Augustine did not describe his final barrier to faith in those terms. It was as if, convicted of his finitude, he became increasingly aware of his fragile hold on the petty principality that remained—his own self. Unable to possess God, Augustine begins to fear that he will be unable to possess himself. But this is too cryptic. We must return to Augustine's own account.

At first, change is very much Augustine's desire. He reads Cicero's praise of philosophy and commits himself to seek wisdom. He will leave behind the mundane world of falsehood and conform himself to truth. As he embarks on this project of discipline and transformation, Augustine's first brush with Christian teaching is a harbinger of his later, more painful struggles. Aflame with desire for truth, he rejects the usefulness of Scripture for his philosophical quest. It cannot compare to "the grand style of Cicero" (3.5). Scripture is far too crude a set of writings. It is entirely different from what the young Augustine thinks worthy of study and meditation. He wants to test his mind with different ideas, different writing, but not with something *that* different.

Augustine's early dismissal of Scripture is but a figure. The real threats of change did not begin to cut into him until after his crucial awareness that he could venerate Jesus as a teacher of wisdom from whom he might learn, but not as a Savior on the cross upon whom he must depend. Everything Augustine had learned about Christianity seemed to grow in plausibility. He seemed to be reaching the goal of his quest for truth. He seems a man transformed by the wisdom of apostolic teaching. "I no longer desire to be more certain of you," he writes of this time, "only to stand more firmly in you" (8.1). But he could not stand more firmly in the way of Jesus. "I was," he reports, "still reluctant to enter into its narrowness." Everything seemed right, but it involved so much, too much. As he reports, the problem was no longer pride; it was fear. "The nearer approached the moment of time when I would become different, the greater the horror of it struck me" (8.9). How could Augustine, how can any of us, survive such a basic personal change?

Augustine's account of the final travails of conversion dwell on this fear. Again and again in the crucial time before his conversion, Augustine begged to become different. He wished to be delivered from the "iron bondage" of his own will (8.5). He wished to be awakened from the numbing haze of his own sin. Yet like someone trying to sleep on Sunday morning, Augustine found himself saying, "A minute. Just a minute. Just a little while longer" (8.5). And recalling his youthful enthusiasm for Cicero's praise of philosophy and the zeal with which he had pledged to do and become whatever wisdom required, he was now overcome with the realization that from the very beginning he had never allowed himself to change. The motto of his youth was "Make me chaste and continent, but not yet" (8.7). This had been his thought from the very beginning, and now Augustine realized that for all his intellectual discoveries and personal insights, he had not changed at all. For all his desire to become different, it was a desire canceled by second thoughts. And how could he avoid such a cancellation? For the more one knows oneself a sinner, the more the escape from sin requires one to destroy oneself, and the more hope for salvation comes frighteningly close to a desire for death.

The dynamics of St. Augustine's conversion do not reassure any of us who might find ourselves sympathizing with his earlier horror of dependence and fear of difference. The division in his soul between the desire to be different and the fearful cry of "not yet" was resolved solely by external forces. The voices of children beyond a garden wall told him what to do. "Take it and read it," they said. Augustine had only to obey, and he did, but not by carefully selecting a passage that he might judge appropriate but by reading the first passage that met his eyes (8.12). The moving forces in this scene come from without. Through his dependence on what was simply given in that moment, Augustine entered into the weakness of submission that he had so feared. In no sense did he discover that he had misjudged the narrowness of the way. He could rise only as he fell upon the divinity of the obedient Son. Nor had Augustine been mistaken about the shock of difference. Real and dramatic changes followed in the wake of his submission. He renounced his planned marriage. He resigned his post as teacher of rhetoric. He began his journey back to North Africa, where he would die as a tireless servant of a world being conquered rather than as conqueror of the world. His mistake was only in thinking that the dependence diminishes and that the difference destroys.

If we wish to think about our age in Augustinian terms, then we must see that our difficulties stem from a rejection of the Christian promise of personal change. We should stop trying to meet these difficulties with demonstrations that Christian teaching really is plausible, or that the biblical text really is historically reliable, or that faith really does not place undue demands upon reason. Instead we should analyze our difficulties in the same way St. Augustine analyzed his own difficulties. At the most fundamental level, we rebel against the God of the Nicene Creed because we assume that dependence on another leads to dominion and diminishment, and a difference as profound as life promised in obedient suffering and death threatens the very basis of ordinary life.

Our Horror of Dependence and Fear of Difference

I cannot show that this Augustinian approach is the best story to tell about why the basic teachings of Christianity are so deeply controversial in our day, for that would entail retelling the history of modernity in some detail and demonstrating how the horror of dependence and the fear of difference more adequately explain important modern criticisms of Christian teaching than the standard Enlightenment story. However, David Hume offers a useful window on modern concerns. Far from a rational critic of Christianity, Hume is more adequately described as a moral critic. For Hume, Christianity is not too incredible; it is too dangerous. This reaction, I think, is rightly keyed to the Augustinian roots of our resistance to Christian teaching.

Among Hume's essays is a brief treatment of the corruptive forms of religion, "Of Superstition and Enthusiasm."[4] As Hume analyzes these "corruptions" he uses Augustinian patterns of thought. Superstition is most troubling to Hume, because it is a form of life based on propitiating dependence. To be sure, superstition is laced with false belief. However, neither the fantastical belief in cosmic powers and unseen agents that might afflict or rescue us nor the irrational anxiety we might have about life after death is the crux of matter. Of all the philosophers of the Enlightenment, Hume was most aware of the ubiquity of ignorance. His freethinking allies lived in a world of moral certitude and speculative fancy just as illusory as the traditional "three-story universe" of Christianity. Seeing this human propensity so clearly, Hume entertained an entirely realistic assessment of the role of ignorance and credulity in human life. He did not strive on behalf of an empire of reason. Instead Hume's philosophy is a sustained attempt to anchor our ignorance to humane patterns of thinking and behaving. As such, his criticism of superstition has far more to do with its inhumanity than with its irrationality. Superstition encourages a "gloomy and melancholy disposition," he writes, exalting supposedly suprahuman powers and persons above the weak and vulnerable human being.[5] This creates an atmosphere of dread and a feeling of unworthiness in which the only shred of hope seems to be in offering "mortifications, sacrifices, presents" to curry the favor of the divine.[6] Superstition is, at root, training in "tame and submissive" dependence, where the natural powers and initiative of the person atrophy and eventually disappear.[7]

This pattern of reasoning recurs many times in the history of modern engagements with traditional Christian claims that God does something "for us" that we cannot do for ourselves. Dogma, so this pattern reasons, violates the autonomy of the thinking person, compelling obedient assent rather than free inquiry. Commandments make us perpetual children of an authoritarian father rather than nurturing us to self-directing adulthood. Privileging Christ as savior distorts the diversity of religious experience by pressing it into a single mold. At each turn, the objections have little to do with what is reasonable or relevant and a great deal to do with the young St. Augustine's judgment that the narrow way of Christianity is a threat. It is not that we imagine ourselves geniuses. Rather, we fear compaction; we worry that the forces of authority and the path of obedience will reduce us to mechanized pawns, robots of faith.

I cannot even begin to suggest how one might respond to these objections. However, I do hope that when someone complains that the church should not require formal confessional commitments from its leaders because such a requirement would violate the "freedom of conscience," we can see that such an objection is best understood in light of the Augustinian story, not the Enlightenment story. The objection is not to a "three-storied universe" or to supernaturalism or to miracles. The objection is to the very idea that being a Christian depends upon anything other than what is going on inside one's head. It is an objection to dependence.

When we stop assuming that the standard Enlightenment story is correct and start paying attention to what people are saying, I think a great many objections reduce to this basic form: it is simply antihuman to think that the most important things in someone's life depend upon anything or anybody other than that individual person. The U.S. Supreme Court is anxious to protect my right to define the meaning of my own life. Surely God, so this reasoning concludes, must be just as vigilant.

Just as Augustine's resistance to grace is motivated by more than a horror of dependence, so also does Hume summarize for us another strand of the modern discomfort with Christianity, the fear of real difference. "Enthusiasm," for Hume, denotes the Christian tendency to get carried away. Filled with inspiration, the believer overreaches. In a frenzied desire to serve God, the faithful consecrate even the blindest and most violent impulses as God's will. We might say that under the sway of enthusiasm the catastrophic language of salvation that runs through the Scriptures takes on a personal and social reality. As Hume reports, "Enthusiasm produces the most cruel disorders in human society."[8] Hume is cautious. He mentions only the various excesses of the left wing of the Reformation as his examples. Yet the basic theme leaps out: Christianity unsettles, and it does so because it both commands and promises that people should and shall be different.

At work here is Augustine's other concern, his fear of the disruptive changes both promised and demanded by discipleship. Even as he hoped for that difference, the young Augustine feared the pain of change; he was altogether unsure whether committing himself to serve God would not set off a violent revolution in his soul in which a part that he still cherished would have to be destroyed.

We also find ourselves anxious about eruptions of social disorder. Names such as Jonestown and Waco evoke a dangerous extremism, and the media drumbeat of "Islamic fundamentalism" tempts us to assume that intense belief is dangerous. However, our inwardly turned culture tends to focus more on the cruel disorders that the redemptive aspiration of Christianity has produced in our psyches. For example, one can hear therapists describe us as suffering from a society overwrought with a Puritanical attitude toward sex. Even very distant echoes of traditional Christian teaching seem to inspire hand wringing about repression.

If I am right about the diagnostic superiority of the Augustinian story over the Enlightenment story, then objections to traditional Christian moral teachings are motivated far more by the fear of personal change than by considered examination of the sociological evidence, or by careful calculations of social utility, or by a disciplined reflection on the conditions for personal well-being. The objections boil down to shocked expression of dismay: Surely you cannot expect me to become different! Our goal is satisfaction and affirmation, not something so destabilizing as redemption.

The Relevance of the Gospel

It is extraordinarily important to realize that Christianity does not dismiss these difficulties; it claims to answer them. The horror of dependence, a signal feature of our culture, is based on an accurate intuition. From battlefield to factory floor, from feverish political rallies to the numbing cannonade of advertising, the past century has ground down many more persons then it has raised up. The fear of difference would seem equally justified. The twentieth century was one of final solutions and five-year plans. We can be forgiven if, like Hume, we find ourselves not wanting to tamper too much with the dry tinder of humanity for fear of a consuming fire. The excesses of aspiration suggest that we should seek an equilibrium of veniality, a life and a society that we can call healthy and normal even if we cannot describe it as pure and excellent.

Thus these difficulties, the horror of dependence and the fear of difference, have to do finally with us, with the brutality and darkness of our so very modern world and with our fragility and vulnerability as persons.

Given the cruel tyrannies and heartless "progress" of modernity, Christian teaching is difficult not because it is the alien imposition of an archaic and now irrelevant or anachronistic expression of the religious experience of ancient Mediterranean Jews and Gentiles. It is a flashpoint of controversy because it has to do with us, and at exactly those points where contemporary life threatens. Christian proclamation and the witness of faith swim in the channels of dependence and difference. The Gospel stories are quite straightforward on this point. Jesus of Nazareth has everything to do with the brutality and darkness of our world that make dependence such a frightful prospect. Caught in the machinery of worldly powers, broken on the difference between life and death, he certainly reveals rather than disguises our fragility and vulnerability. Thus even if we find ourselves unable to accept that such a man is "for us" in a way that saves, even the most resistant fiber in our bodies should be able to acknowledge that he is "for us" in the sense of being "about us." The Augustinian story allows us to see that the difficulty we face is hardly one of relevance; indeed we fear Jesus' relevance. The so-called problem of relevance that has dominated modern theology turns out to be a pseudo-problem conjured up to keep the crucified Lord at a safe distance to be navigated only by the hermeneutically authorized.

Christianity is terribly relevant, but we do not like what it has to say. This is the true difficulty of Christian doctrine. This is the root of our difficulties in reading the Bible. To recall Bultmann one more time, he thought that the greatest myth was that the Son of God became man for our sake and took upon himself suffering and death for our redemption; in his historical criticism Bultmann consistently explained the textual emphasis on Jesus' saving death as a latter editorial interpolation. But what is so mythological about Christ's dying for us? The airwaves are full of people promising to do things for us. If the idea of someone's being "for us" is too incredible for modern persons, then why does every car salesman reassure us that he is "on our side"? He does so because it works. No, we have no trouble believing that others can do things for our sake. But we have trouble with the seriousness and depth of the Christian claim that Christ died for us. Our difficulty is the narrowness of the way that made Augustine hesitate so long. The problem is that in doing so much for us, God's love demands far more of us than we would like, both far more dependence than we think worthy of our dignity and far more difference than we think ourselves able to endure.

Bultmann, like most modern theologians, was entirely right to assume that the single greatest task of theology is to show how the teachings of the apostles can be a living force in our world. The mistake of modern theology has been to think that this task grows out of an impersonal historical or scientific distance that separates Christian proclamation from the concerns of the modern world. Again, the task of rendering effective the Word of God is not the challenge of bridging the gap between the ancient text and the modern reader or between the agrarian values of Scripture and those of postindustrial society.

Here we need to be crystal clear. The distance that separates us from the gospel is spiritual. Thus the very real difficulty that modern theology senses but misdiagnoses is the challenge of bridging the gap between what we want and what God gives us. It is the difficulty of achieving the intellectual, moral, and communal disciplines sufficient to even imagine that dependence is not an assault on our dignity and that the difference of spiritual rebirth does not rend the delicate fabric of our humanity. These disciplines are crucial. For only when we draw near, overcoming the distance we will for ourselves in order to protect ourselves, are the changes promised in Christ realized.

4

The Radical
Orthodoxy Project

Abide in me as I abide in you. Just as the branch cannot bear fruit by itself
unless it abides in the vine, neither can you unless you abide in me.

John 15:4

Distance defines modern Christianity. Unable to participate in an integral life of natural and supernatural belief, civic and religious life, tem-
poral and eternal hope, the modern believer feels torn. If she is "conservative," then the expectations of modern life seem corruptive, and
in order to retain the integrity of faith, many features of contemporary
reality are kept at a distance. Home schooling, polemics against secular humanism, redoubled affirmations of doctrine—all fend off the invasion of modern life and leave room for the development of a traditional
faith. If he is "liberal," then this traditional faith seems archaic and
unconnected to everyday realities. "Revisioning," spiritual eclecticism,
endless numbers of books of so-called critical theology—these and
many other strategies parry the claims of a past orthodoxy in order to

make room for a new and putatively modern form of faith. In both cases, the defining experience is alienation. One is distant either from modern life or from traditional faith, and a great deal of theology and spirituality sets out to justify, even expand, that distance. One side seems to say, "The more recalcitrant and antimodern the piety, the better!" The other side responds, "The more revisionary and modern the theology, the better!"

Modern theologians break into rival schools, debating fiercely over the nature and origin of this chasm between traditional faith and modern life. I have already observed the way some depend upon an Enlightenment story that explains the distance as a natural upshot of scientific progress and rational maturity. The less sanguine can interpret this development as a prideful rebellion of humanity against all obedience. Still others advance theories about the baleful effects of "Cartesian rationalism."

Not only do theologians argue about causes, they also propose different ways forward. A certain kind of liberal will insist that the positive gains of modernity—freedom, critical thought, historical consciousness—must be used to bring out the deeper truths of Christianity. A mature age shall have a mature faith! Those who identify pride as the cause of distance often suggest a shock therapy that angers the liberal. The Word of God must be proclaimed with a clarity that forces choice. Will we be for the gospel or against it? The diagnosis of Cartesian rationalism usually leads to massive doses of romanticism. The deadening abstractions of the intellect shall be counteracted by the warm and life-giving truths of the heart.

The ins and outs of modern theology are important, especially if we wish to understand the theological trends that have dominated the past century of Western Christianity. However, this is not the place for historical retrospection. Instead we need to ask basic questions about our experience of distance and fragmentation. Should we allow the apparent rift between traditional Christianity and modern life to define our life of faith and the theology we practice? Is this distance real, or is it an illusion conjured up by modernity? Must the distance be traversed, or can we leap the chasm with a bold new initiative?

"Radical Orthodoxy" is a theological movement that asks and answers these questions, and its answers are as bold as the questions are basic. In the roughest terms, the radical orthodox reject the distance that defines modern theology. They insist that our alienation from traditional faith stems from a false and nihilistic view of reality. Against distance, Radical Orthodoxy insists that our deepest assumptions about reality, our sense of what makes things what they are, must have a participatory foundation. Things are by virtue of their shared intimacy, not separated isolation. For this reason, Radical Orthodoxy denies that distance must be traversed. A new vision, or better, a newly recovered classical vision, of Christian truth eliminates the chasm that defines much of modern theology. In this way Radical Orthodoxy proposes a genuinely postmodern theology, a theology not at all defined by the problem of distance.

Is Radical Orthodoxy successful? The achievement is uneven. For all the desire to overcome the modern fixation on the distances between "real life" and traditional faith, Radical Orthodoxy re-creates some of the typical patterns of modern theology. Liberal anxieties about the authoritarian closeness and potent particularity of the Christian redemptive vision reemerge. This raises a sobering thought: the modernist tradition and its fixation on distance cannot be overcome by a "new theology," however bold, however postmodern in style and vocabulary. The way forward is spiritual and ascetical, not intellectual and theoretical.

Understanding Postmodernism

Radical Orthodoxy is centered on a group of Cambridge-trained theologians well versed in the latest French poststructuralist theory. The three main figures of this group, John Milbank, Catherine Pickstock, and Graham Ward, have written severely technical and intellectually ambitious treatments of leading postmodern issues. Milbank's *Theology and Social Theory: Beyond Secular Reason* takes up the modern and postmodern construction and policing of an independent secular reality.[1] His essays in *The Word Made Strange* treat a wide range of philosophical, social, and theological concerns, all under the postmodern premise that "we make signs, yet signs make us and we can never step outside the network of sign-making."[2] Pickstock's *After Writing: On the Liturgical Consummation of Theology* contests modernist and postmodernist despair over the redemptive potency of language.[3] Ward's *Barth, Derrida and the Language of Theology* affirms the fundamental role of "discourse."[4] All three joined to edit a programmatic collection of essays, *Radical Orthodoxy: A New Theology*, and this volume, like the preceding books, is sedimented with layers of postmodern reflective habits.[5]

Because of their investment in the theoretics and rhetorics of postmodernism, we can easily imagine that the Radical Orthodoxy crowd is caught up in the postmodern tidal wave that has swept through university culture. The swagger is unmistakable. Pickstock, for example, sets out to overthrow "the sinister project of *mathesis* [spatial manipulation of knowledge],"[6] and *After Writing* begins with an extended skirmish with Derrida over the proper reading of Plato. Milbank's work is full of the jargon-laden sentences that give postmodernism its distinctive atmospherics. Like so much of postmodernism, Radical Orthodoxy promises to embrace finitude, "as language, as erotic and aesthetically pleasing bodies, and so forth," warning that "conservatives" may be dismayed by the joys of "excess."[7] Radical Orthodoxy appears to invite us to another night at the casino of cultural relevance. Get out your wallet. Christianity has never been this much fun.

But however deeply invested Radical Orthodoxy might be in the vocabulary, thought forms, and literature of postmodernism, it rests on a different foundational assumption about what we might call *the glue that holds the world together*. It is Augustine's vision of heavenly peace, made effective in the dynamic and binding power of divine purpose, not Nietzsche's postulate of violence wrought by an omnipotent will to power, that shapes the reflections of the radical orthodox. This difference allows Radical Orthodoxy to interpret postmodern thought without being drawn into its orbit, giving Milbank and company the perspective to expose the ways in which postmodern nihilism makes distance an inevitable mechanism of self-protection.

The best way to explain the Nietzschean postulate that governs postmodernism is to illustrate it. Consider this piece of glue that holds our world together: "Marriage is the union of a man and a woman." One of the signal postmodern convictions is that such a claim is contingent. What makes "marriage" mean "union of a man and a woman" is the fact that dictionaries define the word in such a way, not some underlying essence of "marriage" or an enduring "natural law." Dictionary definitions do not rest on an essential set of immediate truths. We define marriage as we do simply because, well, that is the way we define it. This bit of "glue," like all other bits, is an arbitrary act of will. The fact that we do indeed define words in certain ways is more fundamental than any other fact.

We can easily think that the postmodern conviction that language is arbitrary signals "relativism." Words such as *marriage*, we worry, cannot mean just anything; otherwise we cannot reliably talk about the world as something that holds a consistent shape, something glued together with reliability and constancy. Radical Orthodoxy rightly ignores this reaction to postmodernism, which turns out to be an existential anxiety—a modernist reaction to postmodernism that has little relevance to what postmodernists actually say. After all, the leading postmodern theorists such as Jacques Derrida and Michel Foucault are preoccupied with the fact that words *do* take on determinate meaning. They are concerned to understand "identity"—the fixity of so much of what we encounter in language and practice. They champion "difference" precisely because it is so easily veiled by our confidence in identity. Dictionaries, and the law courts, define marriage as the union of a man and a woman, and our lives are shaped accordingly. The glue is sticky.

The terminology and dialectics of postmodernism are daunting, but Radical Orthodoxy uncovers the basic line of its analysis: violence gives the world its shape and holds it together. Words have determinate meaning and therefore retain influence in our lives, argues postmodern theory, because their meanings are enforced by the exercise of power. Derrida's deconstructive project is devoted to exposing the many moments in which meaning is shaped. He observes, in endless examples culled from the history of philosophy, the ways in which key ideas that have effectively governed Western thought take on meaning because alternatives are repressed, hidden, and deferred. Words, and their stable meanings, are forged out of the flux of language. A blow of violence must be struck—"Marriage means *this* and not *that*."

But the single blow never settles the matter, so we must deploy constant reinforcement to maintain stable meanings. We hold our world together through an ongoing battle against the tendency of our ways of talking and thinking and acting to disperse into alternative possibilities. Identity is defended against difference by building moats and walls that keep the flux of possibility at a distance. Deconstruction, as an intellectual technique, is nothing more than "showing" the original blows and "exposing" the ongoing projects of reinforcement and defense of identity.

Foucault's explanations of the glue that holds our world together evoke a more conspiratorial atmosphere, but the underlying explanation of stability and identity is the same. Social networks of power and interest shape language, society, and even human consciousness. Fixed patterns of meaning are carved into the raw material of our humanity. Our definition of marriage, for example, is part of an elaborate system of repression. What does not fit the mold is cordoned off and separated from society with words like *abnormal* and *immoral*. Foucault's analysis, then, explains why we are not in fact, relativists. Under the impress of power, our world takes on determinate shape and hardened identity. Violent and malicious power is the glue that holds our world together. A Leviathan, impersonal and dispersed across any number of social practices, fixes identity.

Out of this central claim comes the brutally political nature of the postmodern moral agenda. If power defines marriage as the union of a man and a woman, then power can change that definition. Not coincidentally, postmodern theoreticians are eager to exert power: to urge the judiciary to bring to bear the force of the state, to compel curricular changes, to enforce codes of speech. With enough redirection of power, they assume, marriage can come to mean the union of two persons of the same gender. A blow was struck in one direction; a blow can be struck in another. The arbitrary violence of conventional meanings is met by the new violence of postmodern revision. So professors denounce, the role of homosexuality in antiquity is willfully distorted and misrepresented, and the entire university tries to shame the recalcitrant into conformity or to cast them out.

Not surprisingly, then, distance defines much of life. Identity must be protected, and dictionaries ensure the stability of words by lifting them out of everyday usage and giving them official definitions. Nothing about postmodern theory discourages this distance. Deconstruction unmasks the process but redoubles the necessity for each of us to dig moats and build walls of defense. If my identity is to endure, I must lift myself out of the play of differences; I must find a way to cordon off and defend myself against the blows that make things mean first one thing and then, with another blow, something else. Just as Plato disguised and mystified the embedded and unstable nature of his key philosophical terms, I must push away the contingency of my life in order to maintain a clear and distinct sense of self. Distance becomes a strategy of defense against the powers that inevitably wish to reforge my identity.

Overcoming Violence

Faced with the postmodern premise that violence and power are the basis for identity, the glue of that holds things together, Radical Orthodoxy never blinks. Governed by an Augustinian rather than Nietzschean vision, it has no reason to trim and disguise the nihilism of dominant postmodern theory. The dialectical gymnastics designed to make "progressive" violence into the more winsome principle of "difference" are nothing more than a theoretical effort by postmodernism to repress and defer its own assumptions. "The play of differences" can sound like good clean schoolyard fun, but postmodern theory more often recalls the battlefield and penitentiary. An honest Nietzschean acknowledges that the "peace" and "stability" of society, personal identity, and textual meaning are born of domination, and he does not try to disguise this truth with happy-clappy labels such as "aesthetic individualism"—unless, of course, such deceptions serve *his* will to power. The deconstructors find themselves, to their surprise, led by their own metaphysics of identity and difference into the machine of deconstruction.

Radical Orthodoxy does little more than draw aside the curtain that hides this procedure from the view of postmodern fellow travelers. For Radical Orthodoxy, then, Derrida need not be made into a savior nor

Foucault a saint. In the fevered world of contemporary cultural and literary studies, *that* is something different.

Unblinking opposition is possible because, for Radical Orthodoxy, violence and the power of dominion are not necessary premises to explain why the world is stable, why identity emerges out of difference. "For theology, and theology alone," writes Milbank, "difference remains as real difference, since it is not subordinate to immanent univocal process or the fate of a necessary repression."[8] For example, we can study the history of marriage and observe that Christianity substantively changed its meaning by assimilating the relation of men and women to the relation of Jesus Christ to the church. Yet we need not conclude that such change amounted to a contest of power. Things can be understood and inhabited across change and difference without submission to power and dominion.

Christian theology counters the Nietzschean nihilism of foundational violence (in the language Radical Orthodoxy borrows from postmodernism) by advancing a participatory framework, an analogical poetics, a semiosis of peace, a metanarrative that does not require the postulate of original violence. Put more simply, Radical Orthodoxy hopes to recover neo-Platonic metaphysics as an explanation for the glue that holds the world together. Something can be what it is—a unit of semantic identity or meaning, a person, a social practice—and at the same time depend upon and reach toward something else. Or more strongly, something is real only in and through this constitutive dependence and fecundity. For the neo-Platonist, you, or I, or the value of my moral acts, or the meaning of this chapter *is* as emanating from and returning to the One. Distance and all the strategies of defending identity are not at all necessary. Quite the contrary, the *closer* something is to the One, the more *real* it becomes.

For Radical Orthodoxy, the particular neo-Platonic hierarchies of being, Being, and "beyond Being" are not decisive. What matters is the way neo-Platonism treats the world as a differentiated realm of beings and events knit together, not in spite of or against the discrete identities of things but in harmonious order and toward a common purpose. This view, which Radical Orthodoxy consistently argues is advanced and intensified by classical Christianity (especially by Augustine), operates outside the contrastive logic of identity and difference. Identity is neither a wound in the flux of difference nor a vulnerable citadel to be defended. Dynamism and difference—"I am coming from and going toward . . ."—constitute identity. The glue is sticky, but it never dries.

This sounds very abstract, a dialectical posturing that defines the Christian, participatory alternative simply by negation. The reader is tempted into this interpretation, for the typical style of a Radical Orthodoxy essay tends toward poetical-dialectical constructions of antithesis. For example, Milbank announces that theology must elaborate a "meta-narrative of counter-historical interruption of history," a "counter-ethics" and "counter-ontology."[9] But unlike the postmoderns and their continued and very modern dependence upon violence and power, the Radical Orthodoxy crowd promotes a vision of peace. Against the nihilistic conflict between identity and difference, Radical Orthodoxy offers harmonious identity in difference.

Radical Orthodoxy, then, does not reject modern and postmodern assumptions about the foundational role of violence only to exist as a negative critique, dependent upon postmodernism for its *raison d'être*. The neo-Platonic framework so warmly recommended by Radical Orthodoxy offers a theory of identity and meaning based on peace. Consider the role of liturgy as an incorporating force. In an extended meditation on the dynamics of eucharistic celebration, Pickstock wishes to show that the Roman Rite of the Mass is a complex combination of giving and receiving in which the human subject remains identifiable even when incorporated. We need not become "not selves" in order to receive the body and blood of Jesus Christ, nor can we remain simply "ourselves," unchanged and unaltered. (The neo-Platonic note is struck.) Christian liturgical practice assumes that we can be ourselves *and* be enrolled in the drama of redemption. We can participate without either abandoning our identity or guarding it against divine dominion. The glue that holds us together as discrete individuals with personal projects is the same glue that holds us together as a community in common worship. The one intensifies rather than diminishes the other.

This element of liturgy as participation in a divine community has a political and social analogue. Since nothing exists outside the embrace of divine purpose, the Christian vision necessarily gathers up the diverse aspects of human life into its analysis, looking toward a transformed way of living. As Milbank details so effectively in *Theology and Social Theory*, modern attempts to designate a social reality underneath or outside our participation in God's consummating revelation in Christ rest in a primal violence. Distance is the creature of renunciation—"*This* part of human life, the natural, the secular, God shall not have!" In this way does modernity disentangle "real social analysis" from theology. Because God gives himself to us, this designation of the merely human as the proper object of inquiry must always take the form of resistance. To build our earthly city, to identify a "natural human being" on which to base moral and political analysis, we must deform and destroy our actual humanity, which has been created for citizenship in the heavenly city.

Against these efforts to carve out a place free from divine purpose Milbank argues for a conception of social reality governed by the supernatural vocation of fellowship with God. Nothing exists outside this vocation, yet this vocation vindicates and fulfills rather than corrupts our condition as natural, rational, and social beings. Our identity in embodied existence, rational discourse, and corporate life is the same as our identity with God. The one reinforces rather than weakens the other, and we are more ourselves the closer we are to God, not the more distant.

This ambition on behalf of the incorporative scope of redemption explains Radical Orthodoxy's self-designation as "Augustinian." The proponents of Radical Orthodoxy do not simply use the heavenly city as a gesture by which to escape from the dead ends of postmodernism. They want to substitute a Christian and participatory account of the glue that holds the world together for the postmodern and violent account. Only then can theology escape from the gravitational pull of the postmodern commitment to power and violence. Once Radical Orthodoxy escapes, under the guidance of a metaphysics of participation, its proponents can show how the diverse features of human life find fulfillment in God's consummating purposes. The way is open to recover and reconstitute a comprehensive Christian vision.

One of the tragedies of modern theology has been its systematic renunciation of this ambition. The deep end of truth has been ceded to science, while theology swims in the shallow end of "meaning." Aesthetic expression has been relinquished to the cult of original self-expression and "what it means for me." Morality becomes a subset of utility or a creation of private conscience, and Christians are reduced to "sharing their values." An impoverished realm of "spirituality" or "transcendence" remains the rightful property of Christian reflection, and running on these slight fumes, theology drives toward relevance in a world over which it has renounced authority. Radical Orthodoxy is intensely opposed to this renunciation; the whole world is fit for absorption into a theological framework. Christian theology should shape the way we talk about everything. Nothing should be kept at a distance.

Scope, however, is not the only Augustinian ambition lost in modern theology. For every metaphysical, historical, and anthropological adventure of speculation, Augustine devoted even more energy to affirming and defending the irreducible *particularity* of divine redemption in Christ. The scope may be wide but the center is focused, and the pull of the gravity of Christ is profoundly strong. The world is participatory, true enough, but its participatory framework is Christ-formed. The proponents of Radical Orthodoxy embrace the universal scope of Augustinian ambition—redemptive purpose structures the natural world, history, human desire and vision, and truth itself. Like many modern theologians, however, they often express a deep ambivalence about the concrete particularity of Augustinian ambition and the authority it exerts over the Christian life. To this ambivalence we must turn.

The Return of the Modern

Time and again, Radical Orthodoxy blocks any center of gravity from acquiring weight sufficient to control or direct our participation in God. For example, when Milbank engages the biblical text, he consistently translates the particular sense into a conceptual or speculative process. The Gospel stories are for him allegories of a participatory metaphysics. As we grasp this theoretical truth, we come to see how we are "co-creators" of revelatory meaning.[10] Our "analogizing capacity is itself 'like God,'" and instead of being addressed by God, "we have to discover the content of the infinite through labour, and creative effort."[11]

The same implicit repudiation of authoritative particularity occurs when Milbank identifies the church as a process rather than as a tradition of first-order language and practice. The church is at root "a new social body which can transgress every human boundary, and adopts no law in addition to that of 'life' . . . [and] is attendant upon a diverse yet harmonious, mutually reconciling community."[12] Whether the focus rests on Scripture, creed, or tradition, a certain "ideality" seems to govern, a tendency to think theologically in terms of higher, purified, and untainted forms. A formal claim, a "way of being," supersedes the determinate particularity of apostolic teaching and practice.

Milbank's struggle with the doctrine of the atonement illustrates this tendency more precisely. In *Theology and Social Theory* he provides a determinedly conceptual reading of the redemptive significance of Jesus. "After Jesus' death our redemption becomes possible, for two reasons," Milbank reports. "First, we speculatively grasp that sin is negation, arbitrary violence, the refusal of pure love itself, and this speculation is an *indispensable* and yet independent moment of faith." The second element is an equally postmodern combination of theory and rhetoric. "The speculation is only occasioned," observes Milbank, "by the horrifying and sublime compulsion of Jesus's death, whose concrete circumstance makes us feel that here we really 'see' sin, and at the same time the essence of human goodness." Jesus makes possible a reflective pattern, and his life is redemptive because the determinate features of his life stimulate us to "speculatively grasp" that pattern. Only in this "speculative grasp" do we come to inhabit "the idiom, the *logos* of adequate return," and through our adoption of this "idiom," through our "speculative grasp" and consequent new way of thinking and living, *we* make atonement universal.[13]

"Speculative grasp" suggests a general tendency in Radical Orthodoxy to substitute the creative production of theological theory for the redemptive power of Christ. In an essay interpreting the canonical witness to Jesus' saving power, "The Name of Jesus," Milbank explicitly turns from person to process, from the identity of Jesus to an ideality created by his absence. Milbank begins this essay by reading the Gospel stories as internally divided. On the one hand, Jesus is the man who proclaims the coming kingdom of God. On the other hand, we encounter what Milbank calls a "metanarrative" that concentrates on the sacrificial economy of Jesus' rejection, suffering, and death.[14] Viewed carnally, the narrative simply fails, as these elements conflict with each other, leaving Jesus dispersed between the narrative and the "metanarrative," between the historical and the cultic.

But Milbank does not read carnally. He reads spiritually, speculatively. Far from failure, the dispersal of Jesus' identity is the key to salvation. The inability of the text to identify Jesus opens up space for reconstituted human community. The absence of a savior in the text creates the need for us to construct a savior in and through our own interpretive practice. This allows, then, for participatory atonement: the ecclesial practice of unending exegetical openness in which the church creates a savior in and through its interpretive creativity. In this way Jesus saves as the "founder of a practice/state of being," and thus the ecclesial process "must be God himself."[15]

In his contribution to the *Radical Orthodoxy* collection of essays, Ward develops a view similar to Milbank's. For Ward, Jesus' "displaced body" renders him absent, opening up space for "a participation in and through difference that enables a co-creativity."[16]

What is going on here? Radical Orthodoxy is very clear: it wishes to renounce the compromises and half-measures of modern theology and recover an Augustinian boldness on behalf of Christian faith and practice. Yet Milbank's attempts to explain our participation in Christ's redemptive power are easily folded back into modern theology. A passing acquaintance with standard modern views allows us to see that the "poetic atonement" effected "by the horrifying and sublime compulsion of Jesus's death" echoes Kant's account of Jesus' redemptive significance. Milbank's "speculative grasp" may spin with a theoretical rotation, but the relation of Christ to believer differs not at all from Kant's account of the rational will aroused by Jesus, who is the sensuous manifestation of the archetype of moral rectitude. Further, Milbank's "atonement by absence" mirrors Hegel's dialectic. The identity of Christ is lost only to be recovered in the ongoing career of Spirit. To be sure, Milbank's "speculative grasp" is linguistic and enacted, not conceptual in the old-fashioned and purely intellectual way. Nonetheless, for Milbank the purported failure of Scripture to render Jesus present as an identifiable person is the key to its success. Jesus' absence allows for unending interpretive potency and the "blending of differences" that characterizes the salvific process.

This easy plotting of Milbank's accounts of atonement onto two seminal modern thinkers is crucial. The Kantian and Hegelian views of Jesus' saving role lead to two important consequences. First, the fulfillment of a human possibility—the turn to righteousness (for Kant) and the development of culture (for Hegel)—becomes the true source of redemptive potency. In the wake of this turn to a human source, modernity and postmodernity turn toward power. As we lose confidence in a singular voice of conscience or a universal cultural teleology, my conscience wars against yours, and we fight for control of the cultural process. The other consequence of Kantian and Hegelian soteriology is to encourage the alienation from scriptural authority and rejection of the binding constraints of apostolic practice that are common in modern theology. Kantian rectitude or Hegelian history of Spirit supersedes the apostolic language and practice as the font of theological truth, just as they surpass the incarnate form of Jesus by completing and perfecting his redemptive potency. The potency of moral choice (Kant) or a speculative grasp the dynamics of history (Hegel) eclipses the identity of Christ, after which modernity and postmodernity come into their own. Generation after generation of biblical critics and liberal theologians try to pierce the veil of the literal sense of Scripture in order to wrest its meaning from inherited orthodoxy and ecclesiastical authority.

The "new theology" proposed by Radical Orthodoxy repeats the patterns of modern theology, with similar consequences. The articles of Milbank, Ward, et al. have the effect of obscuring and superseding the particular identity of Jesus Christ as the mediator of salvation. As a consequence, they demonstrate an overall ambivalence about the role of Scripture, creed, and inherited ecclesial practice that moves in a modernist direction. Authority shifts out of the particularity of Word and sacrament and into a supervening theory or concept. To be sure, the theory or concept is a practice, an inhabited language, rather than a static idea. Nonetheless, however modified with appropriate postmodern twists and turns, the "speculative grasp" that lives in the generative practices of "reconciling differences" is more perspicuous, more redemptively potent, than the particular form of Christ present in Word and sacrament. "New Being" replaces the crucified and risen Lord as the glue that holds all things together.

Temptations of the Ideal

How could this collapse into modern theology happen? The usual explanation is straightforward. The proverbial educated believer cannot reconcile the pieties of her childhood with the critical methods and realities of modern life. Scientific explanation seems to require a thoroughgoing materialism, transforming spiritual concerns into echoes of social practices, reflections of psychic needs, or simple glandular oddities. Historical inquiry inculcates a skeptical temper at odds with the accepting embrace of faith. Ideals of personal autonomy conflict with traditional patterns of religious conformity and obedience. For modern theology, the job of the theologian is to demonstrate that modern methods and realities do not really conflict with Christianity, properly understood. In short, the modern theologian must "mediate," must show how the educated believer can inhabit both worlds, religious and secular, without loss, without divided loyalty.

Radical Orthodoxy's slide toward the standard moves of modern theology cannot be explained in this usual way. Its relentless critiques of modernity and postmodernity block any such strategy of mediation. Milbank and company want to replace the presumptions of secularity with a Christian account of everything: no distances here across which to correlate. What, then, should we think? Radical Orthodoxy remains loosely put together, defined by strong intuitions and theological thought experiments and lacking a systematic gestalt. The essays collected in the Radical Orthodoxy volume, for example, range widely both in tone and in topic, combining Roman Catholic and Anglican authors who evidence divergent sensibilities, so that generalizations are dangerous. Yet I can offer a nonstandard explanation for the allergy to the particular that makes Radical Orthodoxy paradigmatically modern when handling such crucial theological questions as atonement. It is an explanation that should caution us about the dangers and difficulties of a *radical* orthodoxy of any sort.

The three leading figures of Radical Orthodoxy—Milbank, Pickstock, and Ward—are Anglican, deeply influenced by the piety and practice of Anglo-Catholicism, and this encourages them to replace particularity with theory, identity with ideality. Let me explain. Anglo-Catholicism was born out of profound dissatisfaction with modern Anglicanism, and for complex cultural and theological reasons this dissatisfaction could not come to rest in conversion to the Roman Catholic Church. This put Anglo-Catholicism in a difficult position. By conviction, Anglo-Catholics were committed to tradition. Yet by their thinking, predominant Anglican practice could not provide an adequately rich, catholic tradition, and the Roman Church, as currently constituted, could not provide an adequate institutional basis for faithfulness to the tradition. Therefore a tradition had to be invented.

Of course this invention was denied. Anglo-Catholicism is characterized by an extensive archaeology of patristic and medieval texts and endless recoveries of Catholic-leaning figures in early Anglicanism, as well as extensive borrowings from post-Tridentine Roman theology and sacramental practice. Yet however ancient the pieces, however venerable the raw material, the actual structure and form of Anglo-Catholicism emerged out of an idealized picture of catholic faith and practice. It had to turn to the ideal, for the actual and particular forms of Christian practice—established Anglicanism as well as Roman Catholicism—were inadequate.

Radical Orthodoxy inherits this pattern of ideality. Its theoretical impulse does not serve the usual modernist purpose of finding a pivot point on which to correlate or mediate across the distance between Christ and culture. Instead the drive toward a "speculative grasp" serves to discern the ideal form of Christian truth, to find a basis from which one can faithfully invent a tradition free from the limitations and imperfections of inherited forms. By their own description, the proponents of Radical Orthodoxy are "radical" in just this sense. "Re-envisioning" is required because, we are told, "Christianity has *never* sufficiently valued the mediating participatory sphere which alone can lead us to God."[17] Just as Anglo-Catholicism could not inhabit an inherited tradition—neither Canterbury nor Rome—Radical Orthodoxy cannot receive a theological tradition, at least not directly. The Christian metaphysic must be discerned, the participatory sphere (which *alone* can lead us to God?) must be uncovered, and under the guidance of this ideality, theological imagination and creative theoretical production will perfect and complete that which has been received. Thus the redemptive potency of the Christian witness is unlocked and realized.

The Anglo-Catholic heritage both highlights and explains the proximate basis for the turn to ideality, but Radical Orthodoxy does not simply reproduce a feature of Anglo-Catholicism. It manifests, with an intensified urgency, a problem facing postmodern theology in general. Because mainline Protestant churches are now liberal by tradition, orthodox theological practice becomes an invention, a determined culling from the past, an act of imaginative recovery. For example, Milbank, Pickstock, and Ward wish to recover the confident, comprehensive voice of Augustinian neo-Platonism, a theological vision bold enough to claim all aspects of life as ordered toward God. But as a painful matter of fact, over the last two centuries Anglicanism has been marked by retreat, concession, and diminished confidence. Educated at Cambridge University, in the residue of the past glories of a Christian intellectual, aesthetic, and political culture, the proponents of Radical Orthodoxy find reminders of the scope of Augustinian ambition. But monuments are not living institutions, and Gothic buildings are no substitute for enduring practices. Radical Orthodoxy cannot invent the flesh and blood of a Christian culture and so must be satisfied with describing its theoretical gestalt, gesturing, in postmodern fashion, toward that which was and might be.

In itself this determined resistance to the retreat of the church and the secularization of culture is noble. Radical Orthodoxy *should* attract the attention, and affection, of anyone committed to the power of the gospel. But in the theological practice of "re-envisioning," the modern solutions to the problem of distance reemerge. The theologian is a heroic redeemer, a visionary, a genius. Intellectual virtuosity eclipses ecclesial obedience as the key to renewal. Theology becomes creative and inventive rather than receptive and reiterative.

Intensely sensible of the failures of the modern church and its modern theology, the proponents of Radical Orthodoxy seek to render Christian truth so perspicuous, so clear and evident at the level of theory, that the nihilistic temptation of secularity will be impossible and Radical Orthodoxy's peaceful consequences will be made plain. Here, without doubt, they are driven by ambition: if the actual practice of the churches in our time fails to make the truth of the gospel potent and clear, then theologians, theoretical shepherds of the speculative grasp, shall.

But this ambition is not Augustinian; it is, I would submit, a quintessentially modern ambition to solve the problem of distance with a leap of metaphysical insight. Living in the ruins of the church, Radical Orthodoxy is tempted to transfer loyalty from the *concreta Christiana* to an ideal. That ideal is, to be sure, Christ-formed, but it is not incarnate.

Our Task

If we understand our theological vocations as in and for the church, and if we see and regret and decry the vulnerability of much of Western Christianity to the nihilistic temptations of secularity, then how can we not feel the same ambition? How can we not find ourselves in the same position as Radical Orthodoxy, wanting to "re-envision" Christianity, not to make the capitulation to "science" or "modern realities" easier but to intensify resistance, to put backbone into the church, to make theology *foundationally* antimodern? How can we avoid becoming Anglo-Catholics, not in substance but in ecclesial location and theological practice: alienated from the vast body of our liberal churches, trying to find an ideality under which we can receive and pass on a faith that our churches no longer have the confidence, will, or even basic scriptural and liturgical competence to give us?

Radical Orthodoxy should serve as a warning. The drive toward a "speculative grasp" is no quirk of postmodernism, no oddity of an Anglo-Catholic legacy. It is the habit of any theology alienated from the concrete and particular shape of the contemporary church. For generations, modern theologians felt alienated because of the apparent disjunction between the moral, intellectual, and political imperatives of "progressive thought" and the constraints of classical Christianity. The upshot was a conceptual redescription of Christianity designed to allow for correlation and mediation across this disjunction.

Now a similar alienation seems to be forced upon orthodox theology by the failures of Western Christianity. Christian faith and practice no longer seem to live up to the gospel. But just as the modern alienation led to a theological abstraction from apostolic teaching, so also does an orthodox alienation now tempt us. For if, like Radical Orthodoxy, we accept this disjunction, the consequences echo modern theology: Christian faith and practice must be raised to a level of purified abstraction so that they can be saved from their own failure to make Christ present in the church and in society. But as Milbank's treatments of atonement show, such a move returns to modernist patterns and obscures the particular identity of Jesus Christ. In the end Christ is absent, and only the high labors and creative vision of the theologian can recover his identity and make him present. His identity must be held together with the sticky glue of the "speculative grasp."

Anglicanism has no monopoly on failure. To a great extent the magisterial Protestant churches in Europe and North America, and to a lesser extent Roman Catholicism, have been diminished. Those of us bitten by the Augustinian ambition cannot help but war against that diminishment and its institutional acceptance, even embrace. However, in protest, we must recognize how difficult and narrow is the way of a postmodern recovery of orthodoxy.

Many offer courageous and articulate warnings against the modern "culture of death," and Christian witness does provide an alternative that has weight and substance. Nonetheless, no triumphant vision of peace emerges out of what early-twenty-first-century Christians actually say and do. Christianity, its holy Scriptures, and its ecclesial practice seem unable to hold all things together. Against the weakness of the gospel—in churches that seem not to hear and in a culture increasingly blind—we are tempted by theory. We imagine that by sheer theological genius and intellectual virtuosity we can reconstruct an all-embracing Christian culture, we can uncover and make present the glue that holds everything together. But guided by what might be rather than what is, we come to correct and perfect that which we have received in Word and sacrament. As the editor's blue pencil excises and adds, violence and will to power reemerge. We re-create the distance we wish to overcome as we turn to apostolic teaching and practice with an eye to improvement, correction, and enhancement. If it is weak, then *we* will make the gospel strong. Our theorizing, our "new theologies," will hold together what Christ and his church seem unable to encompass and embrace.

Against this temptation we must keep our noses close to the ill-smelling disaster of modern Christianity, articulate about its failures but training ourselves to dwell in enduring forms of apostolic language and practice. Diminished vision may be the price we must pay. We may no longer be able to see our culture, stem to stern, through Christian eyes. We may no longer be able to see the complex shape of our contemporary churches as a creature of the gospel. We can see only what has been given to us to see. But paying this price is necessary if we are to train our eyes to see the identity of Christ in the witness of Scripture and the practice of the church. For no matter how high we might soar on eagle's wings of theological ideality, and despite our hopes that from such heights we might recover a vision of the full scope of the truth of Christ, we will be disappointed. Christ is in the concrete faith and practice of the church, and only he can give power and potency to a postmodern theology that is genuinely orthodox. The Son holds all things together in the Father.

Thus to escape the patterns of theological modernism, the first task is not to imagine and invent, for this opens up a distance between us and the concrete and enacted forms of our apostolic inheritance. Instead we must train ourselves in that which modernity rejects most thoroughly and fatally: the disciplines of receiving what has been given. We must eat the scrolls that the Lord has given us and dwell amidst his people. Only then will the scope of an Augustinian ambition recover the intense, concrete, and particular Christ-centered focus that gives it the power of good news. Only there, amidst walls ruined by faithlessness, apathy, and sin, can we taste God's peace.

A Church
in Ruins

5

The Theological Vocation
in the Episcopal Church

Judah mourns
   and her gates languish;
[her people] lie in gloom on the ground;
   and the cry of Jerusalem goes up.
Her nobles send their servants for water;
   they come to the cisterns,
they find no water,
   they return with their vessels empty.

Jeremiah 14:2–3

Because theological vision is based upon intimacy with the concrete life of the church, in order to understand the theological vocation we need to come to terms with the difficult situation we face. Without a doubt, the ecclesial working conditions of theology are inauspicious. Denominationalism reinforces divisions in the church. Theological liberalism continues to squander the capital of corporate memory with its many schemes of so-called relevance. Liturgical revision threatens to swing public worship in ideological directions. As corporate and legal models predominate, collective decision making has come unhinged from any distinctively Christian basis. It is not a pretty sight, and one can be excused for drifting toward ideality or theory as the way to reformulate a healthy and vital Christian witness.

However understandable, this drift must be resisted. The theological vocation is grounded in the common life of the body of Christ, and in the church we find the living form of apostolic language and practice. For this reason the first task of theology is clear. We must remain as close to the reality of the church as possible. We must resist temptations to stand at a distance, and this includes the temptation to leap toward a clear and forceful orthodoxy that we might imagine or hypothesize. Only by remaining close to ecclesial life do our theological vocations avoid the subtle (and sometimes not so subtle) turn toward serving the university, an ideology, private spiritual needs, and our own speculative fantasies.

What, then, should we say about the church on which our theological vocations depend? Here we need to be careful. We find ourselves embedded either in a particular church or in none at all. Therefore, to work within the common life of the church entails working within a denominational tradition. My tradition is Anglican, and it takes denominational form in the United States as the Episcopal Church. It is this specific church—not Methodism, not Presbyterianism, not Roman Catholicism—that must be my focus. I am sure that trends in the Episcopal Church characterize a great deal of American Christianity, especially the formerly "mainline" Protestant denominations. But I must work from the specific to the general. In this way I hope to cast some light on the shape and challenge of a theological vocation in the twenty-first century.

I will structure my remarks around the four elements of ecclesial life that a classic Anglican formulary, the Chicago-Lambeth Quadrilateral, identifies as fundamental: Scripture, the Nicene Creed, the historic episcopate adapted to local conditions, and the sacraments of baptism and Eucharist. I will suggest that the first three of these elements no longer function effectively and that the fourth functions potently but ambiguously. In order to better understand why these "fundamentals" are dysfunctional, I will offer some diagnostic suggestions. I will conclude with a brief assessment of the consequences of my description and diagnosis for the theological vocation.

A Descriptive Sketch

Scripture may play a very important role in the personal piety of any number of Episcopalians, and it may continue to be honored as holy, but at present the Episcopal Church has no functional tradition of theological exegesis. Very few institutional decisions are justified, even *pro forma*, by appeal to Scripture. Why this is so is a complex matter. Certainly in part it stems from the fact that the critical reading taught at seminaries is itself internally diverse and marked by an intense scholarly debate that, ironically, makes "objective" exegesis highly subjective. How is one to choose between various historical-critical readings? The fade of Scripture into the distant horizon of church life is also bound up with an overall decline in biblical literacy. One can by no means presume knowledge of Scripture among laity or clergy.

But biblical illiteracy and historical-critical lack of consensus are not in themselves the most profound evidence of the dysfunction of Scripture in the Episcopal Church. More important is the fact that in the increasingly bitter atmosphere of ecclesiastical controversy, when exegetical claims do enter into the public discourse of the church, they evoke denunciation. Traditional, precritical readings are vigorously attacked as "fundamentalist," and critical readings are repudiated as motivated by revisionist ideology. What the Chicago-Lambeth Quadrilateral identifies as a sign of the church universal is often experienced, then, as a sign of the church divided and at war with itself. Scripture and its interpretation are points of contestation and confusion, not consensus and clarity.

This drives the church away from Scripture. Insensibly, but with increasing force, one begins to think that Scripture is part of our problem. So, for example, a rather plain vanilla affirmation of biblical authority made at the 1998 Lambeth Conference was put forth at a later General Convention of the Episcopal Church. It was viewed by most as a vote on the homosexuality issue (or even more complexly, as a vote about African denunciations of American attitudes toward homosexuality). That moment was not atypical. Scripture is now significant primarily as a contested element in power politics. Not surprisingly, then, we begin to turn elsewhere for the Word of God that unifies. Whether spirituality or crisis management techniques, abstract theological speculation or philosophical reflection, something besides Scripture becomes the key to moving forward. For this reason I think it incontestable that the visible life of the Episcopal Church has become fundamentally detached from scriptural reading, and thus Scripture has no significant theological role in our common life.

The second element of the Chicago-Lambeth Quadrilateral, the Nicene Creed, evokes less controversy, and its role is more ambiguous. One of the great proponents of "incarnationalism" and the seminal spokesman for liberal Catholicism, Charles Gore, made a case for accepting a historical-critical reading of Scripture while preserving the supervening authority of the ecumenical creeds to constrain that reading. He failed in his efforts to meld creedal authority with historical-critical exegesis, but he did succeed in perpetuating a general Anglican tendency to conform to ancient formularies. As a matter of fact most Episcopalians, both lay and clerical, are inclined to subscribe to the fundamental theological categories of patristic thought that shape the ecumenical creeds.

This is all for the best, and we should be grateful that a lot of mid-twentieth-century silliness about "Greek metaphysics" and "the three-tiered universe" no longer creates false crises of conscience among most priests and laypeople. However, the creeds serve as an epitome of Scripture and an authoritative exegetical framework. Therefore to the extent that the Nicene Creed is severed from relationship to a living tradition of theological exegesis, it is difficult to see how such a linguistic artifact can function in the life of the church.[1] And given the eclipse of Scripture, the creed has little influence. Our loyalty toward the creeds is more atavistic than living, and this is so because the creeds lack sufficient semantic density to exert influence on the life of the church. This is especially evident in the fact that the creeds are no longer treated as ruling out any theological position or liturgical practice.

The third element of the Chicago-Lambeth Quadrilateral is the *historic episcopate*. This is clearly part of the common life of the Episcopal Church. We have approved the agreement with the Evangelical Lutheran Church in America, *Called to Common Mission*, in which the historic episcopate is affirmed as a sign of apostolic continuity and Christian unity. Yet at the same time, within the Episcopal Church bishops are currently the most visible and pugnacious signs of *dis*unity, and many bishops conceive of their office as prophetic questioners of the faith and officers of innovation rather than guardians of a faith once received. Further, since the 1960s the House of Bishops of the Episcopal Church has been unable to exercise effective collegial discipline sufficient to maintain even the minimal theological cohesiveness of noncontradiction.[2] In the 1990s a number of parishes refused to accept their diocesan bishop's sacramental authority, insisting upon more theologically congenial visiting bishops. The Church of England has formally adopted a system of "flying bishops," and some in the Episcopal Church are now entertaining similar schemes. Further, in an effort to influence the Episcopal Church, so-called missionary bishops have been ordained, and their single function (up to this point) is to demarcate and intensify divisions within dioceses.

Bishops, then, have become signs of personal prophecy and warring theological factions, not apostolic continuity and Christian unity. This may not be unique in the history of the church (see the career of Athanasius!), but it is exceptional. In this state of conflict, then, bishops are very much a part of our common life, so much so that we insist that bishops, and bishops of a very certain, canonically correct sort, are indispensable conditions for full communion with other church bodies. But at the same time we treat bishops almost exclusively as creatures of institutional power, and the office seems to place no burdens on the consciences of its holders. Quite the contrary, episcopal ordination gives a microphone to one priest's personal vision of the faith, and thus bishops embody conflicts within the church, not the unity promised to the church.

The upshot of this self-canceling function is an altogether too typical Anglican sensibility. We know that we must have bishops. Bishops set us apart; they mark our sense that our church is not a creature of contemporary culture but an apostolic institution governed by a logic and purpose other than the corporate (shareholder value) and political (will of the majority) institutions that dominate our society. Bishops are signs of the divine authorization and institution of the church. The office is part of the visible structure of a political body ordered toward the kingdom of heaven.[3] Yet we can say very little, in good conscience, about how our bishops presently serve the evangelical mission of the church. The typical Episcopalian is painfully aware that the episcopal office is easily absorbed into standard patterns of secular power and institutional dynamics. The consequence is a disabling contradiction. The Episcopal Church is committed to bishops, and at the same time the willfulness and disorder that stem from current episcopal practice are so transparent that the weight and cogency of the episcopal sign are undermined. Unlike Scripture and creeds, we seem to have a commitment in our common life that is not just verbally affirmed and functionally impotent; it is actively contradicted and canceled in practice.

Baptism and Eucharist, if we are to trust the retrospective assessments of those who were instrumental in revision, were central concerns and received great emphasis in the preparation of the 1979 *Book of Common Prayer.*[4] That revision has been successful, for at present baptism and Eucharist, not Scripture, creed, and the historical episcopate, have dominated official initiatives and the rhetoric of the leadership in the Episcopal Church. Here we encounter something with living force. These two sacramental signs have emerged as the most prominent and widely accepted markers of ecclesial identity in the Episcopal Church, and they have come to exert a fundamental influence over our common life. However, this influence has been complex and ambiguous.

The current *Book of Common Prayer* provides a fulsome, communal rite of baptism that is linked directly to the Eucharist. It signifies quite vividly the incorporation of the baptized into the communion of saints by the instrumentality of divine grace vested in the people of God. The distinctive language of faith is vigorously emphasized. Indeed the rite is saturated with just the "mythological worldview" that so embarrasses those who have wished to take the side of "modern man." The effect of the renunciations and affirmations that make up the core of the rite is to establish a bright line that separates the baptized person from the generic attachments and defining features of contemporary society. One is not a Christian automatically; it does not happen as a concomitant attribute of middle-class respectability. One is not a Christian privately and secretly. In many ways, then, baptism now functions to enhance the Augustinian ecclesiological assumptions that have animated Anglicanism since the Reformation. Baptism is a visible sign of a divine institution that is distinct from the world in purpose and conditions for citizenship.[5]

Baptism, however, does not only sharpen and brighten the divide between church and world. Within the Episcopal Church it also dulls and obscures. The current emphasis on the distinctive mark of baptism has become a theological rationale for rethinking the role of ordained ministry. Here two streams converge. Egalitarian utopianism decries "clericalism" and treats baptism as the only real line of demarcation in the life of the church. Ordained ministry is critiqued as a postapostolic strategy for preserving privileged roles of power and prerogative in the church. These walls must come down so that *all* can exercise their baptismal ministry to the full potential of their pneumatic gifts. An easy slogan follows: "A truly countercultural church must have the courage to rethink the very idea of sacramental and institutional leadership!" Church-planting gurus are not so ideologically driven, but the upshot is similar: the idea of a seminary-trained cleric on full salary is part of an old, outdated model of ministry that both taxes financial resources and blocks the excitement and commitment of full lay responsibility for church life. Another slogan follows: "A church of truly evangelical commitment must have the courage to rethink the very idea of sacramental and institutional leadership!"

So as the Episcopal Church genuinely receives a heightened sense of the reality of baptism, the distinctive ways in which the church is marked and set apart from the wider society are enhanced. Yet in a burst of enthusiasm for the effective power of baptism, one of the other historically important means for setting the church apart from the world—the ordained ministry—seems less and less plausible and necessary.[6]

The transformed role of the Lord's Supper in the common life of the Episcopal Church is as important as that of baptism. The shift from a preaching service of Morning Prayer on most Sundays to the Holy Communion service was much endorsed and is now almost universal. This has had a marked effect on the consciousness of ordinary Episcopalians.

Activists trumpet the ministry of the baptized, but most people in the pews continue to pay their priest and endorse his or her position of authority over worship. However, there is a broad consensus among clergy and laity that the Eucharist is the most important and "real" thing that the church does. If anything marks the church, the eucharistic liturgy does. Here, the consensus affirms, the Episcopal Church is marked by a *real* sign of divine purpose and efficacy. This consensus is not merely verbal. There is genuine criteriological weight in eucharistic practice. A sentence of the form "We do *x* in communion; therefore we ought to do *y* in church discipline or mission" is not at all uncommon, and it carries weight in debate and deliberation.

Although the Lord's Supper, like baptism, has taken on a genuine functional significance as the distinctive identifying feature of the church, the same blurring tendencies that seem to emerge out of baptismal enthusiasm also grow out of confidence in the reality of eucharistic celebration. Many priests, convinced that the Eucharist is the genuinely effective center of the church, are eager to share it with everyone. So we find that it is now a legitimate theological position to deny that baptism is a necessary condition for communion.[7] Others resist this fundamental divergence from apostolic practice but are very energetic about making eucharistic liturgy more welcoming, more finely tuned to the spiritual needs of diverse populations within the church. New settings, new language, new symbols must be introduced in order to heighten the range and potency of this central defining feature of the church.[8] In both cases what is widely regarded as *the* defining feature of the church is blurred and becomes less well defined. To remove the requirement of baptism weakens the role of the Eucharist as the cultic center of a set-apart society, and this allows eucharistic practice to merge into a wide range of general religious practices now available to the postmodern seeker. To revise set and common forms according to perceived local needs makes the communion rite a sign of congregational rather than wider church identity. It marks differences, not unity. Neither tendency buttresses or deepens the classical role of the Eucharist in Anglican ecclesiology.

Diagnostic Claims

Classically understood, the idea of the *via media* amounts to a claim that after the Reformation the Church of England came to represent a "mere" or ordinary Christianity uniquely transparent (unlike papal obscurantism) to the fullness (unlike Puritan diminishments) of the apostolic inheritance.[9] While I lack confidence in the transparency and fullness of Anglicanism, I admit to harboring the thought that Anglicanism has a special role in Western Christianity. Anglicanism may well be the "telltale" church, manifesting the functional difficulties of being a church in modern Western culture.

Anglicanism is "telltale" because it combines a formal loyalty to apostolic language and practice with a material alienation from the shaping power of that language and practice.[10] I take this formal loyalty to be a necessary (albeit minimal) condition for the endurance of Christianity in the West. I take this material alienation to be the defining feature of the modern Western Christian experience (whether in the mode of resistance or of capitulation). Thus if Anglicanism cannot claim to be transparent to the gospel, it might legitimately lay claim to being transparent to the larger condition of Christianity in the West: the indispensability of inherited apostolic language and practice and the painfully weak cognitive and spiritual potency of that inheritance.

Thus on the basis of my description of our common life, I will make some broadly diagnostic comments. I believe that what I say is true of my church, and with the arrogant conceit of a true Anglican I presume it to be true of a great deal of Western Christianity.

The functional irrelevance of *Scripture* in North American-European magisterial Protestantism is widely acknowledged. Understanding why would involve a complex and fundamental investigation of the history of modern theology.[11] I offer only the following observations. In the first place, the public cogency and perspicuity of Scripture is linked to the public cogency and perspicuity of the church. To the extent that modern Christianity has explained ecclesial life (e.g., denominationalism and Christian division) in terms of spiritual platitudes that dismiss or explain away the plain sociological sense (e.g., a distinction between "invisible unity" and "visible disunity," with priority going to the latter), it should not surprise us that we are habituated to read Scripture similarly. After all, if we do not take seriously the visible and tangible reality of the church, then we should not be surprised that the plain sense of Scripture is no longer taken seriously.[12]

My second observation is that we should recognize that historical consciousness is not the culprit. Historical-critical study may be wrongheaded; it may be hopelessly ideological; it may be boring and irrelevant to preaching. Yet it does not explain the loss of classical Christian commitments to the authority of Scripture. We need to realize that a moral and spiritual animus against the Old Testament, and not historical-critical consciousness, is central to the modern alienation from the authority of the plain sense of Scripture.[13] For this reason the recovery of Scripture as the functional foundation of our common life is not an intellectual challenge. It is an ascetical challenge. It will require disciplines of heart and mind that directly attack our Gnostic hatred of Torah. We cannot countenance election and commandment. The former offends our universalistic egalitarianism, the latter our self-protective spiritual autonomy. Against these sentiments (sentiments that motivate us to adopt the distancing technique of labeling the Old Testament the "Hebrew Bible"—a name that removes the text from the interpretive traditions of both Christians and Jews) we must recover the patristic *halakha*, the disciplines of vision that the Fathers both practiced and commended.

The creeds and the doctrinal reflection they both express and motivate are embedded linguistic artifacts. Without ongoing practices of patristic exegesis, liturgical worship, and ascetical practice, they lose clarity and semantic density. A great deal of the corruptive consequence of neo-orthodoxy has been the ongoing illusion that doctrines are discrete linguistic artifacts that bear semantic weight independent of ecclesial faith and practice. The doctrine of the Trinity does not generate a "trinitarian" understanding of anything simply by virtue of its verbal formulations or conceptual gestalt. The apostolic meaning of the creeds depends upon apostolic scriptural interpretation. The doctrine of the Trinity has force and meaning only in the context of a living exegetical tradition. Here we must recognize a fundamental fact. At the most basic level, the doctrine of the Trinity is about the relationship between the God of Israel and Jesus of Nazareth, not "relationality," or "mutuality," or "self-giving." For just this reason, unless figural exegesis of the Old Testament—presuming that Christ is the subject from Genesis to Revelation—is a fundamental constituent of the ecclesial appropriation of Scripture, the Nicene Creed cannot be inhabited and interpreted with apostolic consequences.[14] After all, unless we can understand how following Jesus as Lord is the same as worshipping the God of Abraham, Isaac, and Jacob, then we cannot dwell in the triune teachings of the church as a mystery that saves rather than confuses.

The fate of *the historic episcopate* in the common life of the Episcopal Church reflects a whole range of practical contradictions of theological commitments. The Episcopal Church evidences a high degree of rhetorical commitment to the reality and trustworthiness of the sacraments. Yet church discipline on matters of divorce has so thoroughly collapsed that the Episcopal Church has effectively renounced any confidence that God offers trustworthy promises in holy matrimony.[15] This is but an instance of a widespread collapse of church discipline across any number of issues. Few churches now have the will or means to structure their public life in accordance with theological principles. Most poignantly and painfully in the American context, the ideological acceptance of denominationalism within the public teaching of the church contradicts that which is signified by the historic episcopate, that which is enacted in the Eucharist, and that which is taught by Jesus.[16] In this way loyalty to the apostolic tradition is falsified in thought and action.

We need to be clear on this point, because it has a great deal to do with the modern sense that inherited forms are empty and impotent. The sociological gestalt of the church is not merely imperfect—a condition entirely in keeping with the Augustinian legacy of most Western Christian ecclesiologies—but it contradicts the theological rationales for its various offices and functions. This bears directly on the effective loss of Scripture and creed as active, formative, and identifying elements of the Episcopal Church. If right reading of Scripture is as much an ascetical challenge as intellectual, and if proper discipline of the soul requires the formative power of the Holy Spirit active in the people of God, then the contradictory and self-canceling practices of the church will inhibit the proper discipline of the soul and our ability to read Scripture rightly. Further, to the extent that doctrines are embedded linguistic artifacts, the failure of the church to manifest a coherent public gestalt will obscure the proper context for understanding and applying doctrine. An alienation from apostolic language and practice follows. The modern and postmodern distance from inherited forms seems inevitable.

The difficulties that impair Scripture, the creed, and the historic episcopate contribute to the ambiguous consequences of the ecclesiological elements that continue to function. Because Scripture, creed, and historic episcopacy are so invisible and ineffective in the Episcopal Church, the ecclesial reality of *baptism and Eucharist* must bear all the weight of a functional ecclesiology: evangelism, social mission, spiritual discipline, doctrinal authority. Clergy and lay leaders inevitably try to deploy this one functional element to fill the void created by the other three aspects. Historical forms of structuring the church become less and less plausible under the pressure of self-contradictory practice, and therefore baptism must be stretched to serve as the sole rationale for church order. When we are unable to see how Scripture and doctrine can yield pneumatic power sufficient to convert and edify, the Eucharist substitutes for proclamation and catechesis. These consequences seem inevitable and debilitating. While baptism and Eucharist may be necessary for an apostolic ecclesiology, they cannot be the sole and sufficient elements without becoming something quite different.[17]

Significance for Our Theological Vocations

For outsiders, one of the most exasperating features of Anglicanism is its intense and inarticulate loyalty to certain elements of the ecumenical tradition. We are patristic without being scriptural. We know that the Nicene Creed is fundamental, but we have not a clue just how and why. We have a distinct sense that ecumenical doctrines ought to shape our common life, but we have little confidence or skill in bringing them to bear on our teaching and deliberations.[18] They function as symbols (in the purely modern sense of the term) and shibboleths (incarnationalism! a trinitarian *anything!*), not as exegetical epitomes and structuring rules for theological reflection. The same holds for our traditions of church order. We insist upon the historic episcopate as a sign of continuity and unity, and at the same time we defend the "right" of Bishop John Shelby Spong to "speak his own mind." So, functionally, the "fundamentals" of Anglicanism are insisted upon, *and* they become largely empty symbols that are widely malleable in application and without criteriological authority.

Debilitating consequences follow for theology. Discernment and consensus on matters of doctrine and order have an ambiguous status. A fragmented common life makes our theological synthesis seem more personal than communal, because the synthesis is made possible by the degree of coherence and spiritual integrity each of us might attain personally even as our churches disintegrate. However, personal vision without communal integrity is unstable. Underdetermined by current ecclesial practice, theological language will seem vague and obscure. Look at any document produced by theological committees and denominational offices in recent years. They bear out this prediction. Consider the status of theology in the academy. Most scholars in other disciplines do not now criticize theology for being rigidly dogmatic (though such crticisms are still being made). Rather, they criticize theology for being flaccid and undisciplined. An unsettled church inevitably leads to unsettled premises in theology, and theology is thus reduced to meaning mongering and pasting together fragments with an aesthetic hope rather than rational confidence in basic categories of analysis.

A theological consensus that emphasizes those functional aspects of ecclesial life—baptism and Eucharist—both cannot save the day. The theological content of baptism and Eucharist, as the sole functional elements, vacillates between the specific elements and language of the rituals and our overall sense of what the church "is." Consensus on the limited and classical questions about baptism and Eucharist sheds light on only parts of our apostolic inheritance. Thus given the need for a wider vision, we drift back toward the insubstantial consensus concerning the other elements (Scripture, creed, and church order). If we try to force baptism and Eucharist to expand to fill this void, then we will do little more than manifest divergent theological sensibilities in the largely symbolic and highly abstract language of "baptismal covenant" and "eucharistic fellowship." Our theological vocations suffer accordingly.

Although an honest appraisal of the dysfunctional condition of the Episcopal Church leads to the conclusion that our theological vision is obscured, I do not intend to condemn the theological vocation as futile. What is difficult, very difficult, is not therefore impossible or worthless. We can and must forge ahead, but under two important constraints that stem from the fact that we must suffer the ruins of the church.

First, we must seek to understand what a dysfunctional church reveals about God's will for the future. As we search for guidance, we must look backwards, not forwards. We are deeply dependent on those who have gone before us. For however troubled their ages, however divided and fragmented their churches, however ill-advised their judgments and odd their assumptions, they lived and thought about the will of God in the context of a common life characterized by a functional exegetical consensus, living creeds, a largely settled polity, and sacraments that were integral parts of a form of life rather than the sole surviving elements. They did not live, as we increasingly do, without a rule of faith that constrains judgment.

Therefore the great theological imperative of our time is *ressourcement,* a return to the sources. This cannot be a piecemeal and creative recovery; rather, it must be a return to the sources that is marked by submission to their premodern methods and forms. To recover a coherent, public theological vision, we must train ourselves to think with premodern theologians whose lives and minds were disciplined by a no-doubt imperfect but nonetheless functional common life.

In this submission to those who have gone before us, we should not worry that our faith and work will be sectarian or anachronistic. We have already been formed on the anvil of modernity. This holds true for liberals who seek accommodation, conservatives who counsel resistance, and those who seek a "third way," either in hopefulness or despair. The discipline of *ressourcement* will shape and correct the raw material of our undoubtedly unique and different contexts; it will not replace our theological vision. Indeed because we live in the ruins of the church, our vision, however disciplined and corrected, will be unlike the vision of our predecessors who practiced theology in a church less ruined, or at least ruined otherwise.

Second, if we do not wish to indulge in theological fancy, then we must recognize how limited we are in room and scope for judgment and action. For a great Anglican figure such as Richard Hooker, the deepest law of ecclesiastical polity was preservative, and all the more so when the church was threatened by centrifugal forces that threatened ruin. Hooker was aware that in the midst of controversies that divide and debilitate the church, "suspense of judgment and exercise of charity were safer and seemlier for Christian men, than hot pursuit of these controversies, wherein they that are most fervent to dispute be not always the most able to determine."[19] Hooker could recommend such a course of action because he was convinced that the church communicates the grace of God as a stable and settled form of life that is visibly connected to the apostolic age. His *via media* was precisely the willingness to dwell in this inherited and stable form, especially when uncertainty and indecision about pressing contemporary issues predominate. For Hooker the first imperative is clear: to receive that which has been given, rather than embarking on a fantasy of constructive theological speculation and ecclesial purification that would only diminish and destabilize.

As the traditional forms of church life today fall into dysfunction, I cannot imagine that we have more liberty of judgment than did Hooker. Indeed, if we are honest about the condition of the Episcopal Church, a condition not unique in Western Christianity, our liberty of judgment is no doubt even less. In the ruins of the church we are unlikely to say anything new—certainly not about human sexuality, certainly not about some new theological perspective that will miraculously integrate disparate views, certainly not about different ways of being a "trinitarian community." Synthesis requires a step back from the *disjecta membra Christiana*. For the dysfunctional elements of church life—Scripture, creed, historic episcopate, baptism, and Eucharist—seem only to confuse us with either silenced authority or willful conscription to any number of warring causes. But the step back is a step in the wrong direction. Our theological vocations are based upon a step forward into that which our Lord has given us to dwell in.

Therefore, whether we like it or not, we are even more deeply bound to that which we have received, and less capable of faithful innovation and development of doctrine, than Hooker and others who suffered the debilitations of the church in centuries past. Should we be faithful, we will be cast back upon the sheer givenness of the apostolic tradition. Disordered to the point of incoherence, the church gives us only its most primitive and basic gifts. Our goal should be to dwell in those gifts. Our scriptural exegesis must be primitive, that is to say, reiterative rather than innovative or exploratory. Our engagement with the creeds must be submissive. We must suffer the contradictions of the historic episcopate. We must persevere in baptism and Eucharist. We must first cherish the stones before we can set about to rebuild the wall.

In all these things, the textured Christian tradition of theological interpretation and church discipline no longer helps order and mediate our relationship to the enduring features of our apostolic inheritance. Theology and discipline have come unhinged from their sources, and the essential features of the church, as I have tried to show, are now largely unintelligible. For this reason, if we will dwell in our church, we will be like children who are untutored and inarticulate, who are given what they need even as they can neither understand nor contribute. We can rebel against this spiritual weakness. But if we are willing to accept the painfully unsophisticated tasks of spiritual childhood—to memorize the catechism as we once memorized multiplication tables, to hear with rapturous joy the literal sense of Scripture as we once listened to stories read at nighttime, to repeat again and again the ancient liturgies as we once repeated our favorite TV shows, word for word—then we will find our way toward a theological vocation proper to those who live in the ruins of the church. Only with this retrospective, receptive, and reiterative disposition can we join with Nehemiah on his reparative return to Jerusalem. For it is written that in our love for the fallen walls of Zion we will find our hope:

> Thou wilt arise and have pity on Zion;
> it is time to favor her;
> the appointed time has come
> For thy servants hold her stones dear
> and have pity on her dust.

Psalm 102:13-14 RSV

6

The Drive Toward Change

I am sure the Liturgy will torment us so long as we continue selfish and divided, therefore I would cling to it.

F. D. Maurice, *The Prayer-Book*

The contemporary moral atmosphere is thick with affirmation. We want programs, opportunities, and social interactions tailored to personal needs. Maybe we imagine ourselves "visual learners," and we are frustrated that the instructor does not accommodate our style of learning. Maybe we are single parents, and we are angry when the elementary school teacher presumes a nuclear family. Maybe we did not change our name when we married, and we are exasperated when coworkers fumble over questions about whether or not we are married. Maybe we are country-club Democrats or African-American Republicans, and we hate the way people stereotype. The possibilities are endless. In fact, a great deal of postmodern moralism disciplines us to suspend judgment and accommodate differences. We work hard to avoid reinforcing social assumptions and expectations. We want to feel comfortable with ourselves, and we want to empower others to feel comfortable as well.

"Don't let anyone tell you who you are!" What is striking is that the resistant and inwardly conserving slogan "Be yourself!" is married to a conviction that social and cultural change is good, even inevitable. The link is not ill-considered. Precisely because traditional societies are devoted to disciplining and forming individuals into inherited patterns, we need to change our society from "traditional" to "modern." We need to change educational expectations, change gender relations, change assumptions about race, family, sex, and so on. In fact, as Nietzsche recognized clearly when he identified the will to power, the only way we can acquire the freedom to *be ourselves* is to *change everything else.* The world must reflect me so that I do not reflect the world. The upshot is a complex attitude toward revision, reform, discipline, and change. We deny the inward need to reform our souls, and at the same time we insist upon the need to reform all outward cultural forms. The solidity of the world must be liquefied so that we can swim freely through life.

In the Anglican tradition, the *Book of Common Prayer* has been an unchanging outward form. To be sure, the common liturgy has been revised over the centuries, and set forms have always been modified, even ignored, in local situations. Nonetheless, this modest plasticity has never become a fluidity. As an anchor, the Prayer Book might drag along the seabed of tradition, but always in order to make it a more reliable tether. Revision in Anglicanism has sought to strengthen and solidify; it has not attempted to reduce the disciplining and shaping power of common prayer.

One experience drove home to me this fixity and influence. I have a vivid memory of meeting with my rector for premarital counseling. My future wife wanted to gently modify some aspects of the ceremony. "Must we have so many prayers that end in the name of the Father, Son, and Holy Spirit?" she asked.

The priest, a man of impeccable liberal credentials and inclusive sensibilities, looked at her in shock. His response was primitive: "But *I* cannot *change* the Prayer Book!"

This reaction was entirely traditional and typical. For most of its history, the Anglican liturgy has functioned as a given fact about which the endlessly changing needs of pastoral ministry must revolve.

One of the most important features of the Episcopal Church in the present age is the loss of this sensibility. Like everything else, the liturgy must change so that we need not. My wife's acquiescence, our age thinks, was a tragedy of conscience, a blow against the dignity of difference. The priest's resistance, we now presume, was mere atavism, a mindless commitment to traditional forms, a Pharisaical devotion to liturgy, a fear of change. We cannot allow the letter to kill; this way of thinking continues. We must embrace the spirit that gives life. We cannot allow an empty ritualism, a slavish devotion to authorized forms, an Old Testament legalism to corrupt the unique and diverse faith journeys of individual persons.

The fact that my wife's difficulties with the liturgy of our wedding were motivated by the fact that she is Jewish has given me pause. The longer I listen to rationales for making the fixed anchor of common prayer into a fluid resource for meeting unique spiritual needs, the more aware I am of the potentially anti-Jewish aspects of the present drive toward liturgical change. The horror of unchanging common prayer is, at root, a rebellion against the Torah. Like all rejections of the law, this does not lead to spiritual truth. It leads to anarchy, conflict, and falsehood.

This rebellion is complex and by no means always conscious and intentional. I have participated in national gatherings of the Episcopal Church, and in that context I have witnessed the drive toward liturgical change, and I can report that ardent proponents of feminist "expansive language" revision, as well as advocates of full inclusion of active homosexuals into the life of the church, provide the most committed support for liturgical change. This should not surprise readers. Feminist theologians regard the traditional communal language of prayer and worship as scandalously patriarchal. Gay rights activists wish to change the way the church thinks about sexuality, and in recent years they have become profoundly aware of how difficult this will be to effect. Because of this they are eager to support an atmosphere of church life in which dramatic changes of all sorts—in theology, doctrine, and practice—are normal and accepted. The underlying thought is simple. The more thoroughly we can revise the liturgy, the more thoroughly we can revise the church's images of God and teachings on morality.

I have interest neither in analyzing the particular rationales for feminist revision nor in discussing justifications for changing the church's teaching on sexual practice. Both have received extensive attention. I have discussed the former elsewhere, and I will weigh in on the latter in the next chapter.[1] But more important, neither theological feminism nor the gay agenda provides a sufficient explanation for the drive toward liturgical revision. Only a minority of national leaders, not insubstantial, but definitely not anything approaching a majority, have an articulate commitment to either feminist theology or the homosexual agenda. Nonetheless, a majority support change. I wish to understand this support. I wish to grasp why successful rectors of large parishes that are getting along quite nicely with the current Prayer Book accept the need for revision.

The Present Climate of Opinion

I detect three elements, each of which contributes to an atmosphere in which fundamental liturgical revision is regarded as necessary. The first is an intense desire to strike an affirmative pose. The upshot is a strong undercurrent of therapeutic tolerance. Most Episcopalians are satisfied with the current Prayer Book, but these same folks are eager to affirm and support those who are not satisfied. The second element is a distrust of the particular. We wish to be flexible and creative, and the constraints of set forms of prayer offend. The content of the current Prayer Book may be fine; as I said, most find it very satisfactory. Nonetheless, the obligatory and restrictive form of classical Anglican worship seems unnecessarily delimiting. Third, like much of modern society, the Episcopal Church simply assumes that outward change is both inevitable and benevolent. A vote against revision is perceived to be antediluvian and futile. It will happen, we are told, whether we want or not. All three elements—therapeutic tolerance, distrust of the particular, and the dogma of inevitable change—compound to produce an atmosphere in which a majority support liturgical revision. We need to understand each in some detail.

Therapeutic tolerance. Tolerance is the executive virtue of our time, and this tolerance is active and enabling rather than passive and merely permissive. Well-socialized Americans respect the expressive rights of every person. This requires us to avoid "imposing" our own opinions on others. When discussing matters of controversy, sentences always begin "From my point of view . . . ," "In my experience . . . ," "I feel . . ." This pervasive solipsism is not the result of a cynical relativism or a well-formed philosophical belief that there are no universal truths. Instead the compulsive deflation of one's moral and theological statements stems from a particularly intense and therapeutic desire to create conditions in which the unique sensibilities of others can be freely and safely expressed. A good leader, we are told, empowers others to find "their own voices."

This ideal of therapeutic tolerance has deeply influenced the Episcopal Church. It is at the core of the much-championed ideal of a "church of no outcasts." By no means is this ideal limited to feminist and gay issues. Every pastor feels the tug of therapeutic tolerance. Consider these examples. The nonbaptized spouse of a devoted new member feels uncomfortable and unwelcome because of the heavy emphasis the tradition places on baptism as a necessary mark of membership in the church. The former Methodist feels that his or her faith journey is being questioned by the expectation of reception and confirmation. The ex-

Catholic is threatened by appeals to the authority of bishops. The ex-fundamentalist bridles at any and all perceived literalism. In an atmosphere of therapeutic tolerance these experiences of exclusion, marginalization, and threat cannot be questioned. The experiences are real, and the church must acknowledge them as such.

The upshot is pastoral discomfort and dissatisfaction. The well-trained and committed priests tries to find ways to explain the boundaries and constraints of the Christian life and the Anglican tradition. Anglican authority is "dispersed." We read Scripture in light of "reason." Reception is just a detail of "canon law." But some people continue to feel uncomfortable, continue to feel excluded. This creates a fundamental scandal. No one should feel excluded or impeded in his or her quest for fuller faith! These feelings must be ministered to; the exclusion and impediment must be relieved. If Tillichian theology and the shibboleths learned at seminary will not do the trick, then stronger medicine is necessary.

I am convinced that no matter how liberal or conservative their personal piety, most Episcopal priests feel this way. They conceive of their ministry as shepherding individuals toward richer, fuller spiritual lives, and they are reluctant to gainsay anyone's self-reported spiritual discomforts and dissatisfactions. If someone is fixated on masculine pronouns, the priest has little room to maneuver. He can get out some feminist theology book he was assigned in seminary and try to preach some sensitive sermons. He can form a worship committee and "explore" ways to "enrich" the current worship of the congregation. He can point to his support of NOW in order to establish bona fides. He cannot, however, tell the unhappy parishioner that her fixation is childish. He cannot tell a woman that the received liturgical language of the church is not subject to change. He cannot tell her that she must work toward a spiritual maturity that recognizes that the language of prayer is doxological, not political. The therapeutic ideal makes this impossible. The priest must affirm and empower. He cannot rebuke and reform.

Always meeting diverse needs, the pastoral task requires a great deal of juggling—Rite One at 8:00 A.M. for the old folks, a Family Service at 10:00, Pomp and Circumstance for the Aesthetes at 11:30. One can well imagine that a successful rector who already is well advanced in the practice of "market segmentation" might be very alive to the benefits of an even more flexible, more open and expansive range of options on which to draw. That successful rector might well be thinking that the church needs to take the leap—new forms of prayer, new ways of ordering the church and conducting worship, new structures for governance and ministry. Only then can the diversity of churchgoers and their diverse needs and complaints find a suitably flexible context for their faith journeys.[2] Only then can liturgy be affirmative.

To the extent that this spirit of therapeutic tolerance animates the church, fundamental revision becomes normal, even necessary. The discomforts and desires for change that motivate feminist and gay advocates are but extensions of a general sense that our current approach to worship and common life is too rigid, too limited, too restrictive. Therapeutic tolerance requires a much more open and more fluid common prayer, one that permits the pastor to trim, tailor, and restructure according to dictates of individualized pastoral judgment.

For a clear illustration of this way of thinking, consider Phoebe Pittingell's introduction to an official set of alternative liturgies. "With some people," she writes, "a major sense of context will spring from life experiences; others look for continuity with biblical and ecclesiastical tradition." Pastoral therapy must address the particular needs of both groups. Far from insisting upon scriptural knowledge and continuity with the apostolic tradition, a flexible approach must give the priest resources to facilitate the spiritual growth of those who find the creed off-putting and Scripture alien. With this in mind, Pittingell sums up the intent of the supplemental materials: "The committee sought language and imagery which would speak to the diversity of people who worship in the Episcopal Church today, both those who are steeped in the tradition and those whose knowledge of scripture and the Christian tradition is fragmentary and to whom much traditional language is puzzling."[3] The vision may be noble. Liturgy is to meet people where they are, but the real consequences are clear. If you like the apostolic tradition, the Episcopal Church will have a liturgy for you; if you do not like that tradition, the Episcopal Church can meet your needs as well.

Distrust of the particular. Any book of common prayer, whatever its content, fixes the public life of the church according to set forms; otherwise the prayer is not common. To a very great extent, contemporary Episcopalians are satisfied with the set forms and inherited language found in the 1979 Prayer Book. Nonetheless, those same Episcopalians are often troubled by the simple fact that the corporate life of the church is bounded and limited. They are embarrassed by the thought that the Prayer Book, however winsome and useful, is *required.* This discomfort is not just a matter of authority—"*Who says* that this must be our way of praying?"—although that too undermines confidence. Rather, the discomfort stems from a profound sense that limitation, constraints, and boundaries are intrinsically antithetical to Christian freedom. So many assume that required forms of prayer have no place in true Christianity.

This rebellion against limitations and requirements—in short, against Torah of any sort—takes many forms. One often hears that the Cranmerian liturgy reflects sixteenth-century piety and thus conjures up a "Tudor deity."[4] One can undertake to show that the vast bulk of the Prayer Book—sixteenth and twentieth century, English and American— comes from pre-Reformation sources, some from the first centuries of Christian worship. This exercise is futile. The point is not, finally, that the Prayer Book is Roman, feudal, Tudor, or anything else. The point is that a distrust of the particular treats *any* set form and inherited language as limited, historical, and distorting. Why should we lock our experience of God into such a small, constricted box?

To give another example, we hear that the *Book of Common Prayer*, and the rigid liturgical sensibilities that it presupposes, reinforces the class consciousness of WASP elites. One can point out that African churches use a Prayer Book more archaic and more rigidly fixed than our own, and those churches do not produce WASP elites. But sociological evidence is beside the point. What matters is the pervasive distrust of the particular. God is so much greater, we insist, than any particular tradition or form of prayer. To require a single approach, or even a limited range of approaches, imposes constraints upon the freedom of the Spirit. We must be open to all things. "Shouldn't we be free," many think, "to experiment with new ways of being the church?" We must "live provisionally" and resist the temptation to sanctify merely temporary and human boundaries.[5]

Feminist theologians frame the issue clearly. Patriarchy is a rather loose concept, but in general it applies to any pattern of strong and spiritually significant distinctions and fixed boundaries. Distinctions between the saved and the damned, between the elect and reprobate, are typically analyzed as strategies for protecting power and sacralizing social hierarchy. The same holds true for the distinguishing marks of ordained leadership. The set-apart minister who possesses unique powers reflects a social model of paternal authority over the family. Against this patriarchy, feminist theologians emphasize solidarity and mutual cooperation. "The division between clergy and laity is not healthy for the development of a witnessing Christian community," we are told. Against standard models of ministry, the feminist style of leadership is "collegial, experimental, experiential, committed to honoring differences, . . . praxis-oriented, collaborative, and flexible."[6] The Christian community should not be preoccupied with marking and maintaining boundaries, establishing and reinforcing ordered patterns of authority and responsibility. The church should be characterized by a *"synergy, serendipity,* and *sharing"* that exhibits a brave "openness to the future."[7] In short, we should distrust the particular. We should reject the ways in which inherited forms of common prayer and communal practice constrain and limit. Thus goes the brief against patriarchy.

Although feminist theologians are very forthright, by no means is distrust of the particular limited to feminist thinkers. The Episcopal Church breathes in an atmosphere of uncertainty about the legitimacy and necessity of structured and differentiating sacramental orders. For example, proponents of open communion rebel against the idea that baptism might be a requirement for receiving the body and blood of Jesus Christ. At the same time, the mark of baptism is exalted in a rally cry: "Ministry of All the Baptized." The distinguishing mark of ordination is then treated as an unnecessary impediment to the full exercise of the many charisms of the faithful. In both cases, the particular ways in which the Anglican tradition marks persons with distinctive and particular roles are called into question. Inherited forms and structures may be useful—again, most find current worship and practice just fine—but they cannot be required. "Perhaps the church has thought baptism necessary for receiving communion," a conventional rector of a large parish might observe. "That belief no doubt reveals a very important truth about the importance of commitment and community, but now we are moving into a fuller understanding of the Spirit. Now we recognize that the insights of the past need not weigh upon us as stultifying law. The past serves to nurture spiritual wisdom. We should love and cherish our inheritance. But we need to be spiritual adults and make our own judgments about what promotes growth in relationship to God."

This rebellion against the very spirit and essence of the law will always find obligation, prescription, and constraint an offense. Guided by this rebellion, given forms of worship must be dissolved into innumerable "choices" that can reflect our inner and spiritual insights. Such a sentiment, however "orthodox" in current conviction, however committed to the current Prayer Book in practice, cannot help but be swept into the drive toward wholesale liturgical revision.[8]

Inevitable change. The greatest and most pervasive reason the Episcopal Church is willing to embrace liturgical revision is the conviction that cultural change is inevitable. Essay after essay simply announces liturgical change as a fact of life. The church has always changed, the writers assume. Life is a constant process of growth, and the church necessarily adjusts and grows. The imperative is immediate: accept change.

This conviction that change is inevitable is so protean that it barely admits of analysis. If a congregation resists changes imposed by a well-meaning priest, the explanation is ready at hand. "Of course they are uncomfortable with change. It is natural to cling to what is familiar. It takes courage and maturity to embrace something new." The priest is sympathetic but undeterred. "Human weakness motivates loyalty to the past; personal strength and maturity produce openness to the future. If we are insecure and worried about who we are, then we seek fixed anchors. If we are confident that we already possess spiritual strength, then we are willing to take risks. The former leads to stasis and immaturity; the latter leads to dynamism and maturity."

Social analysis follows directly. Revision advocates usually assume that communities committed to a particular set of beliefs and an inherited language of prayer are "fundamentalist." That is to say, such communities lack sufficient critical maturity to recognize that past forms are historically conditioned and necessarily limited. Such communities do not want to take responsibility for formulating their own experience of God; instead they comfortably hide under the skirts of past formulations. Conformity predominates; individuality is suppressed. I cannot count the number of times I have heard church leaders reiterate these platitudes.

To vote for revision, then, is to vote for the only possible course of action that is mature and responsible. One *must* revise; otherwise one lives in the childish illusion that nothing changes. One *must* embrace change, because it is a fact of life. Indeed it is a good and blessed fact, for endless outward change prevents us from making "idols." Change saves us from fundamentalism. "If only we could get people to stop saying the traditional Lord's Prayer," says the progressive, "then they would finally see that it is our *experiences* of God, not the *words*, that matter." Change is championed as inevitable and benevolent. The only questions are when, how, and under what principles.[9]

Assessment

What, then, are we to make of therapeutic tolerance, distrust of particularity, and the dogma of inevitable change? In general, these sensibilities are debilitating. They constellate to undermine the apostolic basis for the church's common life, for to run from the Torah is to flee from the One who fulfilled the Law. Let us consider each sensibility in turn.

Classically, the role of the minister has been to order the community of faith according to apostolic faith and practice. What constitutes "apostolic faith and practice" has been contested throughout Christian history. Nonetheless, the ordained ministry has been understood and exercised under the constraints of that contested faith and practice. Now, under the guidance of therapeutic tolerance, the role of the minister has changed, and ministry is seen as the orchestration of faith journeys.

Under such a view, the pastoral therapist becomes the singular authority for dictating communal practice. The upshot is a redoubled clericalism amid rising protests to the contrary. None can gainsay the therapeutic wisdom of the experienced cleric who manages diverse spiritual needs. Should I object to the repudiation of baptism and amass historical and theological arguments, the priest simply responds, "Yes, yes, I acknowledge and respect your traditionalist sensibilities, but surely you must see that I have to respond to the needs of other, less traditionalist members of the congregation." In this way all objections are swallowed up into the quicksand of the therapeutic project, and in that project the priest is has absolute say. Thus Bishop Spong is not speaking "for himself"; he is speaking "on behalf" of those who find traditional Christianity irrelevant. No one can question his right, indeed his pastoral obligation, to undertake such a great and noble ministry in our age of doubt and unbelief.

This atmosphere of therapeutic tolerance not only justifies Spong's impieties, it also makes liturgical revision seem natural and necessary. After all, the therapist must have an open range of tools and techniques. Let us say, for example, that Sioux rituals have helped a Seattle congregation develop a rich and stimulating creation spirituality. Why not include such helpful aids? Or in another imaginary scenario, a church in Chicago finds interreligious dialogue profoundly challenging and enlivening. Should we not allow such an experience to find a central place in its worship?

In all this, the particular details of liturgical revision are not the issue. What matters most is the way this approach to revision debilitates the clerical vocation. It transforms the minister into a spiritual manager and turns the church into a support group of like-minded seekers. For this reason the flight from fixed liturgy signals the balkanization of the church. Freed from a common liturgy that is required, congregations will "reform" their worship to more transparently reflect *themselves.*

This therapeutic project compounds with the distrust of the particular and reinforces the pervasive Gnosticism of our times. We do not want to be limited; we do not want to submit to a determinate form of life that will shape and winnow. We want a formless God who is all things to all people. We want a God who comes to us as we are and affirms us. This desire underlies our discomfort with the tradition of common prayer that has defined Anglicanism. Particular forms of required prayer remind us that God intends us to live in a particular and required way. The narrow limitations of a prayer book remind us that discipleship leads down a narrow footpath. Thus the general sensibility that the Anglican tradition of prayer is beautiful and endearing but not at all obligatory parallels a similar presumption that traditional Christian doctrine and moral teaching are very inspiring but by no means mandatory. Animated by a distrust of the particular, a now habitual Gnosticism finds the very idea of apostolic Christianity a constraining offense.

It is this offense, and not the particular revisions currently circulating, that constitutes a profound threat to the *Book of Common Prayer* and its goal of dwelling in apostolic prayer. If spiritual freedom means maximal choice, then the common life of the church will lack discipline. Worship becomes a collage of particular interests and needs, ever changing as the pastor takes the spiritual temperature of the congregation.

The presumption against fixed and determinate apostolic prayer is reinforced by the dogma of inevitable change. For Marxists of old, history grinds forward, and we can either join the vanguard or be crushed by the wheels of change. Those who throw in their lot with change necessarily fight as midwives of a future that will justify all. The future will redeem that past, rather than the past shaping and redeeming the present. Thus, driven by the dogma of inevitable change, the agents of revision must put their shoulders to the wheel, and as members of the vanguard they need not trouble themselves with the fate of those who resist.

A dismissive attitude toward any who would protest is typical. Urban T. Holmes embodied this insouciance. When he wrote about the conflicts surrounding Prayer Book revisions in the 1960s and 1970s, he expressed certainty that the old forms are withering away and need not be taken seriously. About one particularly articulate critic Holmes wrote, "He is talking about issues and a world in which I do not live."[10]

Such sentiments are widespread. Many "progressive" leaders are frank. They simply say that "traditionalists" should leave the church if they do not like change. Critics should not be answered. They should be counseled about how to live with inevitable change—or urged to find another "world in which to live." The past is dead, so let the dead bury the dead.

Holmes would no doubt mock the men who came to Nehemiah to tell him of the travails of Jerusalem. They were voices of a dead past, not the bright and living future that we imagine easily because it is so plastic with possibility.

The vision of inevitable change leads to a dismissive attitude toward inherited forms of prayer and practice. Consider Ellen K. Wondra's remarkable observations. She notes that Christianity was born out of a profound revision of the beliefs, language, and ritual of Judaism. "Our contemporary processes of discernment and reception are basically the same," she concludes.[11] One cannot help but wonder whether Wondra sees the logic of her affirmation. The upshot of the apostolic revision of Judaism is *a new religion*, one that Jews think fundamentally antagonistic. If our approach is basically the same—and the dominant sensibilities of therapeutic tolerance and distrust of the particular lead me to think Wondra is all too prescient—then we can anticipate a revisionary process that will lead to *a new, post-Christian religion,* one fundamentally at odds with apostolic teaching and prayer.

A Crucial Choice

If my analysis of the underlying support for liturgical revision is correct, then we must acknowledge how deep are the impulses that drive toward change. We are not in the midst of a great groundswell of interest in recovering ancient rites. Revisionary initiatives are not animated by a neo-Benedictine desire to pray the Psalter from dawn to dusk. Revision is not even motivated by a desire to update and enrich the Prayer Book tradition that has defined Anglicanism since the sixteenth century. Rather, we are careening toward an open-ended process of revision motivated by spiritual antagonism. Apostolic Christianity itself seems too constricting and too archaic for the Episcopal Church.

Guided by a therapeutic impulse, a process of liturgical revision, however well intentioned, will institutionalize the demoralizing sense of emptiness that afflicts the clerical vocation. It will make spiritual management even more central to the ministerial task. What prayers do the people of St. So-and-So need? What form of worship is best for this urban flock of marginally catechized, college-educated folks? The spiritual elect may relish such an opportunity to exercise their religious genius. "Finally I can create the worship service I have always known would be effective!" But those who are incapable of such megalomania will feel even more adrift. That much-championed resource "experience" hardly yields abundant and reliable guidance. So the church will be doubly afflicted. Self-appointed pneumatics will feel free to invent new religions; faithful ministers will be forced to reinvent apostolic Christianity as a liturgical "choice." Churches already anticipate this situation, advertising themselves as "inclusive" or "traditionalist" parishes.

We wish to be led by the Holy Spirit into the fullness of life in Christ. Even the most ardent revisionists are propelled by such a desire. Yet a distrust of particularity prevents us from seeing that the fullness of Christ has determinate shape and concrete substance. Most clergy, as I observed at the outset, readily acknowledge that the 1979 *Book of Common Prayer* is a functional anchor of stability and source of spiritual strength, both for them and for their congregations. Nonetheless, these same clergy cannot affirm that the Holy Spirit is leading them and their congregations into this particular fixed life of prayer. The Holy Spirit, we imagine, is using the current Prayer Book to lead us elsewhere, somewhere beyond the particularity of our inherited forms of corporate worship.

That such a sentiment is antithetical to historical Anglicanism seem to go unnoticed, and if noticed is rejected as irrelevant. The defining feature of Anglicanism has been a constant refrain: we order our common life according to the particular, inherited forms given by the providence of God to his faithful people.[12] The unquestioned dogma that change is inevitable now makes this classical Anglican claim impossible to sustain. Just as our liturgy must change, so must our attitudes toward liturgy. Indeed if we truly believe the dogma of inevitable change, our attitudes toward Scripture, Jesus, and God must change. Spong is not bishop by accident. He knows his audience. Christianity must change or die! Jesus of Nazareth must be detached from the moldering irrelevance of ancient documents (Scripture), old doctrines (the creed), and outdated church practices (inherited liturgy).

Should we be surprised, then, that little is left but thin outlines and empty slogans? Should we not see that the priest has no vocation to pass on the faith once delivered? Spiritual therapy is the only task in the quest of "New Being." The only vocation left is to prepare a congregation to be "open to the future." And in that vocation, destroying the authority of the apostolic tradition—the continuing claims of the past—is the positive duty of clergy.

Such emptiness need not be our fate. Liturgical revision is a necessary aspect of the life of the church. However, revision should not encourage the idea that the church must "manage" faith journeys. Revision should not blur and diminish boundaries marked out by inherited prayer and practice. Revision should not adopt the glib assumption that change is inevitable. Instead revision should reinforce and intensify the clarity and particularity of apostolic prayer and practice. It should brighten the boundaries between true and false teaching, between life in an assembly of the faithful preparing for heaven and in a congregation captive to worldly powers. It should strengthen our bonds to the faith once delivered. It should deepen our affection for the irreplaceable apostolic past. Revision should strengthen the anchor of common worship so that we see as clearly as possible that we—not Christian teaching and practice—must change in order to dwell in the fullness of new life.

Postscript

There are two kinds of people who make up their own wedding ceremonies: geniuses and fools. There are few of the former, and that should be a sobering thought to all of us who wish for more "flexibility" and "individuality" in common prayer. Consider this thought experiment.

Your parents and grandparents had the technology to make videotapes of their weddings. Now, imagine viewing those tapes. Do you have any doubt that the "flexible" and "creative" ceremonies would generate snickers of amusement decades later? Do you doubt that a Prayer Book wedding viewed decades later would produce anything other than the silence that reflects awe and gratitude?

My wife and I made no tapes at our wedding, but in the clarity of memory, I look back with complex and powerful emotions. I am grateful to my priest that those emotions are not tinctured by an embarrassed recollection of having made of fool of myself with improvised sincerity and superficial profundity.

And my wife? Marriage has a way of clarifying the fact that we must make choices. We cannot live in the illusions of adolescent immortality and infinite possibilities. For my wife, this has meant a decision for more explicit, more serious, more committed Torah observance. Doing this with a Gentile husband is difficult, and in many ways being married in the name of the Father, Son, and Holy Spirit was a figure for her future of trying to live against the grain. Yet my priest did not add to the difficulties. Quite the contrary, by refusing to say that the prayers we inherit are malleable resources for our current needs, he avoided a modern form of Christian anti-Judaism. Of course, my priest did not agree with the rabbis about the meaning of the law, the nature of temple sacrifice, and the fulfillment of prophecy. But he did not presume that required and set forms deaden and afflict. Even as he read the Torah with Christian eyes, he did not reject its very form and purpose. He did not mock halakhic constraint by dismissing the binding usages of the *Book of Common Prayer*. In his loyalty to the Prayer Book, he communicated the conviction that affirms the rabbinic project even as it wrestles for control over its outcome. Our way toward God must submit to a narrowness of a law of common prayer and communal life; otherwise we are ill-prepared to submit to the free and altogether more severe demands of the Spirit.

7

Sex in the Episcopal Church

Have mercy upon us, O LORD, have mercy upon us,
   for we have had more than enough of contempt.
Our soul has had more than its fill
   of the scorn of those who are at ease,
   of the contempt of the proud.

Psalm 123:3–4

Even the most casual observer of the Episcopal Church knows that homosexuality is a dominating controversy. As a deputy to recent general conventions of the Episcopal Church, I have had more than a passing view. With close votes, homosexual issues generate the moments of highest legislative drama. Special legislative committees are formed to handle the increased passions. Testimony is given pro and con. Forces are mobilized to influence decision making.

The predominance of gay and lesbian issues was especially evident at the 1997 General Convention in Philadelphia. The outgoing presiding bishop, Edward Browning, gave a parting speech, and among the litany of causes he gave gay liberation the longest play. The newly elected presiding bishop, Frank Griswold, was hailed as a moderate because he seemed unwilling to destroy the denomination tomorrow in order to ensure the blessing of same-sex unions. The legislative committee responsible for a wide range of social concerns shut down all other issues until the final days of the convention. We had to deal with all the minutiae of the Episcopal Church's struggle with homosexuality before we could consider things like partial birth abortion or school choice.

The 2000 General Convention in Denver was less outwardly dominated by conflict over homosexuality. The leadership worked very, very hard to keep the controversies about sex from infiltrating every aspect of church business, but everyone was aware of the elephant in the room.

The Episcopal fixation on homosexuality may be old news to most. It is old news to me. But the sheer dominance of the issue at general conventions at the turn of the millennium forced me think through some fragmented ideas I had had for a long while. After all, if we take the concrete form of ecclesial life seriously—the church as it is rather than as it ought to be—then we cannot avoid wrestling with the questions raised by the boiling caldron of ecclesiastical politics. For me, that means wrestling with the questions of why conflicts over the gay agenda have become the defining feature of the Episcopal Church and what my disposition ought to be toward those conflicts.

I have come to the following conclusion. The powerful forces within the life of the church that collide in the debate over homosexuality are *not* theological. The conflict is *not* between comprehensive or articulate theological positions. This leads me to think that theology is not the place to start. More important are the primitive, almost atavistic loyalties that shape our lives. More important is the realm of presumptions not arguments, premises not inferences.

I trace the drive toward revision of traditional sexual morality to the Episcopal Church's class loyalties. This is a descriptive claim that, if true, must inform our reflections upon the current conflict over homosexuality. For the upper class from which we draw a large measure of our leadership is not, I think, really very interested in homosexuality in particular; it is interested—*we* are interested—in sexual freedom in general.

But this is only half the picture. We would not fight if our class interests in sexual freedom were overpowering. We fight over homosexuality because our collective and enduring apostolic loyalties stand as a counterforce. Our commitment to the received tradition, quite inarticulate in many ways, makes it impossible to simply step forward into the progressive Promised Land. This needs to be understood if we are to think clearly about the current crisis in our church.

Finally, although these forces have achieved an apparently equal and self-canceling potency in the current debate about homosexuality, they should not be considered equal in the overall life of the church. Our collective loyalty to received teaching should trump. But this is a cryptic summary, and I must turn from outline to argument.

A Cultural Explanation of Revisionary Pressure

It seems hard to believe that the current desire to revise church teaching on sexual morality stems from a study of the Scriptures and immersion in the theological tradition. As many theologians, both conservative and progressive, have pointed out, the Scriptures are dominated by a repressive sexual ethic. The subsequent theological tradition does not alter that ethic significantly. From Origen to Kenneth Kirk, a severe sexual discipline is endorsed, and debate is restricted to the question whether celibate commitment is a "higher" and "fuller" form of discipleship than monogamous, lifelong marriage. Thus a ribald Martin Luther evidenced an altogether healthy and forthright attitude toward human sexuality, pleasure, and the body. Yet he advanced no modification of Christian sexual morality other than a forceful criticism (by no means original to him) of the presumption that celibacy is more meritorious than chaste marital fidelity.

Of course some might object that our age has witnessed foundational new discoveries in exegesis and theology. We might imagine, for example, that this generation is the first to stumble upon God's inclusive love. This is implausible. Luther's view of the reality of salvation in Jesus Christ is as aggressively inclusive as one might imagine. No sinner, no matter how far gone, no matter how alienated from God, is beyond the saving power of the cross. And yet Luther never imagined that this inclusive love would not inspire a repentance that gladly accepts the disciplines of Christian moral expectation.

Or we might imagine that we are following in the footsteps of Richard Hooker, appealing to the threefold cord of Scripture, tradition, and reason. Yet neither Hooker nor any other Anglican divine until the twentieth century ever said anything about sex that could possibly be called upon to support the dramatically revised moral outlook proposed by progressive theologians today. Thus whether progressive or conservative, nearly all agree that our inherited forms of theological reflection are fundamentally at odds with the progressive agenda in sexual morality.

I can imagine that many would continue to object: there *are* theological reasons behind our turn toward revision of sexual morality. But upon closer examination, what often seems like a reason cannot possibly be so. Consider the following: "God does not make mistakes." This slogan tries to capture a Christian commitment to the intrinsic goodness of creation. This is all for the best, and such an affirmation blocks Gnostic metaphysical assumptions rather nicely. But it is not capable of establishing moral distinctions. Are we to say that what is normal, in the strict statistical sense, is natural? This hardly helps those who would use such an affirmation to overcome condemnations of homosexuality. Should we say that *anything* that people desire is natural and therefore good? After the September 11, 2001, attacks on the Pentagon and World Trade Center, we all discovered that most people instinctively and powerfully desire revenge. Should we therefore conclude that revenge is part of the intrinsic goodness of creation and that we must adjust our moral thinking to accommodate this evident fact? After all, God does not make mistakes. No, the goodness of all creation cannot be the major premise for moral arguments. In the context of the debate about sexual morality, it can serve only as a shibboleth.

I could show the futility of other theological slogans. To say that we need a positive attitude toward sexual pleasure is like saying we need a positive attitude toward arguments. Of course sexual intercourse can produce positive goods, just as arguments produce valuable insights. But unsound assumptions and careless reasoning can lead us astray. The undisciplined mind does not bear reliably good fruit, and a clever propagandist can be a real evil. A lack of disciplined sexual desire is just as debilitating and dangerous. Everything turns, then, on what constitutes disciplined sexual desire, and to affirm a positive attitude toward sexual pleasure gives us no insight by which to answer our question. The same holds true for many other attempts to adduce theological justifications for revisionary changes. "New theological perspectives" usually end up making no sense unless one has already decided the moral issues they purport to illuminate.

There are some theologians who are working very hard to move beyond easy and empty slogans. Perhaps a new and rigorous universalism, a holiness without boundaries, a righteousness without judgment, has captured the spiritual imaginations of some progressive Episcopalians. I need deny neither the hard work nor the universal vision. They may, in the end, carry the day. But I am convinced that such work and such vision are peripheral to the actual forces that are driving the Episcopal Church toward revision. In public debates I do not hear cogent arguments in favor of revision. It is always a slogan that is used to dramatize an appeal to pastoral experience. Such appeals to experience have caused me to ask a key question: What exactly is the "social location" of our pastoral work? What is the actual context for our contextual theologies?

We need to face the facts. Demographically, we are the folks who may not read the *New Yorker* but know people who do. (Let me be clear: "we" refers to "us"—the leaders of the church, not necessarily the rank and file.) We are the people who, even if we did not go to an Ivy League university, would be thrilled if our children did. We are the Bobos, the Bourgeois Bohemians winsomely described in a book by David Brooks.[1] We are lawyers who wear Birkenstocks on the weekends and drink lattes with skim milk in order to stay fit. A lawyer might well work for the ACLU or Legal Aid. Plenty of the people at the general conventions of the Episcopal Church are social workers and teachers, and of course over half are clerics. Money is not the issue. We are not necessarily rich, but status is not income. It is the social outlook that counts. We listen to NPR and subscribe to the *New York Times* even if we live in the Midwest. We read serious books and pride ourselves on being open-minded. We congratulate ourselves for not being materialistic and measuring our self-worth in terms of money. We are spiritually sensitive without being judgmental. And most of all, we are serenely confident that we represent the best and most progressive element in our society.

Sexual liberation is most definitely high on the list of Bourgeois Bohemian concerns. We need to be careful here. The issue is not hedonism in any kind of risky or raunchy sense. On the whole, the well-educated, well-off segment of American society has exploited the collapse of sexual taboos in a prudent way. Sixteen is a tad early for sexual intercourse, we think, but college is a very safe environment for sexual exploration. Unwanted pregnancies? Well, that is a problem, but it can be either avoided through intelligent use of birth control or (and do not say this too loudly) terminated with abortion. Just as we downplay the role of abortion in the regime of sexual freedom, we also turn away from the uglier sides of contemporary sexual chaos. Bourgeois Bohemian men tend not to be violent and shamelessly exploitive. The women tend not to be desperate for just any man. As a result, upper-class people seem able to enjoy a relative sexual freedom that is consistent with eventually marrying and having stable (by contemporary standards) families.

Because of this prevailing experience, advocates of further liberation are not threatening. The gay lobby, while unappealing in some of its excesses, is fundamentally congenial to the sensibilities of Bourgeois Bohemians. The typical Episcopalian is not very likely to be committed to the homosexual agenda in any focused sense. Some urban parishes have made gay liberation part of their social justice platform, though this is really rather rare. But that is not the point. The general relaxation of traditional sexual morality is the decisive element. The experience of many upper-class Americans is that it is OK to sleep around a bit—it did not destroy their lives. So, they reason, the old taboos really were unnecessarily strict, just as gay advocates claim. "Hey," says the Bourgeois Bohemian, "if we can neglect the Scriptures on matters of fornication, adultery, and divorce, then why not on homosexuality?"

This helps to explain why homosexuality is so important in the Episcopal Church. It symbolizes the Bourgeois Bohemian confidence that liberated sexual practices can be prudently and wisely absorbed into a socially respectable way of life. But it does more than just symbolize what has in fact occurred in upper-class culture (and across great stretches of American culture as well). Homosexuality is also important *because it reassures.* The gay agenda looms large in the Episcopal Church because Bourgeois Bohemians are not simply bohemian. We do not want to be rebels. We do not want to overthrow the "System" that has, in fact, treated us very well up to this point. We want to secure recognition and affirmation of our sexual practices. And furthermore, for all our class confidence, we need some modest help in keeping things prudent and under control. We do not want our children to fall into the grossness and recklessness of less refined and less wisely enjoyed forms of sexual freedom.

I do not want to be misunderstood. Such affirmation and pastoral guidance are not desired only by homosexuals. In fact, by my analysis, our deeper class preoccupations have little to do with homosexuality. Plenty of divorced men and women want reassurances that it is OK to enter into the world of "date, then fornicate." Plenty of parents want the priest to tell them that having their son's girlfriend sleep in his bed during a visit over Thanksgiving break is OK. Plenty of unmarried thirty-somethings want to go to church as couples, eager to normalize their lives and test the deeper waters of adult responsibility, and do so without judgment. For us, homosexuality is not about the "heterocentric culture"; it is about joining the Bohemian side to the Bourgeois. It is about reconciling sexual freedom with upper-class respectability and perquisites. The role of homosexuality is simple. If homosexuality is OK, then our transgressions are OK.

This aspiration makes discussions of sex in the Episcopal Church cheerfully pleasant. We wish to see everything in terms of the domesticated and sensible world of the well educated and well intentioned. Sex is most definitely not, in our minds, the world of twentysomething meat markets or the Viagra culture of anxiously aging baby boomers. Premarital sex is all about sensitive college students in long-term relationships that we hope will become marriages. It is not the world of boys bragging about conquests and girls who know that they must "put out" in order to stay on the "A-list." It cannot be; otherwise we would have to confront the uglier sides of the sexual revolution and would begin to feel the necessity of judgments and condemnations that might threaten our happy marriage of sexual freedom and upper-class respectability.

Thus the children of Episcopalians never burn with lust; they are motivated by a tentative and altogether understandable "curiosity." Sex is like the public library: we want our children to feel free to explore their interests. In this way we can reassure ourselves that our commitment to sexual freedom (of which an affirmation of homosexuality is but a part) is just a sensible revision of traditional Christian moral strictness. We keep our eyes focused on a gauzy picture of sexual desire and experimentation domesticated by "commitment."

But we also have doubts. A pessimism about sexual desire and the damage that this rarely disciplined desire does to our dignity, our relationships, and our lives continues to creep into the happy scene. Nabokov rings true, and that is disturbing. Hence the importance of homosexuality once again. If we can all agree that gays and lesbians need only to be encouraged into long-term loving relationships, then we can sleep peacefully (with our girlfriends and boyfriends), confident that we are free from censure and judgment as long as we intend that our peccadilloes will, over time, mature into something "loving" and "stable" and characterized by "mutual respect." Homosexuality, then, functions as a reassuring limit case. If we can bless same-sex unions, then we can reassure ourselves that our collective indulgence can be brought under the umbrella of pious and well-meaning sentiments.

Thus the gay issue has a transcending importance in the Episcopal Church. It serves to sustain the Bourgeois Bohemian dream. We can have everything: sexual freedom *and* the outward signs of moral order and personal honor. This is why the issue is not toleration. We very much *want* public acknowledgment and celebration of respectable gay couples. A thrice-divorced bishop can find reassurance in such success stories. And in the ecclesiastical world of would-be bohemian saints, the dream is even more remarkable. The clergy want more than respectability. They want sexual freedom *and* personal sanctity. For this reason clerics are easily tempted into mysticisms of the orgasm. It is not enough for sexual freedoms to be respectable; those freedoms must be revelatory and sacramental.

Debilitating Consequences of Sexual Freedom

I have fallen into parody, and I can imagine that some might think me profoundly insensitive to the real pastoral needs of the moment. Is it actually possible for a single Ivy League graduate to find a suitable partner with the same class credentials *without* participating in the "date, then fornicate" system? Old moral standards seem hopelessly unworkable. At times I am inclined to agree. I am not at all sure how I will respond to my own children as they become adolescents, then go off to college and live the kind of life that I did at that age.

The problem is that we are unable to see how our distortion of Christianity into a spiritually sensitive response to upper-class American preoccupations—a distortion long ago recognized by critics of the Episcopal Church—creates a significant pastoral myopia. If anything, the sensibilities that animate us are even more exclusively upper class than the *haute bourgeois* mores of an earlier time. In the 1950s a delivery man or shop clerk might wish to imitate the upper classes in order to bring the disciplines of domestic grace into his household (no swearing!) and provide his children with the trained reserve that is necessary for upward mobility. Now the Bourgeois Bohemian culture raises the bar. We have revolted against our class responsibilities. We refuse to endorse and conform to the sexual disciplines that serve the needs of all social classes, and that refusal becomes an important marker of Bourgeois Bohemian identity. Those who would condemn sexual sins do not belong to our club. They are the ugly people on the "Religious Right." We demand various forms of the "liberated conscience" for membership.

So in our day a factory worker, shocked by the crudity and violence of popular culture, is unlikely to think the Episcopal Church an aid in the task of imposing the restraint and discipline necessary to guard his children from the dangers of trying to live out the latest rap lyrics. In fact a growing number of professional parents are similarly shocked, and they draw similar conclusions about the inability of the Episcopal Church to help them say no to the swirling temptations of contemporary culture.

Of course, we endorse fine sentiments. A recent church resolution affirms these values: "fidelity, monogamy, mutual affection and respect, careful, honest communication, and the holy love which enables those in such relationships to see in each other the image of God." But we utterly lack specificity of judgment and the will to translate such high-minded ideals into boundaries or norms for behavior. Three cheers for fidelity and monogamy! We are loath to answer the "who, what, when, where" questions that would translate sentiment into principle.

For this reason the ability to say yes to sexual desire and at the same time instill the indispensable disciplines and restraints necessary for social status is increasingly the luxury of those who can afford to isolate their children in exclusive private schools and other institutions (like the Episcopal Church) where the gentle no of prudence and good taste keeps things from getting out of control. Our stunning complacency about the power and perversion of human sexual impulses is, I think, unique to those of us who have the good fortune to be socialized into the benevolent repressions of well-off suburban life. We think we can tuck new sexual freedoms into the traditional patterns of career and civic responsibility. We are confident that the culture of Volvo station wagons and country day schools can absorb the novelty of homosexuality. And maybe we are right. After all, upper-class culture survived the collapse of taboos against divorce. To be sure, lots of folks were maimed en route, but the children still went off to Yale when the time came.

Because the kinds of people who exercise leadership in the Episcopal Church can sustain class identity amid the rising tide of promiscuity, we fail to see the reality that faces the less prosperous and the less disciplined. Not every twenty-year-old male is a sensitive undergraduate who has been socialized to respect women as equals. We live in a culture in which adolescence is the adult ideal, and our society is full of predatory man-boys. Furthermore, modern American culture does not present sex as a matter of love and commitment. Turn on your television and see for yourself. Our culture of sex is about self-satisfaction, the use of sex to get the upper hand in relationships, and most of all, it is about relentless titillation and the ideal of perpetual stimulation.

To think our popular culture anything but perverse, violent, and driven by fantasies (the Eternal Erection has replaced the Eternal Now) is possible only because we live in the secluded comfort of the emotionally and professionally gated communities of Bourgeois Bohemians. Only the most extraordinary sense of moral and spiritual insulation and security could allow a library board member to vote against installing pornography filters on library Internet connections. "We must protect freedom of speech!" God forbid that our precious freedoms might be sacrificed to anything resembling communal responsibility for decency—to say nothing of morality. The same holds for attitudes toward sex in the Episcopal Church. We are the church for the blessed, and God forbid we should sacrifice our precious sexual freedom for the sake of those who, living without the safety nets of upper-class life, need discipline, not affirmation, and clarity of moral judgment, not sensitive pastoral reassurance.

So I think about the sexual politics of the Episcopal Church with dismay. I am not concerned about the postmodern clichés about heterosexism and fantasies of unlimited erotic self-expression. After all, these kinds of extremism have little place in the Bourgeois Bohemian way of life. They have no real voice in the Episcopal Church, beyond marginal figures at places like the Episcopal Divinity School. Nor do I mean personal shock. I attended those high-tone schools that have always provided a cultural "finish" to the upper classes, and gay rights is now an integral part of the training they provide. "Dikes for Dukakis" was just one more element of the landscape of the Bourgeois Bohemian culture I know so well.

The surprising truth of our accommodations to the Bourgeois Bohemian demand for sexual freedom is the ordinariness of it all. In the past I kidded myself that our class identity as a denomination was the result of historical circumstances and institutional inertia. Now I am forced to recognize that we are drawing inward upon ourselves as a matter of policy. (Again, "we" refers to "us," the leadership class. The rank and file often lack our refined socialization and therefore approach sexual freedom with greater anxiety.) For this reason I find myself despairing: will *anybody* not surrounded by the highest advantages and privileges of our society be attracted to a denomination that preaches sexual freedom with blissful naiveté?

The Counterforce Against Revision

Well, people *are* attracted to the Episcopal Church, and so my despair is at least one-sided, if not misguided. I cannot count the number of graduate students I have met who did their B.A.'s at Wheaton College, where they became Episcopalians. For some our present lack of clarity on sexual morality is appealing. For others it is regrettable. But for none is our collective conflict over sexual morality decisive. By all accounts, they are attracted to our church because of the apostolic density of our worship and the depth of our tradition. They become Episcopalians because they are convinced that such density and depth are a more secure anchor for their faith than the evangelical traditions in which they were raised. In short, these students, like many other adults who have come to the Episcopal Church, are attracted to the other side of the reality of the Episcopal Church that makes our present conflicts so bitter—not any particular theology but our no-doubt uneven but powerful loyalty to our past.

This apostolic loyalty is a defining feature of the present church as much as our class loyalty, but it cannot be explained by social location. For this reason our struggle over sexual morality does *not* mirror the larger culture wars in America. Our leaders are almost entirely on the side of the progressive and liberal elite in our society. In cultural sensibility we are far, far closer to NARAL, NOW, and the ACLU than to the Moral Majority or the Christian Coalition. What percentage of bishops, I ask, are registered Republicans? Who subscribes to *Commentary* or *First Things* or the *Weekly Standard?* Who makes donations to the Heritage Foundation, to say nothing of the Cato Institute or Focus on the Family? Because our class loyalties are so obviously tilted toward the left, I must conclude that the resistant and conservative forces cannot be explained sociologically. We are not split on ideological grounds that can be traced to a broader cultural split.

How, then, should we understand the apostolic loyalty to inherited tradition that offers such powerful resistance to the revisions much desired by Bourgeois Bohemian upper-class culture? To begin to answer this question, consider the Unitarians and the UCC. They do not fight about homosexuality, and this is not because they are great lovers of peace and concord. They do not fight because they have made up their minds. They have largely jettisoned the hindering weight of the Western theological tradition on this matter, as on many others. We fight ("we" meaning "us," the leadership class of the church) because we have *not* agreed that our theological tradition has made a fundamental error in the realm of sexual morality (or for that matter in any other realm).

It is a simple fact that the past continues to exert a living grip on the Episcopal Church, and this explains the energy and determination of the counterforce that resists revision. The upshot is clear for all to see. To the extent that we as a church do not see our vocation as innovative or revolutionary but as reiterative and preservative, we may often share the pastoral experiences that seem to cry out for revision, but we just as often continue to demur from the scale and scope of departure from inherited forms and practices that such revisions seem to require. We—the leadership class—hesitate and temporize, often to the great dissatisfaction of progressive activists who cannot understand why bishops or priests who are so empathic with their cause are unwilling to simply do the deed, take the knife and make the cut from the past.

This preservative hesitation is based on accurate intuitions concerning the scope and depth of progressive arguments. Consider, for example, L. William Countryman's exegesis of Acts 10.[2] It involves St. Peter's vision of God's command to eat the unclean animals, a vision that translates into the inclusion of Gentiles in the baptismal covenant. Countryman reads this as a story that points toward the "end of taboo." We are to see how Jesus Christ breaks down artificial, fear-imposed boundaries, and Countryman draws the conclusion that this supports full inclusion of homosexuals in the life of the church.

Of course this begs the question whether calling homosexual acts sinful is "artificial" or motivated by "fear," but that is not my point. More important are the open-ended possibilities of this allegorical interpretation. Many now think that baptism is an artificial boundary that we establish in order to maintain the "purity" of the church, and so, following Countryman's way of thinking, they insist that all are invited to the Lord's Table. Thus the single most enduring and fundamental aspect of eucharistic discipline—the requirement of baptism—falls by the wayside. Here the scope and scale of revision seem to spin out of control, and a collective loyalty to inherited forms rebels against an emerging chaos of theology and practice.

I want to dwell on this point, because it establishes my claim that the conservative resistance to revision has a different status from progressive calls for change. Insofar as progressives genuinely seek an ecclesially loyal theological justification for revised sexual morality, they must accept the retrospective apostolic burden. Countryman does so by accepting the discipline of exegetical justification, rather than simply waving his hands and dismissing Scripture as an inconvenient impediment to progress (as do many others). He wishes to advance arguments to show revision possible without the loss of any essential doctrine or commitment. The changes are surgical and reparative of the tradition, not assaulting and destructive. Thus a presumptive loyalty to the tradition should be assumed by all, conservative *and* progressive.

But this shared concern does not make their situations equal. We need to recognize that the conservative has a privileged role in this debate. Against the representatives of continuity, the progressive has the burden of proof. Seeming discontinuities must be shown to be just that, apparent but not real. The progressive must show two things: (1) how homosexuality is in fact permitted by scriptural and traditional principles and teachings, and (2) that the reasoning behind this will not endorse a wholesale revolution in the church's faith and practice.

This leads to an asymmetry of argument. The progressive needs to step back from inherited assumptions about doctrine and discipline in order to construct arguments showing how novelties and revisions are consistent with the density and depth of our inherited common life. The conservative need not do so. The conservative needs only to affirm a loyalty to the inherited traditions, give a fair hearing to progressives, and accept responsibility for showing how progressive arguments do not adequately demonstrate that a change would be a change-in-continuity rather than change leading to discontinuity.

To be more specific, I need not defend traditional sexual morality. I can assume it. I need only to show (as I have attempted to do in passing) that proposals and strategies for revision are revolutionary, not evolutionary.

This can frustrate those who wish for a "fair" debate, but the life of the church is not the same as that of the Oxford Union. The conditions for any experiential or pastoral or theological arguments for revision must be established by our collective commitment to uphold the faith and teaching of the apostles, as well as the doctrine and discipline of our church, not by the principles of academic disputation. We are not a church of the "free and open search for truth"; we are a church of those who would follow our Lord Jesus Christ. Insofar as the Episcopal Church, unlike Unitarian churches, has been founded upon (and continues to seek to nurture) a loyalty to received tradition, convinced that this tradition is (in part) indispensable and (on the whole) helpful, we must presume the fittingness of the present way in which we are taken captive by the gospel promise. This means that in any theological discussion of sexual discipline, the burden of proof rests with the party of change. This simple truth must be acknowledged if we are to do justice to our common and collective apostolic loyalty.

Concluding Thoughts in Defense of Ecclesial Conservation

This affirmation of the presumptive authority of the church's status quo can seem stultifying to our Emersonian souls. Surely we must have a vision and experience and personal theology that give life to our faith. I quite agree. But beware of assuming that loyalty to inherited forms impairs rather than empowers. If anything defines Anglicanism, it is the rejection of this assumption and the affirmation of its opposite.

The more I have studied Anglican divines, the more I have become aware that Anglicanism advances no recognizable "idea of Christianity." Is there any body of literature properly called "Anglican dogmatics"? About theology, in the grand sense, the Anglican tradition has never seemed able to agree. Rather, the primary identifying feature of Anglicanism has been its loyalty, often inarticulate, to an ecclesiastical tradition that it has never been able to add up to a tidy sum. Thus Hooker defended no theology; he defended that which Anglicanism has rallied around: the common liturgy given and not invented, an Episcopal ministry self-consciously constrained by past practice, a vernacular Scripture commended to all for the discipline of daily study, and the unruly pile of treatises written by the church fathers.

It is for this reason that, however difficult it might be to characterize the "theology" of Hooker's *Laws of Ecclesiastical Polity*, I can report with confidence that his "method" across all eight books is to refute, point by point, the Puritan claim that these many elements of Anglican life are impediments to gospel faithfulness. They are for Hooker *media divina*, "living facts" (to use F. D. Maurice's winsome phrase) that rightly press upon and constrain our lives in Christ. Their heterogeneity can be overwhelming. Of these "living facts," few are necessary, many are fitting, some have the arbitrary contingency of providential appointment. But for Hooker, the many parts, never unified or validated by a supervening theological vision, rightly constrain our judgment and limit our impetuous desire for purer, more perspicuous, more theologically integrated forms of common life.

In the end, Hooker was a conservative without an "idea of Christianity" or a "systematic theology." But he was not inarticulate. I think he identifies important reasons that we should cherish and endorse the apostolic and retrospective loyalty that we all share and that currently hinders progressive thought on sexual discipline. Hooker certainly never anticipated our debates about sexual discipline, but he was well acquainted with the "improving" and revisionary impulse. He saw that the theological changes endorsed by the Puritan Walter Travers created an atmosphere of flux and unsettled discipline and worship in which (to use the language of John Spenser's preface "To the Reader" in the 1604 edition of the *Laws*) the "fire of envy and malice and heart-burning, and zeal to every man's private cause" easily flourishes.

The idea is quite simple, and it motivated centuries of Anglican resistance to the reformatory project of radical Protestants. Absent submission to established and public forms of church life, private judgment (however sacred for the formation of one's conscience) tempts us to try to take over the church and offer our personal visions as new ordering principles. The danger is not just glorious pontificating of the sort we must endure from Bishop Spong. Given the varied and recondite nature of Christian reality, no one vision seems sufficient to sway all, and therefore "tedious contentions" (again, Dr. Spenser's language) emerge in which one person's personal theology wars with another's. Partisan passions are inflamed. The church is wracked by inglorious conflict.

Loyalty to the inherited tradition does not guarantee anything like homogeneity of thought. As I have noted, anyone seeking to study Anglican "theology" will be rather shocked by the heterogeneity. Nor does that loyalty produce concert in action, as past conflicts over sacramental practice demonstrate. Furthermore, such loyalty and deference to tradition does not lead to stasis, as the evident changes in Anglicanism show. However, this habit of presuming the integrity and the appropriateness of our tradition has served as the glue that has held Anglicanism together. It has been the "home base" for all who would debate or cajole the church to change. And when things start to get unsteady, the collective impulse is to find a way back "home."

We should not regret this retreating and retrospective feature of Anglicanism. The desire to find a way back "home" may be a sign of an unwillingness to risk what is, in the end, not yours or mine but ours, the treasure given the whole church. It is not the result of a weak-kneed fear of change. Thus Dr. Spenser commends to us the prudence of Hooker's conservatism: "So much better were it in these our dwellings of peace, to endure any inconvenience whatsoever in the outward frame, than in desire of alteration, thus to set the whole house on fire." This is as true in our time as Hooker's, and the imperative is straightforward. We should endure the pastoral inconveniences and experiential "contradictions" of traditional sexual morality, inconveniences and contradictions that may have more to do with the social location of our ministry than the depths of our theological vision. We should do so for two reasons.

First, an inflamed church tempts all of us toward ever greater violence toward the body of Christ. This is by no means a danger only among conservatives. The last twenty years have seen countless acts of episcopal and diocesan willfulness among progressives. On both sides, the judgment is simple: better that the whole church should go up in flames than that your or my personal vision of faith should be compromised or refused.

Second and just as important, as my brief summary of Countryman's exegesis of Acts 10 tries to suggest, revisionary ambition throws so much up for grabs that we may well discover that revision of church teaching on sexual discipline will "set the whole house on fire." Hooker was aware that when the house starts to burn, the flames easily burn out of control. Shall we require baptism? Do we need ordained ministers? Are all boundaries illegitimate? What is and is not permitted? Do we even need a common book of prayer?

A surgical change in matters of sexual discipline may be possible. Our inherited tradition is extraordinarily complex, deep, and durable, and someone may find arguments that make sense of a change-in-continuity in this matter. But I think we are kidding ourselves if we do not see that a wide and violent range of revisionary pressures could easily erupt. There is a very good chance that once unhindered by loyalty to the past, surging forces of ideological revision will be very destructive. Just look at the pallid liturgies currently produced to meet ideological standards. They are as spiritually sanitized as our cheery view of sexual desire.

But I do not want to end on a note of warning, but rather hope. Our loyalty is not merely protective; it is productive and the source of our joy. John Henry Newman was a great lover of reason and a master of ideas. However, he recognized that a notional grasp is not a real engagement. Ideas, even ideas of Christianity, are not motive, for they lack full, personal force. For this reason the brute givenness of the Christian tradition, its particularized forms and determinate shapes, need not be regretted, need not be raised up to the level of thought in order to be exercise its proper potency in our lives. "Revelation," he writes in one of his Oxford University sermons, "meets us with simple and distinct *facts* and *actions*, not with painful inductions from existing phenomena, not with generalized laws or metaphysical conjecture."[3] That which we have been given in this church—our prayer book, our polity, the vernacular Scripture that is now the possession of the English-speaking world, our mild and humane moral discipline, the patristic inheritance—these things are the *facts* and *actions* that have the fullest power to convert our hearts and minds.

Our apostolic loyalty might hinder our moral instincts and compromise our pastoral freedom in many ways. Our collective loyalty to the inherited traditions of our church will not necessarily help us deal with the Bourgeois Bohemian desire to join sexual freedom to social respectability. Nonetheless, I think that we must recognize that this loyalty, however silent and inarticulate, brings us ever closer to the actual and palpable instruments of God's sanctifying love, the "living facts" that have been built up by generation upon generation of those who have dwelt in the power of *the* "living fact," our incarnate Lord. Our ideas of Christianity, our experience of God, and our personal theologies cannot transform our hearts. They are consequences rather than causes. Rather, it is the exquisitely particular, richly detailed, and dauntingly complex thing called the Christian tradition, ours in its Anglican hue, that shapes us rightly and faithfully. Christ shapes us by drawing us into conformity with his body. *Lex orandi, lex credendi:* the law of prayer is the law of belief. This great truism is a living truth only when we give a privileged place to apostolic loyalty and conservation. For we must be shaped rather than shape if we are to bear in our bodies the marks of Jesus (see Gal. 6:17). Acknowledging this greater receptive discipline and accepting the constraints of the tradition should be at the foundation of any deliberations about the particular matter of sexual discipline in the contemporary church.

The Imperative
of Intimacy

8

Toward a Postliberal Ecclesial Spirituality

> The time is coming when people will not put up with sound doctrine, but having itching ears, they will accumulate for themselves teachers to suit their own desires, and will turn away from listening to the truth and wander away to myths. As for you, always be sober, endure suffering, do the work of an evangelist, carry out your ministry fully.
>
> 2 Timothy 4:3–5

Without doubt spirituality is a growth industry. A quick visit to the local bookshop shows that the "inspiration" section has far more titles than sections of theology or biblical studies. Seminarians often list spirituality as their first priority. Parishes want to hire priests with "strong" spirituality. An ability to guide others to a "deeper" spirituality is now a bullet point on resumés. One feels as though the labyrinth will soon become an indispensable feature of church architecture. Spirituality is like good weather: it is hard to see how you can have too much. Given its ubiquity, how should we read this sign of the times? What does it say about our supposed secular age that spirituality is so much in fashion?

Whether St. Teresa's *Interior Castle* is as often read as bought, or more important, understood as often as read, I do not know. Indeed I cannot venture any empirical observations about spirituality and its role in contemporary church life.[1] So instead of trying to capture this important but amorphous thing called "spirituality" by survey and description, I wish to undertake an exercise of defining spirituality in terms of its function, and with this definition I will analyze its role within the life of the church.

I hope to achieve three goals. First, for all the hype about our *postmodern* condition, the felt need for spiritual growth tends toward characteristically *modern* strategies, and these modern strategies continue to define contemporary ecclesiastical discussion and pastoral work. Therefore a formal and functional definition of spirituality will allow me to give a precise account of what makes modern Christian spirituality modern. Second, spirituality is not a simple fad; it speaks to a genuine and felt need for a deep and reliable source of spiritual power. A functional definition yields some observations about the situation in our church that makes modern spirituality such an important and influential factor in addressing this need. Finally, typically modern approaches to spirituality fail to relieve the present thirst for closer and more effective contact with the gospel. I hope to use this account of spirituality to explain why this is so and to suggest an approach that is not modern and therefore offers hope of greater success.

Spirituality Defined

The daily round of work seems flat and insufficient. Domestic life is comfortable but uninspiring. Introspection yields the same tired clichés. For these and any number of other reasons, people read books, go to workshops, attend lectures, take lessons in martial arts, join prayer groups, seek out a spiritual director. They want *more:* more depth, more vibrancy, more engagement, more insight, more commitment. People want what the Johannine literature calls "life." Spirituality, then, is anything—books, techniques of prayer, styles of worship, therapies—that brings life, in this Johannine sense.

This same basic desire and need obtains in the ecclesiastical realm. Like the daily round, the life of the church, what we might call the first-order language and practice of apostolic Christianity (Scripture, liturgy, doctrine, and ecclesial structures) seems dull and lifeless. Sunday services seem merely routine. Creedal affirmations seem archaic and abstract. The Scriptures seem at once overly familiar and strangely alien. Church governance seems an empty exercise in institutional maintenance. Just as the facts of everyday life seem to require something *more* in order to give life, so also do the facts of church life seem to require *more*. "Christian spirituality," then, denotes the many and various efforts to find life in the *concreta Christiana,* the aggregate of first-order language and practice that constitutes the visible forms of Christian life. It is any undertaking designed to bring depth and significance to what has been centrally important to Christianity for centuries. It is the attempt to wrest from the apostolic inheritance the *more* we faithfully believe it has to offer.

This can sound too abstract, too formal. I offer a passage from the Gospel of John to help clarify. In the third chapter, a Pharisee named Nicodemus comes to Jesus in order to interview him. Nicodemus acknowledges Jesus' spiritual authority, affirming that he is a teacher from God. Jesus then offers a saying: "Very truly, I tell you, no one can see the kingdom of God without being born from above" (John 3:3).

In the brief colloquy that follows, Nicodemus raises difficulties. "How can anyone be born after having grown old? Can one enter a second time into the mother's womb and be born?" (v. 4). Jesus elaborates by teaching that one must be born of water and the Spirit in order to enter the kingdom of God. Nicodemus then asks, "How can these things be?"

Jesus' teaching clearly foreshadows a first-order element in the life of the church, the ritual practice of baptism, and Nicodemus's final question is the animating question of spirituality. How can the sorts of things that Jesus teaches, and the church enacts, be real and effective? How can something like baptism be full of the potency of God for new life? Nicodemus's question "How can these things be?" signals his need. He cannot see how Jesus' teaching meshes with everyday life; he cannot see how it has the potency of a real transformation. He needs something to get him to see the import, the life, in what Jesus is teaching.

To step back and speak formally, spirituality is *whatever* helps in answering Nicodemus's question. How, for example, can things like the ritual of baptism or the ancient texts of Scripture or the ecclesiastical institutions of our church be a power and potency for new life? How can mere ritual transform lives? How can the historically distant words of others communicate the divine to us in the present? How can structures of power and hierarchy bring us to communion with God? These are simply more specific forms of the question "How can the basic stuff of Christianity have the power of life?" Thus defined, spirituality is based on the x that closes the gap between what the first-order language promises and what we can see and inhabit in apostolic Christianity as the power of life. Thus we might meditate on the formative power of ritual.

We might memorize Scripture in order bring it closer to our daily lives. We might study the history of Anglicanism in order to appreciate the origins of and purposes for inherited forms of ecclesiastical governance. At each turn we try to close the gap, try to get closer to that which gives life.

An analogy to method in science helps. Scientific methods are those practices or disciplines that allow the scientist to isolate and identify the relevant features of an experiment and, in so doing, to wrest from nature some aspect of its structure and function. Method brings confusing phenomena into focus, and as a result we come to see the life, so to speak, of reality. For the statistician, the double-blind trial is the x. The placebo allows us to factor out the innumerable psychological and social influences that compound with the effects of a new drug or treatment. For the chemist, experimental method is the x. Repeatable experiments allow us to determine when phenomena are related as cause to effect.

In a similar fashion, spirituality is a method, a practice or discipline, that brings the confusing phenomena of inherited Christianity into focus. By virtue of some x, we come to see the point and purpose of baptism, the intent and meaning of Scripture, the religious significance of institutions.

Modern Spirituality Analyzed

With this formal definition, we can analyze the methods of modern spirituality. A great modern Anglican figure, William Temple, provides an exemplary instance. Temple was an influential figure. He represented what we might call the "thinking and progressive" theology that dominated twentieth-century Anglicanism. His impulse was restorative, not critical. He wished to bring others to see how much Christianity has to offer; he did not wish to strip away the first-order language and practice in order to arrive at a Christian minimum that might be acceptable to the "modern mind." In this sense Temple sought what pastors and theologians have always sought: to bring others into fuller participation in the life of the church and the truth it teaches and enacts. Nonetheless, the method Temples uses, the x he uses to lever us toward the life that the apostolic inheritance has to offer, is distinctively modern.

Consider, for example, one of Temple's early sermons, titled "Religious Experience."[2] His topic is the dialogue between Nicodemus and Jesus, and his theme is our theme: spirituality. According to Temple's reading of the third chapter of the Gospel of John, Nicodemus cannot understand Jesus because Nicodemus has a false view of God's power of life. Here is how Temple develops the contrast. "For the Lord and his disciples," Temple writes, "religion was first and foremost not doctrine, whether traditional or rationalist, and not ceremonial."[3] In other words, religion—and for Temple this word means a living and genuinely spiritual faith—is *not* constituted by first-order language and practice. Nicodemus's mistake, according to Temple, was to look to things like doctrine and ritual for life. Instead Temple insists that the power of God for life is found "first and foremost" in "a personal experience."[4] Religious experience is the x that brings us to see and dwell in the Light that is Life. Religious experience is the lever of spirituality; it opens up for us the mysteries of faith that are genuinely present but too often hidden in the things we do, say, and read in church.

With this distinction between religious experience and doctrine and ceremony, Temple is equipped to undertake the project of reengaging the gears of modern life with the language and practice of the church. Do his listeners find the doctrines of the church distant and irrelevant to the pressing moral and social issues of the day? Fear not, reassures Temple, the ancient doctrines betoken the same experience of love that is, he insists, the deepest motive for progressive and life-giving social and political commitments. Do his listeners find the ceremony of the church archaic and constricting? Look again, urges Temple, for these rituals express the same experience of awe and submission that characterizes great art and high morality. This experience, for Temple, is tied to "personality."[5] In all the "higher" endeavors we seek to transcend the daily round, the mute world of scientific facts, the workaday principles of utility and efficiency, and in so doing we seek "personality." In short, we seek life in the Johannine sense, and the task of the Christian is to find and champion the power of "personality" that emerges from all genuine and life-giving experience. As Temple concludes, "it is the life so lived which has in it that religious experience by which in the end all doctrines must be tested, and from which in the end the solution to every problem comes."[6]

For our purposes, what is important is that we see the *form* of Temple's spirituality, for that form is distinctively and ubiquitously modern. Temple is aware that classical Christianity seems dead and lifeless to many of the "best minds" of his time—the intellectuals, the poets, the progressives. When faced with apostolic Christianity and its claims to have the power of life, the best and the brightest ask, "How can this be?" To answer this question, Temple identifies the x that can serve as the fulcrum for levering vibrancy, vitality, and passion into the first-order language and practice of faith. The x is religious experience in this sermon, but for modern spirituality the x could be any quality, capacity, or value. It might be mutuality or community. It might be ultimate concern or the desire for transcendence. No matter what the specific x, the same pattern predominates. We must refocus our attention away from the first-order language and practice and turn to the x that illuminates the deeper, more essential, more universal and personal dimension of faith. If we turn toward this x, then we can *see* how our apostolic inheritance has the power of life. The x illuminates, and as Temple forthrightly affirms, it is the test of that which gives life and that which does not.[7]

John Shelby Spong is no William Temple. He is not interested in reinfusing the distinctive language and practice of Christianity with a renewed potency. Nonetheless, Spong's basic approach follows that of Temple. They differ only in Spong's pessimistic assessment of the capacity of our apostolic inheritance to manifest the potency for life that Jesus promises. Where Temple thinks he can use the x to bring out the real power and efficacy of apostolic Christianity, Spong uses the x to show the irrelevance and even debilitating immorality and irrationality of the first-order language and practice of the church. A great deal fails the test. Little survives the method of the x.[8]

It is very easy to caricature Spong.[9] Yet Spong's project is not atypical; it follows the basic pattern of modern spirituality. The initial assumption is the same. Apostolic Christianity finds itself a weakened force in our culture. This seems an inescapable fact, much commented upon by both unbelievers and believers. Many have sought explanations. Perhaps the rise of modern science is the crucial change. Perhaps the mythic structure of the premodern world—the hoary three-tiered universe—no longer has a hold on our imaginations. Perhaps modern persons no longer fear eternal judgment. Perhaps our therapeutic culture has erased the experience of guilt. Whatever the cause, to use Spong's image, in a broad, cultural sense Christianity is "dying."

For this reason, liberal or not, all see the need to reinvigorate and renew the power of life in the *concreta Christiana*. Some strategy of spirituality must be undertaken. To do so, the proponent of modern spirituality appeals to some x that will lever us toward spiritual enrichment. This x (a phenomenology of religious experience, a philosophy of existence, a refined moral sensibility, an appeal to richness, depth, and meaning) is the light that shines in the increasing darkness of traditional forms. That which seems lifeless needs to be seen from a new perspective so that the hidden treasures might be found. That which is darkened by anachronism, or routine, or mythological thinking, or superstition, or whatever other labels one wishes to put on the diminishing and obscuring aspects of the Christian tradition, must find a new source of light so that hidden truths might be seen. Some x will bring us to see what Nicodemus could not see: the power of life. It is not at all surprising, then, that someone like Spong would wish to be done with the dead weight of that which is dark and lifeless and have a simple religion of the x.

Our Current Situation

A religion of the x turns out to be a very silly affair. For Spong it reduces to tired slogans from 1950s theology—"New Being," "the Courage to Be," and the like. Not by accident did the more serious minds and more serious souls such as Temple see the x as an aid to dwelling more fully and more faithfully in the faith of the apostles, and not as the object of faith.[10] Yet Spong is a sign of the times. Why undertake all the heavy lifting to find spiritual significance in first-order Christian language and practice? Should we not allow for some well-considered triage in order to cut away the lifeless parts of the Christian tradition? After all, only a fool tries to rescue that which is beyond recovery. With this line of reasoning, Spong can claim to take the only reasonable approach. Why should pastors exhaust themselves preaching Christ crucified when New Being is so radiant with life?

The danger of Spong rests in that fact that the debilitated, lifeless *concreta Christiana* tempts us to look elsewhere rather than, with Temple, looking again at the first-order language and practice of the apostolic tradition. This temptation is strong because the lifelessness of Christianity is more than a cultural phenomenon. The problem is more than anachronism and mythological thinking. The problem is not just that cultural elites are increasingly alienated from Christianity, out of both ignorance and disdain. Recent developments within the church have added a new and intensifying twist.

For complex reasons, in the last thirty years the intraecclesial plausibility of apostolic Christianity has collapsed in the Episcopal Church USA. The first-order language and practice of the apostles are now the center of conflict in our church rather than the source of common life. Should the patriarchal images of traditional liturgies be used to celebrate the Eucharist? Should baptism be necessary for the reception of communion? Should ordination be necessary for eucharistic presidency? Should we bless in the name of the Father, Son, and Holy Spirit? These are now open questions, and the language and practice that we have inherited seem to have no clear power to provide answers. Indeed apostolic language and practice generate the problems, not solutions. Let me give examples.

First, consider the effective power of Scripture in the church today. However much any of us might devote ourselves to Scripture, it is certainly a fact that this central text exerts little influence. To be sure, most people, most of the time, have gone about the affairs of life without great regard for the teachings of Scripture. But what is striking in the present context is the way the very core of Christian life and practice is alienated from the Bible. I remember the shock I experienced as a deputy at my first general convention of the Episcopal Church USA. I listened to seven sermons and speeches by bishops. Only one had even a tangential relationship to the Bible. It was not simply that the Bible went unquoted. Rather, the sermons focused relentlessly on the x that would guide us toward whatever the preacher imagined to be a fuller life in the Spirit (respecting our differences, acknowledging "otherness," recognizing the hermeneutical circle, and so on). The words and phrases of Scripture were treated as dysfunctional, and not surprisingly, for the current difficulties facing the church do not concern the putative conflict between the Bible and natural science. The darkness of the present age comes from internal struggles over the text. Does it authorize women's ordination? Does it require us to address God as Father? Does it condemn homosexuality? Does it establish the polity of bishop, priest, and deacon? The Scriptures have become the site of contest and conflict rather than the instrument of adjudication. Therefore the x of modern spirituality takes Scripture's place as the device for disclosing God's power.

So even if Scripture exerts influence over our hearts and continues to have a central place in our worship, when we reflect upon the current life of the church, we find ourselves asking Nicodemus's question: "How can these things be?" How can Scripture be the Word of God when it is set aside by the religious professionals who always have had a vested interest in scriptural authority, when it seems mute before the most pressing issues within the church's life, when it is now thought to be the very source and cause of conflict and difficulty in ecclesiastical affairs? After all, to the extent that First World Anglicanism is concerned about patriarchy and uncertain about sexual morality, the brute particularity and clarity of Scripture create confusion and blindness rather than clarity and light.

To be sure, throughout the centuries theologians have struggled to make sense out of the unruly diversity of Scripture and to bring it into coherent relationship with worldly wisdom. Aristotelian philosophy posed problems in the thirteenth century; theories of evolution created difficulties in the nineteenth century. In this sense Scripture has always been a "problem." However, this problem is now intensified. In current debates Scripture is so deeply implicated in the perceived impediments to fuller life (patriarchy or homophobia or fear of difference or ethnocentrism—take your pick) that it is ruled out as the source of a possible solution. We default, then, to an x, and the silliness of Bishop Spong's religion of the x is waiting in the wings.

The same might be said about baptism. One need not be an unbeliever or scoffer to find oneself in Nicodemus's position. The liturgy of baptism focuses on dramatic renunciations and promises of new life. Nonetheless, Anglicans blend into contemporary society with such ease that the rites of baptism cannot help but seem empty and impotent. The baptismal covenant is much on the mouths of our leadership in the Episcopal Church, but more often than not, the covenant is with the world—defending creation, fighting for social justice, building an egalitarian, inclusive community. It is not a covenant with the God of Israel. So, if we are honest about this, we must ask Nicodemus's question: "How can this be?" How can baptism be a real source of new life?

Of course, we should recognize that Christians have always and everywhere blended into society with troubling ease. The Augustinian basis of Anglican ecclesiology grows out of this fact. Yet, here again baptism is not just weakened by human failings; it comes to be seen as the very source of the church's woes. Thus in the United States many argue that the requirement of baptism for the reception of communion creates the boundaries that Jesus came to tear down.[11] Just as we too easily separate male from female, white from black, sexually pure from sexually impure, so also do we mark those who are "in" the church and those who are "out." So instead of serving as the sacrament of new life, baptism is treated as a barrier and impediment to the new life of inclusive community centered in the eucharistic self-offering of God in Jesus Christ. The rejection of apostolic practice follows: anyone who wishes to receive the sacrament of the bread and wine should be invited to the altar. Thus the impotence of baptism is redoubled. Not only does it seem to fail as a rite of transformation, but more important, it comes to be seen as a Christian practice *that stands in the way of full life in the Spirit.* Again, apostolic Christianity is the source of the problem, not the source of the solution, and to the x we turn for help and guidance.

The Catholic order of our church provides a final and striking illustration. One can have little doubt that the egalitarian sensibilities of Americans have always made the office of bishop somewhat implausible. Mine is a culture of Congregationalists. Nonetheless, most of the time bishops could claim to ensure, however imperfectly, continuity, order, and unity within the church. This is no longer the case. Bishops are now flashpoints of controversy and symbols of the current disunity of the Episcopal Church. Bishops take up causes within the church, ordaining gays and lesbians to the clergy without regard to the constraints of mutual consultation and deliberation. Bishops function as ecclesiastical aggressors, deepening and intensifying church divisions, as the recent ordination of "missionary" bishops to the United States self-consciously intends.

Again, the point is not that contemporary bishops fail to be saintly, intelligent, and cooperative. The history of the church is full of malfeasance, ill will, and vicious politics. Rather, the point is the redoubled lifelessness of the episcopal office. In the United States, bishops now recognize how divisive is their office, and thus they interpret their call as "managing diversity." This means devolving as much apostolic authority as possible onto the local parish, allowing each to make decisions according to the perceived spiritual needs of the locale. The less a bishop acts like a bishop, the more hope we have for avoiding heartrending battles over doctrine and practice within a diocese. We get our Congregationalism through the back door. Certainly, then, Nicodemus's question is pressing: "How can these things be?"

In each case, we need to turn to spirituality. As we have seen, modern spirituality was developed to overcome the darkness and obscurity that modernity imputes to Christianity. However, times have changed. Faced with debilitation created by the church itself, modern spirituality now easily leads away from rather than into the apostolic faith. The x seems the only point of sanity and security amid the dissolution of the church's common life, and therefore, often without being fully aware of the process, church leaders nurture a religion of the x. The means toward spiritual renewal becomes the end. The approach championed by Temple dissolves into the spiritual nostrums advanced by Spong.

To combat this tendency and the temptation of the religion of the x, evangelicalism and Anglo-Catholicism offer alternatives. They reject the methods of modern spirituality and its turn to the x. Evangelicalism and Anglo-Catholicism set out to show how the first-order language and practice have sufficient power to lever us into a life-giving faith in Jesus Christ. The x upon which we must rely for leverage toward new life cannot come from outside. It must be a constituent of the *concreta Christiana*.

Although evangelicalism and Anglo-Catholicism reject the turn to the x in modern spirituality, they assume the same modern pastoral challenges. A. G. Hebert is typical. He writes, "The present age, with its manifold divisions, confusions, and distractions, can hardly be an age of theological synthesis. There are many questions which we are not capable of answering satisfactorily."[12] Hebert recognizes that the collapse of Christendom makes Christianity intellectually and culturally marginal. He is confident, nonetheless, that the common life of the church offers a durable "fact" of sufficient coherence and integrity to anchor a life of faith, even in turbulent post-Christian times. We should advance into this "fact" in order to dwell more fully in its power. Such is the spiritual method of Anglo-Catholicism. The evangelical makes nearly identical assumptions, differing only in the "fact" that anchors the Christian life amid the storms of modernity. For the evangelical, Scripture is the great "fact," and we should embrace its testimony as the reliable key to divine power and truth.

In spite of self-conscious resistance to the modern default to a spirituality of the *x*, evangelicalism and Anglo-Catholicism are becoming increasingly implausible for the same reason that modern spirituality is becoming increasingly post-Christian. Both powerfully and effectively address the spiritual challenges of Christianity in the context of modernity. Both advance effective techniques for bringing people to see the life in apostolic teachings and forms that modern society finds dead or deadly. Yet neither is capable of addressing the ways in which the church *itself* seems to obscure and weaken the very core of its life and practice.

Evangelicalism is able to engender a living faith, but it can no longer presume a functioning communal form. Jesus is the resurrection and the life, and that life is bound up with his kingdom. At some point, no matter how intensely devoted and personally transformed each of us might be, without a kingdom in which to dwell apostolic Christianity becomes a private and personal reality that is fragmented and detached from its public expression. Because of this, an Anglican evangelical faces three unappealing choices: (1) deny that contemporary Anglicanism is tortured by fundamental conflicts and contradictions, or (2) deny that the church is necessary, or (3) come to terms with the impotence, emptiness, and contradictions in the contemporary church. For the evangelical, the third option is painful. Scripture promises real and effective transformation of our common life. Thus if we acknowledge the deep failures of the church, then we most come to terms with the implied impotence of Scripture to engender that which it promises. It seems unable to form and sustain the community of faith. Nicodemus's question is apt indeed. How can these things be?

The Anglo-Catholic follows a different path but ends up at the same point. Augustinian ecclesiology prevents the despair that stems from the moral, spiritual, and even doctrinal failures of ecclesiastical leaders. Yet when the very sacramental life of the church becomes the focus of contest (lay eucharistic presidency, eucharistic reception without baptism), when ancient doctrine is regarded as a positive impediment to faithfulness (patriarchal language, the very idea of binding doctrine), only a total retreat into the brute and magical efficacy of sacramental forms can preserve confidence that the church is an effective instrument of grace. Like the evangelical, the Anglo-Catholic is forced to acknowledge that its spiritual method is falsified by the impotence and confusion of sacramental practice. The Anglo-Catholic ends up asking Nicodemus's question: How can these things be?

In the end, the modernist, the evangelical, and the Anglo-Catholic face the same problem. Decisive though the differences might be, all face the emerging problem of intraecclesial dysfunction. How can these forms of spirituality help us find light in the darkening conflicts within the church? They answer Nicodemus's question only to be faced with Nehemiah's: "Why should my face not be sad, when the city, the place of my ancestors' graves, lies waste, and its gates have been destroyed by fire?" (Neh. 2:3).

An Ancient Spiritual Director

Have I painted myself into the corner of a room? I have argued that we cannot deny that the power of Christianity is weakened, not only because of the broad cultural changes of modernity but also by virtue of a dysfunction in first-order Christian language and practice. I have argued that in this context of redoubled weakness, modern spirituality tends toward a religion of the x, while the major alternatives to this approach, evangelicalism and Anglo-Catholicism, are unable to provide spiritual guidance in a church that undermines itself. Modern spirituality suffers from a tendency to supersede and eventually reject this first-order language and practice. Spong is waiting in the wings, promising to make our sad faces happy by trimming away nearly all of the first-order language and practice that so pain us with problems and conflicts. The evangelical method tends toward an implicit denial of the necessity of the church, denouncing current apostasies while denying that the failures of the church in any way undermine the cogency and perspicuity of Scripture. Anglo-Catholicism tends toward a paradoxical sacramental idealism that endorses loyalty to a church nowhere in evidence. Given these failures, where can we turn?

I do think I have painted myself into a corner, but I think it is the right corner to be in. Nehemiah wept and then turned toward Jerusalem, a city he knew had been laid to waste. We should seek a spiritual method that helps us follow in the same path. For help I turn to Origen, a great theologian of the early church. He was utterly preoccupied with our desire to see and dwell in the power and potency of the first-order language and practice of the church. For that reason he is rightly thought of as a figure who gives spiritual guidance. Yet Origen, who lived in the third century, is also a decidedly premodern figure, and wherever he may lead us, I am confident it will not be into the neighborhood of either Temple or his unfortunate descendant Spong. Moreover, unlike the methods of evangelicalism and Anglo-Catholicism, Origen anticipates the internal obscurities and lifelessness of the *concreta Christiana*. Thus he helps us find life in the very lifelessness of Christian language and practice.

Origen was one of the most extraordinary figures in early Christianity. He was a bona fide celebrity. His intellect was extraordinary. His personal sanctity was much admired. However, the deepest source of his fame was his ability to open up the mysteries of Scripture for his students. More than any other figure of his day, he seemed to have the ability to bring others to see the power and potency of the first-order language and practice of apostolic Christianity. He was able to answer Nicodemian questions that are as ancient as they are modern. "God is love, yet the Psalms say that God destroys the enemies of the faithful: how can this be?" "God sent his only begotten Son to save the world, and yet he allows evil to exist: how can this be?" "God prohibits lying, and yet Abraham, the father of our faith, lies to Pharaoh about Sarah, his wife: how can this be?" I cannot explain the particular answers that Origen gives to these questions. Instead I want to concentrate on what Origen says about the source of such questions and the proper method for answering them.

Origen was convinced that the power to give life comes from "no other source," as he writes at the very outset of his *Treatise on First Principles*, "but the very words and teaching of Christ" (1.preface.1).[13] Now for Origen, and for the fathers in general, the words and teaching of Christ are not limited to the words and deeds of Jesus. The law of Moses and the prophets—what we now call the Old Testament—are, for Origen, "of Christ." Further, the teachings of the apostles after Christ's ascension into heaven are also part of the "very words and teaching of Christ." In sum, Origen treats what I have been calling the first-order language and practice of the church as the sole and sufficient basis for our participation in the life-giving power of God. Thus Origen makes an unequivocal affirmation as forceful as any made by a modern evangelical. "There is no possible way," he writes, "of explaining and bringing to man's knowledge the higher and diviner teaching about the Son of God, except by means of those scriptures which were inspired by the Holy Spirit, namely, the gospels and the writings of the apostles, to which we add, according to the declaration of Christ himself, the law and the prophets" (1.3.1).[14]

In this sense, for all his allegorical invention, Origen was most definitely not a modern liberal. For Origen there is no *x* outside of apostolic Christianity to which one can appeal in order to renew or rejuvenate apostolic Christianity. He was someone Spong would no doubt denounce as a fundamentalist. Yet Origen has another side to his teaching, equally important but more difficult to grasp. He consistently argues that the singular and sufficient basis for our participation in the life-giving power of Christ—that is to say, the *concreta Christiana*—is full of all sorts of difficulties, puzzles, and obscurities. The power of Christ has a strange and enduring impotence that cannot be ignored or wished away.

Echoing St. Paul, Origen often refers to the "stumbling blocks" that Scripture places before the reader. What faith knows to be the sure and certain path is littered with the darkness of offense and contradiction. These difficulties constitute what Origen calls the "carnal sense" of Scripture. For example, if we concentrate on the lies Abraham tells to save his skin, we are reading carnally, for it is difficult to see how Abraham's example edifies. Or if we focus on the contradiction between the Synoptic and Johannine treatments of the day of the Passover and Jesus' passion, then again we are focusing on the carnal meaning. In both cases we are reading the literal sense in a carnal way, for our approach makes the first-order language a barrier rather than a medium for dwelling in the spiritual power of God's Word.

Far from shying away from these difficulties and pretending that a carnal reading is somehow a willful and obvious mistake, Origen gives great lists of seemingly "impossible" passages. Some are patently "mythological" (for example, the passage for Genesis that speaks of God walking in paradise); some are clearly culturally limited (for example, Jesus' commandment to his disciples not to possess shoes); and some are morally repugnant (for example, the Septuagint rendering of Genesis 17:14, in which the child uncircumcised after the eighth day must be destroyed). In these ways, and others, Origen very forthrightly allows that the Scriptures can be, on their face, impotent. That is to say, these sacred writing do not grab the intelligent and intellectually responsible reader by the collar and carry him or her to immediate and unimpeded spiritual wisdom. Quite the contrary, the Scriptures are difficult and puzzling, and a carnal reading, a reading that cannot edify, all too often seems very natural, even necessary. It is, after all, hard to see, using another of Origen's examples (4.2.2), how the elaborate instructions concerning the construction and decoration of the tabernacle can bring us to see and dwell in the saving power of Christ.

For our purposes, the many ways in which Origen handles these difficult passages, most especially his controversial use of allegory, are not important.[15] What is more fundamental and crucial is his underlying approach, for Origen does not treat the stumbling blocks of Scripture as unfortunate and regrettable. He does not try to explain them by distinguishing between *kerygma* and myth, or between historical context and revelation, or between what Temple called "doctrines and ceremonies" and "religious experience." In other words, Origen does not approach the apparent impotence of Scripture (how can dietary laws have spiritual significance?) by appealing to some *x* outside of Scripture (for example, a general theory about taboo) in order to either alleviate the difficulty or inject religious meaning into seemingly irrelevant or repugnant passages. The solution to carnal reading is not a spiritual reading governed by what I am calling modern spirituality. Rather, Origen regards these puzzles and difficulties—what appear, at first reading, to be self-defeating and impotent passages in Scripture—as *central* to the saving significance of apostolic language and practice. It is not *in spite of* but *because of* their surface impotence that they are important. The difficulty imposed is itself a form of sanctifying power; it is a hindering force that stops us in our tracks and turns us toward the power for life in Jesus Christ.

Here is how Origen explains this affirmation of the weakness of Scripture. "Divine wisdom," Origen writes, "has arranged for certain stumblingblocks and interruptions in the historical sense . . . by inserting . . . a number of impossibilities and incongruities, in order that the narrative might as it were present a barrier to the reader" (4.2.9). In other words, God has not given us a way to him that is immediately radiant with spiritual potency; instead divine wisdom has interposed barriers and difficulties—ruins, to echo my larger theme—that make our apostolic inheritance seem impotent. For Origen, this is no sign of divine perversion. Instead these ruins are themselves elements of a divine pedagogy. The conundra and contradictions lead the reader to feel the futility of carnal reading, and the very dryness of this approach forces us toward a proper approach, which Origen calls spiritual reading. As he says, "By shutting us out and debarring us from" a carnal approach, God "might recall us to the beginning of another way, and might thereby bring us through the entrance of a narrow footpath, to a higher and loftier road and lay open the immense breadth of the divine wisdom" (4.2.9). In short, the impotence of certain parts of Scripture has its own kind of power. These parts force us onto the right path, the narrow path, toward the life that God promises us in Jesus Christ.[16]

For just this reason Origen never wishes to step outside apostolic Christianity. Those moments of impotence and ruin—the stumbling blocks that divine wisdom has placed at the very heart of the apostolic witness—have their own decisive and indispensable power precisely *as* difficult and alienating passages. They drive us back to the narrow footpath of dependent submission to "that rule and discipline delivered by Jesus Christ to the apostles and handed down by them in succession to their posterity" (4.2.2). In short, the first-order language and practice of the church provides all the leverage one needs to find spiritual meaning in any particular passage of Scripture. It is just that this leverage is not always "positive"; sometimes it is "negative." We must suffer the ruined carnal sense in order for God to prepare us to receive the spiritual sense.

Thus we should not try to ignore or correct or deny the spiritual dryness of the *concreta Christiana*. The difficulties are quite real—Leviticus really is given over to many cultic requirements—and these difficulties present us all with severe spiritual challenges. How can this be the promise of Jesus Christ? Where is the power of life in such things? But precisely as such, the difficulties and impediments are constitutive of the very saving power of Jesus Christ. The impotence we perceive *is part of* the potency of new life that is promised, for it forces us to submit ourselves to a lifetime of obedient searching in the very *concreta Christiana* we might so quickly abandon as inauspicious and lifeless. The weakness forces us to look again rather than to look elsewhere.

Thus, Origen works within the corner into which my analysis has painted us: he both acknowledges the apparent lifelessness of first-order language and practice and refuses the default to the *x* that defines modern spirituality. Like the evangelical and Anglo-Catholic, he will not turn to any other power, but unlike both, he gives guidance amid the weakness and ruin of the apostolic inheritance.

A Postmodern Spirituality of Articulate Submission

Origen's theological vision is extraordinarily rich. His famous and sometimes notorious reflections on God, time, matter, and the human soul are all keyed to our ever greater immersion in the pedagogy of salvation that draws us into divine life through stumbling blocks and suffering.[17] However, I must break off my discussion of Origen and return to our situation and the spirituality we must adopt if we are to acknowledge the present impotence of apostolic Christianity, in our culture and in our church, while avoiding the modern spirituality that tempts us to look elsewhere for spiritual leverage.

Origen can guide us, for the impossibilities and incongruities he identifies honestly in Scripture have their analogues in the life of the church. The eclipse of Scripture as a whole as the animating principle of ecclesial life is no less a stumbling block to our ability to see our church as holy, catholic, and apostolic than a particular vengeful verse of the Psalms. The disassociation of baptism from Eucharist is as mystifying as the most obscure book of the Bible. The way bishops currently function is no less "impossible" than any contradiction in Scripture. In each case we should follow Origen's lead: we should submit ourselves to these stumbling blocks and impossibilities, these ruined walls of the church, for even in their weakened form they are integral parts of the "rule and discipline delivered by Jesus Christ to the apostles." Modeling our approach to the current life of the church on Origen's approach to Scripture, we should know and acknowledge that our church *does* hide the gospel. It has public impotence and embodies painful contradictions. The church really is in ruins. But we should also trust that this veiling of the power of life is part of the pedagogy of the Holy Spirit that will bring us to life. The impotence and weakness guide us toward the narrow footpath.

Ephraim Radner has called this spirituality the way of constricted penitence.[18] Radner focuses on the ways church division weakens the gospel. We affirm the unity of the church in the Nicene Creed, but we live in a marketplace of religious denominations that make mockery of Christian unity. Surely we must ask, with Nicodemus, "How can these things be?" Like Origen, Radner refuses to answer this question in such a way as to deny the scandal and offense of disunity and division. At the same time, like Origen, he treats the scandal and offense as part of the pedagogy of divine election. No more than Nehemiah does Radner turn away from Jerusalem, even in the moment when its walls and gates have fallen. Nehemiah returns to dwell amid the rubble in order to worship the Lord and in this repentant service to restore and repair the holy city. And so Radner argues that we must dwell in the darkened and debilitated forms of our churches. We must look again amid the lifeless contradictions of first-order language and practice. We should not look elsewhere. Our spiritual method, then, should be articulate submission to the stumbling blocks of redoubled weakness in the life of the church. For the *concreta Christiana*, however disjoined by ecclesial dysfunction, are the scattered stones of the temple. They must be the very materials of renewal.

This spiritual submission to the impotence of the church is not a silent quietism. We must be articulate. Origen insists upon identifying the many impediments that Scripture presents. He does not turn away from the difficulties; he tries to overcome them. So also must we throw a spotlight on the many ways in which modern Christianity in general, and Anglicanism in particular, has encouraged faithlessness and made apostolic Christianity implausible. We should not hide from ourselves and others the ways in which the church—and by no means the Episcopal Church USA alone—has become a stumbling block to the gospel.

But our articulateness must lead toward rather than away from submission, for surely Origen is right. Only "the rule and discipline delivered by Jesus Christ to the apostles" has the power of life, and only in the church does that rule and discipline—however masked and hidden in the incongruities and impossibilities of the present age—endure. The first-order language and practice of the church, however lifeless and ruined, is, as Origen insists, the only possible way to life. Indeed its very lifelessness is part of God's wisdom, for it has the power to force us to enter more fully and more deeply into the narrow path. As Origen writes of Scripture, "If our books had attracted men to belief because they were composed with rhetorical skill or with philosophical cleverness, our faith would undoubtedly rest in the skillful use of words and in human wisdom, not in the power of God" (4.1.7). The Lord humiliates even our most high-minded and spiritual striving, and he does so that we might see his power in those mean things he has chosen as the way for us to come to him. This is as true of our life in the church as of our reading of Scripture: we must labor amid the ruins of our apostolic inheritance in order to find divine life. Only when we suffer the burden of carnal contradictions—Zion brought low—can we begin to see the true blessings of spiritual understanding.

None of us are likely to want to adopt Origen's spirituality of articulate submission. We do not like the idea that the power of God in Christ is hidden, not just by the faithlessness of his followers but by the wisdom of God. We are, after all, not very different from Nicodemus, and we fear the narrow path of Nehemiah. We respond well to visible signs of power, while that which is hidden and veiled, debilitated and destroyed, baffles and demoralizes us. But what we want is not what we are given.

Jesus' brief colloquy with Nicodemus ends with a sharp reminder of just how hidden and veiled is the redemptive power of God in Christ. They were talking about new life, water and the Spirit, and Nicodemus's last remark is that crucial question "How can these things be?" Jesus has the final word. "Just as Moses lifted up the serpent in the wilderness," says Jesus, speaking now to every reader and not just Nicodemus, "so must the Son of Man be lifted up, that whoever believes in him may have eternal life" (John 3:14-15). The Son of Man, on the hilltop outside the city, naked before both Jew and Gentile, will be lifted up, and this will reveal the power for new life promised by water and given in the Spirit. Surely this is a truth we all know: God so loved the world that he gave his only Son that whoever believes in him should not perish but have eternal life. It rolls off the tongue as an oft-repeated epitome of the gospel. Yet what could be more hidden, what could be more opaque, more difficult, more "impossible" than the power of life in that dead and lifeless Palestinian Jew crucified in the first century? How can this be? How can *he* have the power of eternal life? Nicodemus's question, a question asked again at the foot of the cross by passersby, is not only answered by Jesus, its burdensome force and urgency is redoubled.

On this crucial point St. Paul never trimmed or denied. He was articulate about the apparent impotence of the gospel of Jesus Christ. He was forthright in naming it as a stumbling block and scandal. But he never imagined that life could be found in any way other than submission to the narrow footpath of the way of Jesus Christ. Origen does nothing more than follow the spirituality of St. Paul. Surely, then, we should follow on that same narrow footpath. We should be forthright and articulate about the scandal caused by the ruins of the church. We cannot rebuild walls we deny have fallen any more that we can rise with a Lord we deny has died. Yet we should submit ourselves to the scandal of this increasingly lifeless body, not glorying in faithlessness (Shall we sin that grace might abound? By no means!) but confident that the immense breadth of divine wisdom, as Origen says, gives life in and through those things of the Lord that hide and veil.

We should return to rather than flee from the "impossibilities" of ecclesial life, its impotence and lifelessness, and do so with Isaiah's prophecy in mind:

> They shall build up the ancient ruins,
>   they shall raise up the former devastations;
> they shall repair the ruined cities,
>   the devastations of many generations (Isa. 61:4).

We should not seek any other city, however redolent with spiritual power and life it might seem. For in the ruins of Jerusalem, in the pierced, dead, and ruined body of our Lord Jesus Christ, in which we now dwell far more literally then any of us might have imagined, the Lord brings us to see, as only eyes cleansed by tears of repentance can, the omnipotence of his cruciform love.

9

The Daily Office

Will not God grant justice to his chosen ones who cry to him day and night?

Luke 18:7

Open the *Book of Common Prayer* to its first rites. There you will find a demand and promise of remarkable ambition: the unending cycle of daily prayer. The features of this daily prayer epitomize the spiritual drama of the Christian life, both in goal and in focus, for the ambition to mark each day grows out of a faith in Jesus Christ as the Alpha and Omega. We are to dwell in him, and to do so each day must be brought captive to Christ.

We should not imagine that this ambition is optional or peripheral to the Christian life. Daily communal prayer, or what the Anglican tradition (following the lead of the larger Western tradition) calls the Daily Office, serves as an engine of intimacy. In order to explain this function, I want to consider both the basic forms and verbal details of the Daily Office as it is currently available in the *Book of Common Prayer*.

An opening sentence for Morning Prayer expresses the need for daily prayer: "Watch, for you know not when the master of the house will come, in the evening, or at midnight, or at cockcrow, or in the morning, lest he come suddenly and find you asleep" (Mark 13:35–36). We are warned, rightly, against our tendency to sleep-walk through the life of faith. Prayer morning and evening responds to the exhortations found in the book of Isaiah: "Awake, awake, put on your strength, O Zion! Put on your beautiful garments" (52:1). The Daily Office stands as the primary means by which the church might make us wakeful and watchful. It is in this sense an order of vigilance. The demand of the Daily Office echoes the word of Jesus who is speaking not only to Peter but also directly to us when he asks, "Are you asleep? Could you not keep awake one hour?" (Mark 14:37).

Yet this order is more than a spur or goad; it is also a consummating celebration, for the master of the house has come. "Who can fail to do you homage, Lord, and sing the praises of your name?" asks a canticle for Morning Prayer, itself drawn from the book of Revelation (15:4). (A canticle means, literally, a "song"; however, in the liturgical tradition, a canticle is a song or prayer, other than a psalm, usually drawn from the Bible, that serves as a regular element of worship.) The sweet honey of the Psalms nourishes, and the diadems of prayer, taken from Scripture and sanctified by centuries of use, glorify God. To awaken in prayer is to put on strength. For this reason the Daily Office is not only watchful and vigilant but receptive and doxological. The purposes of the Daily Office are as pentecostal as adventine, as consummating as expectant. Awakened in prayer, we receive that which we hear. Eyes open, we do not just see; we get up and go with Jesus (cf. Mark 14:42). Our minds and hearts walk down the pathways of ancient prayers, many of which defined the boundaries of Jesus' own religious practice in the first century. Thus do we live in Christ, and he in us.

That we should be encouraged by the *Book of Common Prayer* to allow ourselves to be awakened by and absorbed into the fixed forms of its daily prayer says a great deal about how Anglicanism as a whole conceives of our being taken captive by Christ. Indeed the shaping method of the Daily Office marks the outlines of a doctrine of the Holy Spirit, embodying in practice what is often only partially expressed in Anglican theology. For the mission of the Spirit is to bring Christ to us and us to Christ. The Holy Spirit is the agent of intimacy, the divine matchmaker. The ambition of the Daily Office is, then, a direct reflection of the ambition of God's redemptive purpose. Based upon recitation and repetition, the routine of daily prayer shapes us into a determinate, focused way of discipleship, a way fitting to those who would follow the narrow way of the cross. In this way, our lives are drawn into the obedience that is the unbreakable and intimate bond of the Son to the Father.

For this reason Morning and Evening Prayer should be our source for reflection on the concrete and doxological pneumatology that is, I think, the greatest strength of Anglicanism.[1] It is much more reliable than all the contemporary loose talk about the Holy Spirit and the Gnostic dreams of modern theologians. We do well to set aside our books of Anglican theology for a moment and learn from the Daily Office, for it is a discipline far older, far more reliable, than fevered images of "incarnational" or "inclusive" or "nondogmatic" Anglicanism currently abroad. Indeed the Daily Office and its path into the mystery of Christ is far older and more reliable than Anglicanism itself.

Encompassing and Apostolic

The ongoing and daily cycle of prayer is as old as the Judaism from which Christianity sprang. Within the Psalter, the prayer book of the Old Testament, we hear the author of the 119th psalm declare, "Seven times a day I praise you" (v. 164). Whether or not ancient Judaism followed a strict sevenfold pattern, prayer ordered by the hours of the day was common to synagogue life during the life of Jesus. The author of the Gospel of Mark highlights the hours of watchfulness in the verses mentioned above. We are to watch in the evening and at midnight, at cockcrow and at dawn. The imperative to watch is not generic; rather, Mark's watchfulness is keyed to just that ordered cycle of prayer that, however demarcated and numbered, constitutes the watchfulness of Israel.

The early church did not rebel against the encompassing ambition of a day marked by prayer. To the contrary, the Acts of the Apostles records that the baptized attended the temple services "day by day." The fire of the pentecostal spirit leads directly into a routine of worship that praises God (see Acts 2:43–47), and so the early followers of Jesus never tired of the daily round of prayer. They wished to draw near to the Lord, to treasure up his commandments so that they might be written on the tablets of their hearts (see Prov. 7:1–3). Thus did the early church feed on the patterns and practices of daily prayer as an infant upon the milk of her mother.

Practiced in many different ways in early Christianity, daily prayer took on a formal structure in Western monasticism. It was ordered by seven "hours," which we know by the names Lauds, Prime, Tierce, Sext, None, Evensong, and Compline. This pattern of prayer, called the Divine or Daily Office, constituted the work of the monk. However important field and winery might be for the body, scriptorium and library for the mind, the sevenfold marking of the day in gathered prayer defined the monastic life to which St. Benedict gave his *Rule*. To the extent that monasticism nurtured the dominant spiritual and intellectual currents in Western Christianity, the Daily Office also defined the church as a whole. Indeed nonmonastic clergy were encouraged to perform various abbreviated forms of the Daily Office, and breviaries of all sorts proliferated throughout the Middle Ages. So fundamental was the encompassing framework of daily prayer that rebellions against the dominant Benedictine model of monastic life never questioned the necessity of the Daily Office. Mendicant Dominicans and Franciscans renounced the cloister, but they did not renounce the discipline of the hours. No matter how much the *devotio moderna* of the late Middle Ages deviated from the monastic ideal, the day remained marked by an order of prayer.

The sixteenth-century production of the *Book of Common Prayer* did not create a new Daily Office. Instead the work was primarily editorial. The component parts of the seven-hour Daily Office were ordered around the two foci of matins and evensong, already emphasized in ancient practice. The morning and evening hours were expanded through the addition of elements from the other hours of the day, and then the resulting compendia were reduced by eliminating repetitions. The present form of the Daily Office is largely unchanged from this sixteenth-century shift from seven to two liturgical "hours."

The most recent revision of the *Book of Common Prayer* has added orders for Noonday and Compline, which distantly echo monastic practice. Furthermore, there have been alterations in rubrics, modifications of language, and provision of additional canticles. Whether one judges these changes wise or foolish, necessary or superfluous, across revisions recent and remote the Daily Office of Morning and Evening Prayer remains strikingly continuous in logic and purpose. The words of prayer are drawn from Scripture or from the ancient liturgical memory of the church. Therefore both in form and content the Daily Office is fully loaded with the weight of apostolic practice.

Because the method of the Daily Office is apostolic, its encompassing ambition may be received as a gift rather than a burden. Here the word *apostolic* is not a synonym for *scriptural*. Our baptismal promise is drawn from Acts 2:42: "They devoted themselves to the apostles' teaching and fellowship, to the breaking of the bread and the prayers." The New Testament serves as an indispensable form of apostolic teaching, the polestar by which to navigate both the Old Testament and our own times. Without doubt the apostolic witness finds its center of gravity here. However, this apostolic teaching is linked with fellowship, the breaking of the bread, and the prayers. The oral, and then written, record of Jesus and of the origins of an ordered community of discipleship is set within a form of life marked by moral and ritual observances. Thus our faith must not only return again and again to the canon of Scripture; it must also lead us into an ever-deeper immersion in the prayer and practice of the faithful who have gone before. We must reread their testimony and dwell in their form of life.

For this reason we cannot view the prayer book and its order of Morning and Evening Prayer simply as a human tradition that we might enjoy or alter according to present need. Thomas Cranmer did not consolidate the sevenfold Divine Office in order to reassure those fearful of change. He did so because he wished to be faithful to his baptismal promise. He wished to continue in the apostles' teaching, fellowship, *and* prayers. Retaining the language and logic of inherited prayer was for Cranmer a decisive way to tether the faith and practice of the English Church to the apostles, to the faithful in Jerusalem who were going to the temple day by day. Cranmer's goal was to secure the deepest and most fundamental form of "apostolic succession": to pray as have those who have come before us.

The received order of Morning and Evening Prayer does no less in our own equally volatile times. Its apostolic continuity releases us from the fear that in our ambition to watch and wait, receive and glorify, we are unawares being submerged under pious illusions. These ancient forms tether us to Jesus Christ rather than the passing fads of our age. Visibly connected to ancient practice, the Daily Office has a power that rests in the holiness of words and prayers sanctified by the blood of the martyrs and freighted with centuries of faithful use. The apostolic weight of these formulations makes it a blessing to be driven and drawn by such a power.

Impressive and Expressive

If we say that the Daily Office is encompassing in ambition and apostolic in origin, then we should say that it is impressive in effect. Unlike baptism, this regular pattern of recitation and listening does not project us into a complex ritual enactment of birth and transformation. The extraordinary way the eucharistic liturgy engages us as both originating agents and passive recipients is absent. To be sure, the Daily Office involves birth and transformation, activity and passivity. Our recitations of psalm and canticle are verbal enactments that make the Word of God a living force. Our listening to a sequence of readings from Scripture is a hearing and harkening that both gives birth to faith and transforms how we understand our lives. Nonetheless, the range is narrow. The ambience is verbal; the Daily Office is ears and voice, not mouth and taste, forehead and touch. But what is lost in range is gained in intensity. The effect of daily prayer is highly focused, and with focus comes force. As Richard Hooker noted against critics who believed that ordered prayer distances us from the gospel, the narrow constraints of daily prayer, fixed in content, is "imprinted with much more ease in all men's memories."[2] The words press upon us again and again with relentless force, and as a consequence our souls are given apostolic form.

The narrowness of the Daily Office is plain for the eye to see. It is dominated by recitations of canticles and psalms. In Western monastic practice, the gathered community recited the entire Psalter each week. When they compressed the seven-hour office into the two rites of Morning and Evening Prayer, the sixteenth-century Reformers constructed a sequence of psalms keyed to a monthly cycle. (This sequence of recitation is preserved in the Psalter printed in the prayer book. See the headings that run from "First Day: Morning Prayer" to "Thirtieth Day: Evening Prayer.") The current lectionary for the Daily Office organizes the Psalter in a seven-week sequence. Whether once a week or across seven weeks, this cyclical repetition of psalms is decisive. The purpose is unequivocal: the psalms are to become so intimate to us that they come to constitute our primary language of prayer.

The same holds true for the canticles that punctuate the Daily Office. They are largely drawn from Psalms, and from other portions of Scripture that echo the petitionary and doxological patterns of the psalms. Morning Prayer opens with a compound petition that explains the intent behind this repetition. "Lord, open our lips and our mouths shall proclaim your praise." That praise is "of the Lord" in senses both genitive and possessive. The psalms and canticles are praise of him, and they are words he enunciated in his own voice; they are his praise given to us for our use. The Scriptures were on the lips of Jesus, and so might they be on our lips morning and night. Our recitations, then, return to the Lord the very word he gives to us, and as the canticles cut deep channels in our memories through constant use, the circuit of gift, reception, and thanksgiving closes. What is given to us by him becomes the fit means for giving thanks to him. In all this, the purpose is impressive. Our religious imaginations are stamped with the scriptural patterns of the canticles. In repetition we are absorbed, shaped.

For those of us shackled to a culture of personal originality and expressive spontaneity, the repetitive impress can seem overwhelming. We can resist the Daily Office and its tight mold, thinking the recitations a replacement of the inner promptings of our own religious feelings by the ancient insights of the psalmist. We can rebel against words frozen in the fixed canon of Scripture. We can fear the narrowness of this way of daily prayer. However misguided, this response is at least accurate in its discernment of the doxological pneumatology of the Daily Office. There can be little doubt that the repetitions ensure that the very words of our apostolic inheritance find their way into our souls and, once there, come to dominate. The Daily Office is in this sense the womb of our new life in Christ. It gives us our religious imagination, our verbal patterns of prayer, our very ability to articulate need and joy. If we regret this, then we regret one of the great gifts of the Holy Spirit: the voice of faith.

If we resist this impress because of a love of novelty or rebellion against fixed form, we should beware. For the method of the Daily Office rises out of a central truth about how the Holy Spirit brings us to Christ. In Christ the good news of God's love takes the fleshly and determinate form of the man Jesus of Nazareth. He is fixed to a rigid pattern of events. The vocation and prophecies of Israel define his life. His suffering is foretold. His life comes to the bitter boundary of death so that the Scriptures might be fulfilled. In faith, the Holy Spirit brings us new life, but not an uncertain or open newness. Instead new life in Christ is always found through drawing near the defined and delimited man Jesus of Nazareth. The power of the Holy Spirit brings life, because that power allows us to stand with the centurion who looked upon Jesus as he died upon the cross and to say, "Truly this man was God's Son!" (Mark 15:39).

Therefore whatever we might want for ourselves—room and scope for experimentation, the freedom to shape our own destinies, reversible choices and tentative commitments—the way of Jesus Christ winnows. He ventures all in the narrow way of the cross. The Daily Office trains our lives of prayer toward the same intensive concentration. The repetitions bind us to a narrow way. For just this reason, and not because of any particular religious genius or symbolic virtuosity found in the psalms or canticles, the cycles of repetition are crucial. The relentless givenness and ever-increasing familiarity of the central elements of the Daily Office shape us; we are given the impress of a way given and not chosen. Thus does the Holy Spirit work upon us.

This work is all-important, for as we draw near to him, he comes to dwell in us. Here the doxological dimension is central, not ancillary. The psalms train us in the very prayer of Jesus, for it is to the Psalter that he turns on the cross. As we are absorbed into the Psalter, our religious imaginations are fused to his. Just as important is the way the repetitions of psalm and canticle shape us to find our way forward through rather than around, above, or underneath the given form of the scriptural witness. We say these words of Scripture again and again, and this guides us to look again into the apostolic witness rather than elsewhere. And the effect is significant, for when we look up from the Psalter and cast our eyes on the cross, this life of prayer has trained us to look into the fathomless depths of his crucified form rather than compulsively searching for brighter, more pleasant alternatives. The impress of the fixed and given forms of daily prayer prepares us for the narrowness of the way. We do not shape that good news to fit what we imagine to be our own spiritual needs. We are shaped by the good news of Christ.

We do not fall into the way of Christ up to Golgotha with fatalistic abandonment. We retain our distinctive place and mission in the world; we continue as agents in the world. His impress, like the impress of psalm and canticle, shapes us as persons marked for his service. In his Spirit we are called, but we are also sent. Once we have received the impress of psalm and canticle, passion and cross, there is no limit to the degree to which our lives, our world, may be loaded with the electrical charge of his determinate form. The Daily Office is guided by this truth. As we move from the repetitive center of the Daily Office, its cycles of psalms and canticles, we become less passive recipients of the divine impress, less raw material molded by recitation. We shift from abandoning ourselves to fixed form to receiving him within the unique and diverse structures of our lives. The expressive mission of faith begins to take form in us.

Listening to Scripture is the first step in this shift. Here we find ourselves more active. This seems counterintuitive. Sitting to listen silently to Scripture appears to be more passive than participatory. But this confuses behavior with consequence. One cannot think, analyze, react, and respond while standing and reciting. Speaking words aloud, we give ourselves over to the task of enunciation. Little is left in reserve. In contrast, the very passivity of listening makes room for all manner of inner response. Listening takes little effort, and as a result, a great deal of scope is left for deliberation.

In this space for engagement, we are gathered into Christ in the uniqueness and individuality of our lives. The two-year cycle of lectionary readings from Scripture keeps us off balance. The psalms and canticles become familiar, but the diversity and heterogeneity of Scripture continually strike new and discordant notes. The historical books of the Old Testament and the narratives of the Gospels present us with words very different in genre and function from the visions of the prophets and the exhortations of St. Paul. The voice of judgment, command, and condemnation; the calls for repentance and amendment of life; the promise of new life; the vision of God's consummating judgment—the voice of Scripture is a seminal word that we receive in our own individuality and distinctiveness.

In these ways our sitting and listening is a moment of learning and discernment. We may feel the shock of relevance in St. Paul's admonitions to the Corinthians two millennia past or in Amos's denunciations still more ancient. Our listening may be a moment of intense personal emotion in which the uniqueness of our life crosses into the world of Scripture. Our grief over the recent death of a loved one intersects with the story of Jesus' raising of the child, and the resultant thoughts can never be anticipated. Thus where the words of the psalms and canticles live in us with familiarity, no matter how well we know the Scriptures, the sheer breadth of this gracious word lives with an ever-new impact. We might say the Venite (the canticle drawn form Psalm 95 that is known by its first word in Latin) numerous times in a single week; it becomes a center of gravity around which our changing life orbit. Thomas's question to Jesus, David's confrontation with Goliath, the prophetic words of Isaiah come only every other year. They intersect with our life. This yields an active moment: we must discern and decide about what we have heard.

The potentially disruptive, unsetting effect of listening to Scripture in the Daily Office warrants the return to recitation in the most repeated canticle of all, the Apostles' Creed. This we say every time. No matter how deeply personal and highly individualized might be our engagement with God's Word, we rise to say the Apostles' Creed. The ancient formula is a synopsis of our trinitarian faith. God is like *this,* and just so are we blessed. Here the closed circuit of psalm and canticle is reestablished. Shocked dislocation, personal insight, and interpretive novelty may characterize our listening to Scripture. But these shards of individuality are reenrolled into the apostolic and determinate form of our common Christian life. The Word of God that has intersected our lives with seeming serendipity just moments before ("My goodness, St. Paul is talking to *me!*") now dwells within us with the permanence of the One who suffered under Pontius Pilate, was crucified, died, and was buried.

The Doxological Structure of Mission

The purpose of the Daily Office is not to rest quiescent in the truth of the triune God. God's Word is seminal, and the expressive moment has enduring significance. The Comforter comes to us with reassurance but also with mission. The Daily Office concludes on this note. In the prayers that mark the final portion of both Morning and Evening Prayer we do more than listen, discern, and digest. We inhabit the given form of our life in Christ with fullness. These prayers, called "collects" in the Anglican tradition (the name comes from the original Latin term, *collecta*, used to describe short, concise prayers that punctuate larger elements of public worship), the Daily Office guides us toward the fullness of this expressive dimension of our faith. In that sense the prayers render us. They are the moments in which we begin to let out that which has been formed in us by psalm and canticle, that which has awakened in us through hearing the Scriptures.

The beginning of this structured expression of faith is the Lord's Prayer. The most familiar moment in the Daily Office because most repeated, the Lord's Prayer is the hinge on which the extraordinary process of giving ourselves over to fixed repetition *turns into* moments of intense subjectivity and personal involvement. The Lord's Prayer is both impressive and expressive, and each to an extreme degree. Ubiquitous in liturgies, repeated on countless occasions, far from numbing us, the Lord's Prayer is very often the first prayer to our lips in moments of private trial and anguish. It is said by all and frequently, yet with personal conviction and conveying a diversity of individual concerns.

Indeed so personal, so intimate is this most common of prayers that no amount of lobbying by professional liturgists and exhortation by progressive pastors can dislodge the archaic language from the minds and lips of the faithful. "Trespasses" may seem awkward, even false to the true Christian meaning of sin, but through uncounted recitations this word has become loaded with lifetimes of our regrets and failures. We do not say "Forgive us our trespasses" as if it were for the first time, fumbling over the meaning of the word. We use the Lord's Prayer against the background of our very vivid understanding of the meaning and scope of our sinfulness. The remarkable tenacity of the old form of the Lord's Prayer testifies to the subjective and individual, the personal dimension, which is brought forth by repetition of shared prayer. The old form of the Lord's Prayer is dear to contemporary Christians; it is the word that is near them, in their hearts and on their lips, precisely as something said again and again. The impressive fuels the expressive. Novelty and invention disperse us; prayer repeated a thousandfold concentrates us, sharpening rather than dulling the expressive power of our faith.

In the collects that bring the routine of prayer toward its end, this logic is recapitulated. The impressive force of Christ empowers and transforms, and both elements are directly proportionate. Each collect begins by identifying the unique and determinate form of divine life, the originative fact of the revealed Lord. We pray *because* God has taken a powerfully present and concrete form in Christ. In him we know to whom we should pray. The narrowness of the way ensures that we can clearly identify our Lord. Then our lives are *brought into* the orbit of divine life. In the focused person of Christ there is room and scope for our lives and concerns. Finally, the collects close with a formulaic return to the person of Christ, now pronouncing that *through* him our particular needs may be articulated and heard.

The narrow patterns of psalm and canticle, like the narrow way of God to us in the passion, death, and resurrection of Jesus of Nazareth, are a beginning and end that give us life precisely because of, not in spite of, the concentrated impress of their sharp outlines and determinate shape. We must give ourselves to this fixed form, both the man Jesus of Nazareth and a life of encompassing, apostolic, and impressive prayer. This doxological path anchors and animates our live. The impress of Christ, and of the tradition of prayer he both accepted and redoubled, has the force and urgency to drive us to express our mission in the world through prayer and service.

The collects that draw Morning and Evening Prayer to a close outline the work of Christ in our lives and in the world. "Drive from us wrong desires," asks the Collect for the Renewal of Life, "incline our hearts to keep your law" (BCP, p. 99). The Collect for Friday is emphatic: "Grant us your servants so to follow in faith where you have led the way, that we may at length fall asleep peacefully in you and wake up in your likeness" (BCP, p. 123). These collects ask for that which the method of the Daily Office demands and provides: the formation of our lives according to the encompassing and impressive way of Jesus Christ. This is an ever-urgent mission. We are to move toward a more perfect faith, "that our lips may praise you" and "our lives may bless you" (BCP, p. 123). The Holy Spirit glorifies the Father, and does so by bringing us into the way of his Son.

We should not imagine, however, that the Daily Office speaks only to personal piety. The Christian life is not solitary. The Holy Spirit does not work upon us by inward and private means. The church is the indispensable source and focus of discipleship. Custodian of the apostolic witness, the church draws us into the way of Jesus. The collects emphasize this work of the church. "Send forth upon us the Spirit of love," petitions a collect from Evening Prayer, "that in companionship with one another your abounding grace may increase among us" (BCP, p. 125). Through mutual support and exhortation, the Holy Spirit sanctifies the faithful as a gathered people. Marked by baptism and ordered toward fellowship in the bread and cup, the church is structured as a life of committed and mutual service.

This fellowship is not a means to any higher and further end, not to personal growth or social justice, not to spiritual insight or inclusive community. A collect from Morning Prayer expresses this clearly. "Receive our supplications and prayers," asks the collect, "which we offer you for all members of your holy Church, that in their vocation and ministry they may truly and devoutly serve you." The circle of prayer and mission is tightly drawn. Our mission to each other is to pray on behalf of others. More important, we pray that each of us, absent and present, might seek to serve God more fully, that each might join his or her voice to the voices of angels and archangels and with all the company of heaven, singing together the hymn "Holy, holy, holy Lord, God of power and might, heaven and earth are full of your glory." In short, the mission of the church is to become a more perfect fellowship, bound ever more tightly to the end of drawing near to the Lord in songs of praise. Thus to pray for and with others is to pray that we should fall, both as individuals and as a community, into the narrowness of his way.

The Christian mission to the world is no different. Collects from Morning Prayer ask that the Lord "may bring those who do not know you to the knowledge and love of you" and that God will "bring the nations into your fold" (*BCP*, pp. 100–101). The collects from Evening Prayer strike the same note: "Let the whole earth also worship you, all nations obey you, all tongues confess and bless you, and men and women everywhere love you and serve you in peace" (*BCP*, p. 124). All must come captive to Christ. We may bridle at such "triumphalism," but it is nothing more than the cosmic dimension of the impressive force of the recitations of psalm and canticle. Creation and human history have a determinate, fixed destiny. Christ is the end point of all things, and the world must take on his impress in order to be fulfilled; the cosmos must be Christ-formed in order to find its full expression.

As an instrument of the Holy Spirit, the church has a decisive role. As St. Paul teaches, "The creation waits with eager longing for the revealing of the children of God," for "creation itself will be set free from its bondage to decay and will obtain the freedom of the glory of the children of God" (Rom. 8:19, 21). The glory of the children of God is found in their participation in the Lord of glory, in Jesus Christ, whose way in the world is marked out with utter clarity. To the extent that the church is shaped by the impress of Jesus Christ—and this is the surpassing ambition of the Daily Office—it is gathering all things toward their consummation. The proper expression of the longings and groanings of all things, including our own, is the impress of his narrow way.

The expressive moment of the prayers culminates with the rubric that allows for intercessions. Prepared by recitation, animated by listening to Scripture, and trained in petition by the collects, the believer is authorized to articulate his or her need, concerns, and hopes. The venture of the Daily Office, like the venture of God in Christ, requires this moment for unanticipated and individualized prayer. All things are stamped by the impress of Christ, carved into proper shape and form by the hydraulic forces of communal prayer, and under that impress the true shape and purpose of all things, precisely as distinctive and individual, finds power and voice. As we draw nearer to Christ, this impress must come into active engagement with all aspects of our lives. The intercessions are the workshop of this process. Our prayers, then, silent or spoken, are wrought from the raw material of our intrinsically diverse lives by the sharp blows of divine love, made weighty in the fleshly form of Jesus of

Nazareth and delivered effectively in the fixed and sensuous patterns of recitation, lection, and collect. Our prayers are necessarily personal; yet, without contradiction, they are motivated and shaped by the apostolic prayers of the church. We express ourselves because of, in, and through him. Just as the Lord's Prayer is his, and because he is for us ours as well, so also must our intercessions be genuinely our own but his as well.

Final Recapitulation

Morning and Evening Prayers close with a Prayer of General Thanksgiving. This prayer fuses the impressive and expressive. We thank God for all the blessings of this life, but above all for his redemption of the world in Jesus Christ. We express our thanksgiving and praise and in so doing identify precisely the fixed anchor of divine love, whose impress we seek. We thank God for drawing us into Christ's narrow way. However much we may be engaged with the diversity of worldly obligations and responsibilities, pleasures and joys, we can never say, "We pray, O Lord, that having grasped the mystery of Christ, we may get on with life." His way is fathomless, and we can never plumb the depths of the cross. Just so, we can never turn from psalm and canticle, thinking we have dwelt fully and finally in the truth of this narrow way of prayer. The Daily Office has no end, precisely because God's way to us in Jesus Christ continues to the end of the age.

This close conjunction of expressive and impressive moments is recapitulated immediately. We seek to show forth God's praise, to express our thanksgiving. The General Thanksgiving exhorts us to do so in our lives as well as with our lips. Not only should our life of personal prayer fall under the impress of Christ, so also should our actions. We not only pray that God give rest to the weary, bless the dying, soothe the suffering, pity the afflicted, shield the joyous, we pray that *we will do so* as well. The impress of Christ is active; his form bursts forth into our lives as well as onto our lips.

Yet here again the doxological pneumatology of the Daily Office is crystal clear. Our expressive engagement with the world in no way distances us from Christ. Christian morality is not a negotiation between churchly ideals and worldly obligations. The way of Christ does not overlay everyday life; it is not something that requires "mediation" or a "dialectic" of transcendence and immanence. We show forth the Lord's praise in our lives by giving ourselves to his service. We may fail to do so; indeed we certainly fail. However, we must not translate our inability to entirely give ourselves over to his impress as justifiable. We must never treat the distance between him and us as somehow right and fitting.

Here the Daily Office circles back upon itself. To express our faith in Christ entails giving ourselves to his service, both with our lips and in our lives. We must receive his impress in order to faithfully express his holiness and righteousness. Thus our moral vocations, like our prayers, must always find their impetus *because* of Christ, must have the uniqueness of circumstance and responsibility *brought into* his divine life, and must be followed *through* the narrowness of his way. This means, at the very least, that our moral life must be as fused to the recitations of psalm and canticle as our religious imagination. The way of Christ through the world, in both speech and action, is always a narrow way, fixed by sharp boundaries. Just as we share in his prayer when we say the psalms he said, we may also share in his obedience to the will of the Father. His narrow path— "Not my will, but thine"—can be ours without alienation or diminution.

This, then, is the pneumatological pattern of the Daily Office. We are shaped by the impress of recitation and activated by the reception of an ever-new Word. This impress of apostolic prayer and teaching allows us to express prayer for ourselves, the church, and the world that leads back to the sharp outlines of the cross, that follows the pattern by which the Lord comes to us in Christ and we to him. The consequences of this pattern for the Christian life is clear. However diverse our experiences and responsibilities, however distinctive our imaginations and unspeakably personal our fears and despairs, the life of faith has a necessarily fixed form that gives us the power of expression.

To be sure, we must beware of Anglican arrogance and conceit. Nothing so specific as the Anglican form of Morning and Evening Prayer is necessary. That pattern of discipline is both ancient and wholesome, and we should cherish the prayer book's judicious preservation of the Daily Office. But its purpose is to make us Christians, not Anglicans. Its goal is to anchor us in a language of prayer that makes the deeper, utterly necessary form of Christ more visible, and certainly other forms of encompassing, fixed, and apostolic prayer may yield the impress of Christ as well.

What is crucial, then, is the ambition and focus of this tradition of prayer. It trains us for discipleship. Our abandonment to psalm and canticle, lectionary and collect prepares us for our crucial and far more taxing abandonment to the narrow way of our Lord.

Drawing Near in the Daily Office

We live in an age in which the narrow way of discipleship is a scandal. We decry dogmatic conformity and claim to celebrate diversity. We covet novelty and make a cult of creativity. We have readily at hand any number of evasions of the narrow way. We imagine that we must distance ourselves from the apostolic tradition in order to be "open to the Holy Spirit." We eagerly chastise commitments to ancient prayer as "idolatry." We beat away the claim of psalm and canticle by pretending that these inherited forms of prayer are not God's praise given to us but are expressions of the religious imaginations of pious ancients. We raise a smokescreen of ambiguity by claiming that a properly "incarnational theology" is open to God in all things and therefore we should not limit ourselves to things that are labeled "Christian." These slogans and many more are as easy as they are ubiquitous.

We articulate the same evasions in our moral lives. Surely, we think, we have worldly responsibilities that must have their own place in the life of discipleship. We live across a highly varied grid of duties and obligations. We must vote intelligently. We must serve on committees, do our job well, love our children, and care for our parents. Surely, we think, our mission to the world must somehow negotiate with these moral concerns. And in an ether of "sensitive moral judgment" we mix and match Christian teachings with our moral intuitions. We want to pirouette across the stage of world history, retaining our worldly roles while genuflecting to the altar. We hide behind shibboleths about the "Anglican way" of Scripture, tradition, and reason as if those who preceded us in the faith were engaged in a great balancing act.

However real and pressing might be our worldly context, we must look again and more closely at how much of what we take for granted actually shifts in the sands of our unstable culture. Yesterday's civil rights hero is today's multicultural goat. Yesterday's antipoverty gospel is today's paternalistic failure. Yesterday's gentleman is today's sexist bore, or worse. Who knows what tomorrow might bring? If we think the subtle texture of our worldly responsibilities may serve to anchor our faithful witness, we are fools whom our fickle world shall mock the moment we settle into the certainties of our social witness. We must find the anchor for mission elsewhere: in Christ. We should not entrench ourselves on the floodplains of our times. We must throw ourselves upon the narrowness of Christ. Only then may we walk among the worldly powers in freedom.

The Daily Office trains us rightly. At every turn, with the shocking fixity and unvarying patterns of its prayer, the Daily Office issues the central challenge of Christianity to our world: God has done something decisive and final in Jesus Christ. Therefore to get to what is "good news" we must go through him. To affirm this entails repudiating the pious flatulence that claims we do not know where the Holy Spirit is leading us. The good news of God's power and might is in Christ. Therefore the

Holy Spirit is always, always leading us into his narrow way, for only because of Christ, and through Christ and in Christ, do we have life. If we are to speak of the mission of the Holy Spirit, then we must make Christ the Alpha and the Omega. We must dwell more deeply in his way. There is no other mission of the Christian in the world.

Because Christ is not an idea, or a sentiment, or a feeling, his way has weight and edge. He is a person, and like every person, he did very specific things, and very specific things were done to him. As our Savior, Jesus is all things to all people—he awakens us, shapes us, and enlivens us—but he is not all things and is not all people. However much we might wish to place the Christian witness to Jesus in a fog of historical-critical speculation or to throw everything up for grabs with various theories about the universality of "faith experience," we do know Jesus. Scholars can debate pericopes and sayings, raise up endless theories about original audience and the Mediterranean matrix for ancient Christian teaching. Nonetheless contemporary believers, like believers through the centuries, have a remarkably clear view of Jesus. Good Friday and Easter Sunday are strange and alien *because of* the clarity of the events. He may throw our lives into utter turmoil, but this man from Nazareth who died on a cross on Golgotha and rose from a tomb outside of Jerusalem is quite vivid. The fleshly weight of his humanity and the sharp outline of events that defined his life and death give Jesus Christ purchase in our souls.

The work of the Holy Spirit is singular: to shape us under the weight of Jesus Christ, and through us to bring the whole world under his lordship. The church is central to this work, and the Daily Office is central to the church. As a daily pattern of prayer dedicated to Christ as Lord, Morning and Evening Prayer exhibits the encompassing ambition of the Holy Spirit on behalf of Jesus died and risen. Grounded in the prayer and prophecy of the Old Testament and saturated with the New Testament witness, the Daily Office's apostolic heritage testifies to the way the work of the Holy Spirit always emerges out of and returns to Jesus Christ. Fundamentally shaped by recitations of psalms and canticles, this narrow way of prayer trains us as disciples of the narrow way of Christ crucified. Receptive in hearing Scripture and expressive in collect and intercession, participants in the Daily Office are launched toward an ever wider gathering of all things to the Lord. In all four ways—encompassing, apostolic, impressive, and expressive—the Daily Office works upon us in just that way in which the Holy Spirit does the work of Christ in the world.

10

Reflections in Aid
of Theological Exegesis

You who once were far off have been brought near.

Ephesians 2:13

Students of our revered scriptures must be taught to recognize the various kinds of expression in holy scripture, to notice and memorize the ways it tends to say things, and especially—this is paramount and vital—to pray for understanding.

St. Augustine, *De doctrina Christiana*

The challenge of theological exegesis is not altogether different from other situations of reading and listening. The difficulties of interpretation rest in the problem of hearing what is said. For a number of reasons we are often very distant from what is spoken, and as a consequence it is difficult to hear. For example, my daughter is often in the basement reading a book, and she only vaguely hears me yell for her to go and clean her room. She hears but does not hear. As parents know, one must be rather close to children in order to get them to pay attention.

When we read the Scriptures, of course, the text is not on one floor yelling while we are distracted on another. Yet the situation is similar. The text has something to say, or more precisely, as a written artifact it is forever saying what it has to say. We, on the other hand, often fail to hear. Even when the Scriptures are open before us, as near as the desktop, we remain at a distance. What is being said is not always clear. Like my daughter, we often respond to Scripture's word with a pregnant "What?"—or worse, a disinterested "Whatever."

At the most basic level, hermeneutics are the disciplines of attention that help us overcome this distance. After all, Hermes was a messenger. He bridged the chasm between the gods and human beings. He traveled the distance from divine speakers to human listeners. For this reason, no matter how much theoretical heavy machinery is brought to bear on the problems of interpretation, hermeneutical reflection is always practical. It involves acquiring the knowledge and skill necessary to reach the goal of listening: to hear what is being said. It is, in a sense, the knowledge and skill of a traveler, someone who can find a way to overcome the distance that often mutes, obscures, and even silences. Any biblical hermeneutic worth its salt, then, will provide guidance for negotiating what I call the "problems of distance." It must inculcate the knowledge and skill necessary to get from where we are to what the Scriptures are saying.

This chapter advances the following thesis about the hermeneutical task of bridging the distances that separate us from the Word of God. The most important and debilitating distance should be understood spiritually. For all our worries about history, as well as those about the limitations of finite language and culturally conditioned texts, our difficulties in relation to the biblical text are not historical or metaphysical. More precisely, those difficulties are but subsets of the fundamentally spiritual reason that paying attention to Scripture is such a challenge. The Word of God is near to us, but even as it is before our eyes and on our lips, *we* are far. Only the cure of our souls will bring us to hear the Word of God.

But now *I* am speaking cryptically and at a distance. What, exactly, do I mean by "historical," "metaphysical," and "spiritual" distance?

The Distances of Time and Finite Form

The notion of historical distance is familiar to anyone who has taken a course in modern biblical criticism. The idea is simple. My difficulties in communicating with my daughter are not only a matter of trying to make my voice reach the basement family room. Sometimes I will chastise her for failing to perform a certain task. She will respond, "Since when I am supposed to do *that?*" With exasperation I ask her why she cannot remember what I told her only yesterday. For a ten-year-old, one day seems sufficient to erase memory! For the modern reader of the Bible, the challenges to memory are even more severe. The Scriptures were written a long time ago, and as a result the context, the semantic use, and the very languages of the texts stand at a distance. This makes it easy for us to confuse anachronistic readings with accurate readings as we substitute assumptions about the present for the realities of the past.

A great deal of the angst of modern Christian biblical scholarship rests in the historical distance created by the passage of time and the challenges it poses. One of my colleagues is emphatic: the distance is nearly unbridgeable. The New Testament, he insists, was written in a "high context" social matrix of Mediterranean agrarian culture. It cannot be understood by students raised in a "low context" Northern European industrial culture. His way of formulating the historical problem of distance is idiosyncratic, but the basic judgment is widespread. The currents of history carry us so far from the original context that only heroic efforts allow for recovery. In order to pay attention to what is actually being said in Scripture, rather than projecting onto the text what we imagine or would like it to say, the hard work of traveling back in time must be undertaken. Theoretical aids, schemes of reconstruction, ambitious expeditions of textual archaeology—these and many other vehicles carry the biblical critic across the distances created by the passing of time.

The metaphysical problem of distance receives less articulate attention among historical critics, but it is even more pervasive and threatening to modern readers of the Bible. Here the difficulty rests in the fact that the depths of meaning are fundamentally greater than the limited forms of speech. Finite signs and utterances cannot capture the fullness of what is said. I can just hear my daughter saying, "Dad, if that is what you mean, then why not just say it?" The problem is exacerbated when words seek to speak of God. How can the infinite be represented by the finite? How can spiritual truths take effective form as carnal or fleshly sounds in the air formed by our throats, or marks on the page formed by our hands? How can the array of ancient texts that we call the Bible, written by and for members of a small tribe of ancient people and the messianic movement they spawned, be the Word of God?

More often than not, modern interpreters treat this metaphysical distance as the nub of difficulty. What we often refer to as "historical context" is not just a challenge to our historical memory. It is also a challenge to our religious imagination. To cite a now widespread example, many contemporary readers are anxious to separate the patriarchal form of the biblical witness from its spiritual message. The finite form of the witness, wrapped in the historical and cultural limitations of its own cultural milieu, must be distinguished from the timeless and spiritual message it seeks to communicate. Just as I must reformulate my expectations so that my daughter "gets it," so also must the biblical interpreter reformulate the message of Scripture so that the modern reader "gets it."

Like traveling across historical distance, the distance between representation and that which is represented must be traversed. New words must be spoken, even new texts written, so that the eternal Word might shine forth in our new age. For most twenty-first-century academics, the word *hermeneutics* refers to theories of communicative interaction that analyze our efforts to parse meaning from medium and thus guide effective interpretation. A general account of what words and texts can and cannot do directs the journey from what is said to what is meant. The itineraries vary. For some, we must navigate the difficult terrain that separates the finite form of signs from the fathomless depths of consciousness (Riceour) or from effective power of texts (Gadamer). For others, we must renounce such a journey as futile and instead prepare ourselves to be pilgrims devoted to following the swerves and twists of semiotic play (Derrida) or the forward movement of communal consensus (Rorty). For still others, we should gird our loins for the adventures of strong misreading (Bloom) or discipline our souls to endure the prison of language (De Man). In each case, metaphysical distance defines the journey.

My descriptions of historical and metaphysical distance give the impression that these are uniquely modern problems. This is not so. The church fathers were very sensible of both. Origen did not assemble the text-critical apparatus of multiple versions of the Old Testament, the Hexapla, in order to meditate. He did so because he was very aware of how history can corrupt the texts. The passage of time requires the transmission and dissemination of the written word, which is the visible form of memory, and in this process copyists make mistakes that must be identified and corrected. Origen's judgment about how to discern and remedy these mistakes may lack the reliability of modern methods, but he certainly understood an important aspect of the historical problem of distance. In the same way, Irenaeus did not commend the succession of teachers stretching from his time back to the apostles in order to provide a foundation for later catholic polity. He did so in order to identify the reliable basis on which believers can bridge the distance between his own time and the apostolic age. The public memory of the community, expressed in the doctrine of qualified teachers and buttressed by signs of holiness, provides effective guidance to our efforts to gain accurate knowledge of apostolic teaching.

The metaphysical problem of representation and the distance it entails was even more pressing for the fathers. At a systematic level, St. Augustine famously distinguished between signs and things, and in so doing gave conceptual form to the problem facing all biblical interpreters, both ancient and modern. Not only is there an inevitable slippage between signs and things, as we all experience in both the multiple referents of words and their varying uses, but more important, the "thing" of which Scripture seeks to speak is God, and God transcends all signs. As Augustine says, when he speaks of God he enters into the paradox of not saying what he wishes to say, for he wishes to speak of the unspeakable.[1] The reality of God is so much greater than the finite forms of language that the truest thing that can be said is that he is ineffable. The metaphysical problem of distance knows no clearer expression.

Without doubt, then, the ancient church was sensible of the historical and metaphysical problems of distance. What the Scripture says is difficult to hear. Time separates us from what is said, and the finite form of all signs and texts makes the Bible a peculiar instrument for speaking about God. However, to say that the fathers were sensible of the historical and metaphysical problems of distance does not mean that they approached them in the same way as most modern readers. Indeed the solutions they offered are very different from the ones we typically think appropriate. We want historical methods to solve the problems posed by history. We want metaphysical theories of meaning to solve the problems posed by the fact that we use words to talk about things, texts to communicate realities. In contrast, the fathers offered spiritual or theological guidance for navigating the distances created by time and the finite form of language. For them the challenges of interpretation, many as they are, revolve around a spiritual problem: the distance between sin and righteousness.

For this reason the fathers treated the difficulties posed by history, as well as divine transcendence of language, as particular manifestations of this more fundamental distance between the ways of the world and the ways of the Lord. For example, Irenaeus does not dwell on the evidential value of public transmission of apostolic teaching. Instead he draws a sharp contrast between the willfulness of heretical innovation and the obedient submission of orthodox teachers to the doctrine entrusted to their care. Reliable guidance across the distances of time requires affiliating oneself with the community of the faithful whose public life manifests a visible continuity with the apostles. We must adopt the rule of faith of that community if we will draw nearer. Thus what we might now call canonical interpretation, guided by the living magisterium of the church, preserved in its creeds, and alive in the consensus of the faithful, is an appropriate and accurate gloss on Irenaeus's method for preparing ourselves to hear the testimony of Scripture.

St. Augustine's approach to the distances created by finite language is no less theological in character. For Augustine, the soul seeks that which transcends time and finitude. Such a journey, however, is beyond our power. Augustine takes the metaphysical problem of distance very seriously indeed. "We would not be able to do this," he continues, "except that Wisdom Himself saw fit to make Himself congruous with such infirmity as ours."[2] The Incarnate Word journeys to us so that we might journey with and to him. "He wished to assume flesh," writes Augustine, "not only for those arriving at their estate but also to prepare the way for those setting out at the beginning of their journey."[3] His form is fleshly, and encoded with the signs and language of prophecy, he dwells amid the limitations of finitude. Following Jesus' path, we acquire the habits of a traveler along his way, habits of faith, hope, and love, and thus are we carried across the metaphysical distance from creature to Creator.

Biblical Assumptions About Time

The ways in which the fathers analyze our hermeneutical situation can seem impossibly "precritical," so we adopt the assumptions of modernity. Surely historical distance cannot be overcome with the waving of some magical wand, as if prayer and fasting could substitute for the critical tools of modern textual analysis. The problems of historical distance must be treated independently of so-called theological exegesis. The limitations of historical context must be acknowledged. Something that scholars like to call "historical consciousness" cannot be gainsaid. Responsible exegesis must depend upon intellectual and not spiritual discipline. Similar reactions worry that the fathers' spiritual turn ignores the real and enduring problems of representation. Surely we must not confuse words about God with God. Surely we should avoid being idolaters of the letter of Scripture. Unless we gain some sophistication about words and their function as representations, then we will confuse what is said with what is meant.

I cannot begin to answer these objections, common as they are. A full-scale defense of patristic hermeneutics would require a genealogy of modern historical inquiry, as well as close analysis of how the metaphysics of representation was understood by the fathers. The fathers inherited and modified a complex and sophisticated Platonic tradition that nests with the Old Testament's dual structure of polemic against idolatry and affirmation of the power of divine presence in both temple and prophecy. Unpacking this interaction of Platonism with exegesis requires heavy lifting in the realm of metaphysics.[4] I have a perhaps unhealthy tendency to spend a great deal of time in the theoretical gymnasium. To avoid overtraining, I wish to set aside, for the moment, concerns about representation. Instead I will digress to consider a theological assumption behind the usual historical-critical objections to precritical exegesis. This assumption is best described as historical pessimism, the assumption that time is a curse (or a blessing, if one wishes to wipe the slate clean) because it creates an unbridgeable gap between past and present. The passage of time wears away at our connection to the past, and the erosion is unstoppable. This assumption needs to be examined, for the Scriptures themselves advance a theological judgment at odds with the modern view.

Consider the way the Lord blesses Noah after repenting of the desire to end the cycle of generations. The blessing opens and closes with a commandment: "Be fruitful and multiply, and fill the earth" (Gen. 9:1, 7). The passing of generations turns the unmarked passage of time into human history. Genealogy is the archetypical biblical form of encompassing the distance from past to present. Clearly, then, the Scriptures neither deny nor efface the passage of time, and in that sense the biblical witness affirms and promotes "history," as innumerable modern commentators on the Old Testament have noticed. Nonetheless, unlike modernity with its pessimism, the Scriptures do not treat historical distance as corrosive and corruptive; it is the medium of spiritual life, not an alien impediment. The space between past, present, and future creates room for blessing and curse. Time can be filled up and held together by covenant and faithfulness.[5]

In the Old Testament, faithfulness is bound up with memory. However, the mnemonic challenges are not simply technical or intellectual, as if proper critical techniques might suffice for, or even be relevant to, the problem of historical distance. My daughter forgets that I have told her to clean her room on Saturday mornings because she would rather read or play. We fail to remember because we are tempted to forget, and in this sense the ability to bridge the distances of time depends on moral and spiritual discipline, not intellectual techniques.

Second Kings 22 and the discovery of the book of the law suggests such a situation. The scene is very much about "history" and the distances it creates, but the sentiments are antithetical to modern historical sensibilities. In Jerusalem, we read, a lust for evil has darkened memory and corrupted the disciplines necessary to keep the past ever before the eyes of the present. A series of bad kings mark the eclipse of the past. Yet a good king now reigns, and he commissions workers to repair the house of the Lord. There they stumble upon the forgotten book of the law. Hilkiah, the high priest, brings the rediscovered book to King Josiah. His reaction is telling. He does not muse on the odd religious views of an archaic culture; he does not consult with critics to discern the *Sitz im Leben*. Instead "when the king heard the words of the book of the law, he tore his clothes" (2 Kings 22:11). He is a good king, and he has the eyes to see that which is written, ears to hear that which is spoken. The passage of time is a challenge to memory, but it was the reign of bad kings that caused the book of the law to be lost. Furthermore, it was because King Josiah was devoted to the repair of the house of the Lord that the book of the law was recovered and, more important, understood. Thus the drama of sin and righteousness determines connection to the past, and we might do well to reflect upon the possibility that, should we turn in reparative devotion, we may rediscover and understand that which recent centuries have buried and obscured.

St. Paul's reflections on the fate of carnal Israel assumes and deepens the view of history we find in 2 Kings. The passage of time creates a stage for the drama of God's promises and the outworking of his redemptive will, not only in the triumphs of memory but also in its failures. For St. Paul, the mysterious unbelief of Israel conforms to the Old Testament pattern of blindness and forgetfulness. Quoting from Isaiah, Paul interprets the Jewish rejection of Jesus as the consummating form of Israel's blindness. The organs of memory—eye and ear—are disabled (Rom. 11:8). Yet for Paul, the very distance of carnal Israel from the fulfillment of the promises that are its birthright—presently cut off—allows for the nations to enter into the drama of history. They are grafted onto the genealogy of Israel that, as promised to Noah, will fill up the distances created by time and its passing. "I want you to understand this mystery," writes St. Paul: "a hardening has come upon part of Israel, until the full number of the Gentiles has come in" (Rom. 11:25). Israel's inability to hear, as did King Josiah, the word that, however distant in time or form, "is near you, on your lips and in your heart" (Rom. 10:8), establishes the very conditions for the elongation of time. Time and the historical distances it creates are, for St. Paul, the gift that Jewish unbelief gives to the Gentiles. Or more precisely, this time before the end of all time is God's gift, which he gives mysteriously through his providential hardening of the heart of carnal Israel.

I do not intend these brief exegetical digressions to be sufficient for understanding the scriptural view of time. Nonetheless, I hope both cast doubt on the historical pessimism that characterizes much modern scholarly reading of the Bible. From the perspective of the Scriptures themselves, history does not necessarily or inevitably distance us from the word of God. In 2 Kings, as in much of the Old Testament, history offers both the opportunity to draw near and the risk of falling away. For St. Paul, the continued passage of time after the fulfillment of God's promises in Jesus extends and intensifies that opportunity, as one form of falling away makes possible another form of drawing near. Thus the distances created by time are very real. Neither the author of 2 Kings nor St. Paul has any interest in denying the reality of historical time. Quite the contrary, both insist upon its reality, both as the medium for memory and as the stage upon which divine promises find their fulfillment. What is important, however, is that in both cases the distances of time are set within the broader problem of spiritual distance. What matters most is the relation of our souls to the Lord; the crucial issue is the distance at which we stand from that which is near.

Two Exegetical Techniques

If my brief meditation on the biblical view of history has given you cause to reconsider the typical modern pessimism about time and its passing, then I would be pleased. If you are beginning to suspect that, as the fathers so consistently taught, questions of historical distance, like those of metaphysical distance, are best considered under the greater and more fundamental problem of spiritual distances, then we have come a good way toward rethinking the notion of biblical hermeneutics. Yet neither the biblical view of history nor the patristic account of the fundamental distance that separates us from the Word of God adds up to hermeneutics. As I indicated earlier, to have a hermeneutics is to have the disciplines of hearing that help us overcome the distance between what we hear and what is said, and these disciplines are just that, disciplines or practices that train our ears and eyes. Hermeneutical skill does not stem from investigation of the biblical views on any particular subject, even a subject as central to modern interpretation as history. Nor does that skill result from sympathy with the larger, spiritual outlook of the fathers. Instead if you are beginning to think that the fathers are right, that the difficulties of interpretation revolve around a fundamental problem of spiritual distance, and if you wish to address the exegetical challenge at that level, then you must acquire the skills of reading that characterize patristic exegesis. You must read as did the fathers.

I can no more guide you toward the acquisition of patristic skills of reading than I can offer a full-scale defense of precritical exegesis against critical objections. Indeed I can be of even less help, for the acquisition of a skill requires the tutelage of a master, not the observations of a scholar, and I am no master of the particular methods and techniques of reading that characterize patristic exegesis. Nonetheless, I can offer two brief performances, one keyed to the problem of history, the other directed to the problem of representation. Both are methods of spiritual reading that have dominated the exegetical practice of Christians for centuries, and they have been so influential and long-lived because they succeed in overcoming distance.

Figural reading is one way the fathers traversed the distances that separate us from the text. Just what is involved in figural reading is a matter of endless debate. Nonetheless, Christian figural exegesis has a recognizable form. Jesus Christ functions as the disclosing antitype, and he illuminates the meaning of events both before and after his life, death, and resurrection. This illumination occurs because events or persons have a shape or form that outlines a common "figure." One common instance is the deliverance of Israel from the Egyptians through the Red Sea. The deliverance through water prefigures redemption in Christ, a redemption sealed in our passage through the waters of baptism. Here an event in the past, separated from the reader by the distances of time, is brought near through figural conformity to events in the present. An event in Exodus is drawn through Christ into present ecclesial practice. In this way figural exegesis overcomes distance. What happened to the Israelites has happened to each of us.

The Red Sea/redemption in Christ/baptism figural constellation is widespread in precritical exegetical works, but its very conventionality tends to disguise the dynamics of figural reading. Better, then, to undertake something more adventurous. Consider this particularly powerful figural interpretation that I draw from the work of Ephraim Radner.[6] It involves three historical moments. The first is the division of Israel into northern and southern kingdoms, the weakening entailed in this division, and then the slow slide toward defeat, enslavement, and exile. These events serve as the background for the prophetic books, and they in turn are central to the Christian interpretation of the identity of Jesus as the Christ. Moreover, this sequence is not simply historical background to particular prophetic passages that are fulfilled. The sequence of division, diminishment, and exile is recapitulated and intensified in Christ: his betrayal, the scattering of his disciples, his diminishment and affliction in arrest, and his God-forsaken death. In Jerusalem, Jesus alone is the remnant of holiness, reduced to death by the afflictions due to the unrighteous.

Here the second historical sequence of events—the fate of the man Jesus of Nazareth—enters into an illuminative relationship to the first historical sequence. The relation of type to antitype discloses more fully the redemptive suffering of those few faithful who, bound to the body of Israel, were borne into the captivity that is rightly due to the unfaithful. Now the power of the covenant is more fully visible. The union of the righteous to the body of the nation, like Jesus' union with carnal flesh, cannot be sundered, and this union subjects the righteous to an undeserved and yet redemptive suffering. Under the burdens of exile, the remnant carries forward the disciplines of memory that make possible the return to Jerusalem and restoration of the temple, just as Christ, enduring the final burden of death, rises and makes possible our return to the Lord in restored worship. Furthermore, to pursue the figure, neither return simply restores; both intensify and sharpen the disciplines of holiness. The books of Ezra and Nehemiah are characterized by a redoubled rather than relaxed restoration of cult and Torah. St. Paul as well preaches the power of the risen Christ as spiritual worship and discipline that intensifies and fulfills.

The power of figure does not just extend from Christ backwards to the history of Israel. It extends forward to the history of the church. The church is Christ's body, and as such, it participates in the figural sequence of exile and restoration. This forward lean of figure is primitive to Christian interpretation of present times. First Peter, for example, is addressed to the "exiles of the Dispersion" (1:1) who "suffer various trials" (1:6), all of which purify and refine so that a remnant of holiness might be called out of the darkness and into divine light (1:9). But the figure does not jump from Old Israel to New Israel. For the author of 1 Peter, Christ is the illuminating center of the figural sequence. The desolation of trial, the afflictions of exile, should be embraced. "Rejoice," exhorts the author, "insofar as you are sharing Christ's sufferings, so that you may also be glad and shout for joy when his glory is revealed" (4:13). Israel, Christ, and church are three historical moments in figural relation.

First Peter establishes a pattern of reading that invites subsequent interpreters to place the history of the church into the figural sequence. The fathers did this at every turn. We can do so as well. As Radner suggests, the divided churches in the West, fragmented by the Reformation, suffer the same fate as the two kingdoms of ancient Israel. One need but visit a German or a French or an English church to feel as though 1 Peter speaks to the present. Truly the few who gather are exiles in the Dispersion; they are a remnant clinging to the disciplines of memory that keep Christian faith alive in the enclosing darkness of a post-Christian culture. As I have said again and again throughout these chapters, the church is in ruins.

For just this reason Radner urges us to complete the figural sequence. We suffer the failures and weaknesses of our churches. Yet such afflictions are none other than the suffering that shapes the church into the body of our Lord, so that it might share in his suffering. Still further, if we press the figure from present into future, then we can look to the narratives of Ezra and Nehemiah for a pattern of ecclesial resurrection in Western culture. Given this pattern, we should hope that the church will come to weep bitterly in penitent confession of faithlessness, and in redoubled zeal for holiness it will put away its foreign wives and children.

We need to be clear about how this figural sequence functions. In the first place, this way of reading is *not* a matter of matching up prophetic passages with christological fulfillments that are in turn connected to specific ecclesial doctrines or practices. Instead this figural approach takes historical events and brings them together. The division of Israel, the conflict between the two kingdoms, the diminishment and decline that follows, the captivity and affliction, the persistence of a remnant, the return and redoubled restoration—this entire sequence enters into a illuminating relation to the present sequence of events in the Christian church in the West, and it does so through the prism of the passion, death, and resurrection of Jesus. They share a common figure or form that makes events that are historically distant come together.

Of course they do not merge. The historical sequences are very real. Neither a second-century reader who thinks Ezra and Nehemiah and the Synoptic Gospels are utterly reliable accounts of what actually happened nor the most sophisticated modern reader who has all the latest critical tools at her disposal has ever imagined that these two sequences of events are not separated by the distances of history. Nor do any imagine that the more recent history of the church is any closer in time by virtue of figural interpretation. The point is that their figural association allows the reader to bridge the very real and enduring distances of time through an interpretive coordination. Each historical sequence says the same thing about the way of faithfulness. As the crucified Messiah reveals, to suffer afflictions due the unfaithful is the vocation of those who would serve the redemptive will of God.

For this reason, figural reading is the essence of Christian "historical" exegesis. The illuminating form of Christ provides the basis for understanding how the word of God is revealed in events and practices that stand at a distance from each other.

Intensive reading is another and very different skill that was no less dominant among the fathers. Unlike figural interpretation, which deals with patterns and sequences that make up historical events and practices, intensive reading focuses on the semantic plenitude of particular scriptural signs or episodes. Patristic commentary on the Gospel of John is paradigmatic. Origen, for example, gathers up many meanings of *logos,* and he does so not to sift through them and settle upon a single and univocal meaning, but in order to arrange the many meanings around the christological focus of the Johannine text.[7] In this way Origen engages the problem of metaphysical distance. He follows the many threads of meaning, never reaching the destination but always making progress across the difference between representation and reality, between the sign *logos* and the One who is signified.

I do not propose to reproduce Origen's reflections. Instead I wish to illustrate the intensive approach by considering a verse in the Gospel of John that I have long found puzzling. It involves a play of pronouns, and it comes from the sixth chapter. Jesus teaches that he does not do his own will but the will of the Father. In this discourse the will of the Father, very much the crux of the passage, is semantically ambiguous. "This is the will of him who sent me," says Jesus, "that I should lose nothing of all that he has given me, but raise it up on the last day" (John 6:39). The passage perplexes me because *all* and *it* are words or signs that represent something central to Jesus' message. Yet they are pronouns that hold the place for something else. They are the open variables in an equation. Some x is given to Jesus. He shall lose nothing of this x. He shall raise up this x at the last day. Precisely because they have semantic openness—pronouns are wonderfully fungible parts of speech—the passage generates more questions than it answers. What is given to Jesus, and what will he raise up?

The immediate context of the passage suggests the proper referents for the pronouns. The very next verse tells us that all who believe in the Son shall have eternal life and that Jesus will raise them up at the last day. By this reading, "all" and "it" refer to the faithful. This reading is reinforced by Jesus' emphatic affirmation of the saving power of his flesh and blood later in the discourse (6:54). The Father has given followers to Jesus, and the Father has given Jesus the power of redemption, manifest in the eucharistic ritual. Joined to his body and blood in the sharing of the consecrated bread and wine, we participate in his death and resurrection.

The reading seems right, but I am not sure that we have cracked the nut of this puzzling verse. Why would the verse say that the "all" given to Jesus is an "it" that he will raise up? I do not wish to suggest that we are not given to Jesus and that he will not raise us up on the last day. I only wish to point out that the particular and carnal form of the signs used, that is to say, the difference between impersonal and personal pronouns, invites further exegetical reflection. Perhaps the Father has given Jesus the power of life. Then, with this as the x in the passage, we can see that nothing of the power shall be lost, even if Jesus is betrayed, arrested, and crucified. This reading is also strongly reinforced by the immediate context. Jesus is the bread of life. Unlike the manna in the wilderness that sustains a few and only for a time, Jesus gives life to the world (6:33). Therefore on the cross, on his last day, he raises up the power of life. His flesh and blood are for all and forever.

These pronouns can shift yet again. Maybe the x represented by "all" and "it" is neither the faithful nor the power of life. Maybe the x represents the flesh that the Father gives to the Son by sending him to us as the incarnate Lord. The Son will lose nothing of this gift, and for just this reason the Eternal Logos will experience destitution, suffering, and death. Nothing of carnal life is left out or lost. All of "it" is raised up on the cross in the form of the dead man whose flesh is pierced. For just this reason you and I, flesh from flesh, are neither left out nor lost in the risen Lord. Christ will let go of nothing. As he bears the marks of the nails and the wound of the spear—nothing of the flesh is lost, not even its lean toward death—he raises us to light and life.

The point of this kind of reading is not to decide which referent is the right one. Instead the skill involves allowing the very distance between sign and signified to motivate us to undertake interpretive effort. In this case I drew attention to the way the semantic openness of pronouns can open rather than close questions. This openness does not frustrate. Instead the difficulty of settling on a particular interpretation forces us to look again and again at the possibilities. Looking again and not elsewhere is the reason the fathers did not view metaphysical distances created by representation with regret; such ambiguity stems from the plenitude of sense that is an inevitable consequence of the fact that the words of Scripture are effective but inadequate signs. They are inadequate for the reason St. Augustine identified: they seek to speak to us of the ineffable mystery of God. Yet they are effective, because these signs are not mute and sterile but vocal and fecund. The "failures" of representation—in this case, the "defect" of the semantic openness characteristic of pronouns—lead us toward the fathomless depths of that to which all the scriptural signs point: the mystery of Christ. Thus the metaphysical distance between sign and signified is no more collapsed by intensive reading than historical distance is collapsed by figural reading. Exegetical travel is undertaken, and that which seems impossibly distant comes into view in just the right way.

The Ascetical Core of Theological Exegesis

Hermeneutical skill is the ability to understand words; it requires the virtues that sustain travel across the distances between what we hear and what is said. I hope that my brief illustrations of figural and intensive reading have provided a small degree of insight into classical Christian methods for overcoming distances. If we acquire the ability to see figural sequences, then we can travel across the distances of history. If we cultivate an appreciation of the plenitude of sense, then we can travel along the distance between sign and signified. These skills, however, are not isolated. In both cases a spiritual discipline undergirds the practices of reading.

On the central role of spiritual discipline, Origen is perhaps the most lucid and direct of all the fathers. As I observed in chapter eight, Origen is as emphatic as the most hard-nosed evangelical preacher. The Scriptures are the singular path toward truth. Yet unlike a great deal of modern conservative reaction to the very real problems of historical and metaphysical distance that have come to dominate academic study of the Bible, Origen is no proponent of easy perspicuity. The Scriptures are full of obscurity, contradiction, and offense. The distance between us and the text is very real indeed.

However, for Origen such distance is not a curse. Quite the contrary, our distance from the Scriptures is part of the pedagogy of salvation. The more sensible we are of the distance between what we hear and what God wishes to say, the more accurate will be our sense of the arduous and difficult nature of traversing that distance. Reading rightly will require the surest of guides, and here, for all his interpretive inventiveness and potentially dangerous theological speculation, Origen is utterly opposed to the complacent strategies of reading that seek to find relevance or that depend on the inner resources of the reader. The ability to traverse the distance, the power to read rightly, rests only in the primary facts of ecclesial life, however obscure and difficult. Only as we are formed by the common life of the church, its ancient teachings, its ceaseless prayer, and its patterns of self-discipline and mutual service can we read rightly. We must draw near in order to see clearly. This is the most fundamental form of the patristic theory of hermeneutics.

The present age founders on the problems of history and representation because we are unwilling to enter into the spiritual discipline necessary to travel the distance between what we hear and what is said. The ways the fathers read Scripture are alien because their discipline is now alien. We no longer submit ourselves to the common life of the church, not only because our modern souls fear authority, not only because intellectual life has come untethered from ecclesiastical reality, but because Western Christianity has a severely fragmented common life. The prayer of the church is cacophonous. Its doctrines are defined in the spirit of mutual condemnation, not mutual service. What Origen thought indispensable we now seek to re-create through ecumenical endeavor. Not surprisingly, then, the practices of spiritual reading are suspect; the communal conditions for their disciplined use exist only in part.

Equally important, spiritual reading gains little traction because the moral and ascetical practices that the fathers thought essential to the Christian life are now divorced from intellectual training. Who would imagine that fasting might contribute to exegetical insight? To a certain degree, modern historical study has inculcated moral discipline. Pursuit of truth requires the courage to consider all the evidence. Moreover, loyalty to truth engenders humility, especially the humility of a historian who knows that historical judgment traffics in likelihood and possibility, not certainty and necessity. Yet even these virtues are in decline. Postmodern "methods" put few demands upon the souls of their practitioners or the students they train.

Nothing could be further from the patristic atmosphere of interpretation. For Augustine, the ambiguities and uncertainties that finite signs produce do not yield a "play of difference." We cannot turn what is hard into something easy. Instead interpretation is difficult, and for Augustine "this situation was provided by God to conquer pride by work and to combat disdain in our minds, to which those things which are easily discovered seem frequently to become worthless" (*De doctrina Christiana* 2.6). Here the patristic outlook is clearly expressed. Hermeneutical discipline is no different from spiritual discipline. "The mind should be cleansed," writes Augustine, "so that it is able to see [divine] light and cling to it once it is seen. Let us consider this cleansing to be as a journey or voyage home" (1.10). To read rightly will both require and lead to humility; it will both require and lead to a love of that which God wishes us to hear.

This assimilation of hermeneutical skill to spiritual virtue can seem pious and preachy. It is both, but that is because piety and preaching seek to bring us to exactly that which words seek to achieve: understanding what is said. I conclude with an exchange that typifies this truth. When I graduated from college, I lived in New York City, near Harlem. One day, on the way home from the subway stop, I tarried briefly to listen to a man harangue a small group that was gathered at the corner. His voice was filled with urgency; his eyes were aflame. What he said I cannot reconstruct, but I vividly remember the way he ended nearly every sentence. He would call out, "Do you hear me, brothers? Do you hear me?"

He had no doubts about the volume of his voice. He was not wondering whether his listeners had their hearing aids turned on. He was asking them if they would allow what he was saying to gain leverage in their lives. Were his listeners with him? Would they undertake to travel with him toward that which he saw and sought? This was the hermeneutical challenge he posed, and it is, I think, the most fundamental challenge of anyone who wishes to hear something genuinely important and true.

Our relation to the Scriptures is no different, for they seek to speak the most important and pressing truth. Few wish to hear. Most wish to stand at a distance. No technical or intellectual aids will bring us near. Only spiritual discipline will carry us toward something that, though crowned in glory, is flavored with the bitter taste of vinegar and gall.

11

The Marks of the Nails

I read the opening of Genesis
and was filled with joy,
for its verses and lines
spread out their arms to welcome me;
the first rushed out and kissed me,
and led me on to its companions.

St. Ephraim the Syrian, *Paradise Hymns*

If, as I have argued, we dwell in the ruins of the church, then our spiritual condition is influenced accordingly. We suffer a disorientation and dryness that limits the scope of our vision. As the walls of the church are thrown down, we are forced to live among the disordered stones. Yet, this condition, however arid, is not empty. To suffer the ruined church is to suffer divine things, and the stones, however fallen, are living. They are potent with the power of God. For this reason, even as we must face a winnowing vocation, we should cherish the *concreta Christiana*, especially the words of Scripture. In the ruins of the church we may not be able to survey the whole of Scripture as from the high walls of Jerusalem, but as we draw near we can listen to God's Word in its particularity.

I propose, then, to end these reflection with attention to the words of Scripture. I will not approach this exegesis thematically or theologically in any grand or systematic sense. I am convinced that, in the ruins of the church, our approach to Scripture must be primitive. Just as Nehemiah returned, we can recover a theological exegesis of Scripture by drawing ever closer to the words.

Thus, to the First Letter of John I turn. This letter helps us understand how drawing ever nearer to the cruciform ruin of the church is not at all inconsistent with a resurrection hope. The many stones of meaning in this extraordinary text, stones that have no obvious architecture and are difficult to see as an ordered whole, have living power. In 1 John we find possibilities, marks of the nails, that are potent with the joy of resurrection. But I am rushing ahead. First we need to consider the way of reading suggested by this remarkable text.

The First Letter of John has a rather strange influence on readers. The letter contains a number of memorable verses and compelling images. For example, we read, "Love one another, because love is from God; everyone who loves is born of God and knows God" (4:7). What preacher would not prefer to preach on this verse rather than Paul's exhortations to subordination or Matthew's directives to pluck out eyes and cut off members? Other verses percolate in our memories as particularly poignant and apt summations of important truths of the Christian faith. Should we feel faithfulness slipping into the spectral realms of sensibility or mere rote confession, we might call to mind 1 John 3:18, where we read, "Let us love, not in word or speech, but in truth and action." Or should we be anxious about the moralizing tendency of all this talk of "deed" and wish to emphasize the *sola gratia* character of salvation, our memories light upon one of the most joyful exclamations in the New Testament: "See what love the Father has given us, that we should be called children of God" (3:1).

The same force characterizes the sheer directness of the imagery of 1 John. We hear of the "word of life" (1:1); we read that "God is light" (1:5) and "the darkness is passing away" (2:8); we are warned not to "love the world" (2:15) or to "walk in darkness" (2:11); we are taught that those who are born of God have "boldness before God" (3:21) and that those who "have the Son" also "have life" (5:12), which is "eternal life" (5:13). These images and phrases—the antithesis of light and darkness, the variations on themes of birth and life, the sheer volume of the formulations dependent upon the action of love—remain with any reader of 1 John. Yet, and this is what is so strange about 1 John, if you ask anyone what the letter is *about*, you will likely evoke platitudes—"it's about love," "it's about eschatological conflict"—or embarrassed silence.

Full of memorable formulations of crucially central and true Christian beliefs and written with a keen sense of the importance and power of vivid images, yet strangely opaque when taken as a whole—this is the distinctive way the text of 1 John sets the terms of interpretation.[1] These terms suggest that we should read 1 John as perspicuous and fecund. It is a text that says what it wishes to say with a crystalline sharpness, with words fully forged, and a text that sets out to say more than it says, a text with depths sufficient to absorb all our attention. If we fail to read in this way, then we fail to respect the form in which the text quite self-evidently presents itself, a form that makes even the most casual reader aware of the odd conjunction of memorable turns of phrases, lucid inferences, and sharp images with a frustratingly obscure sense of the whole. So let us approach the text without assuming that this odd conjunction is a mistake or problem to be overcome. Let us leave behind the various historical-critical strategies of looking behind or beyond the text, strategies that always seem to end up wearing an interpretive hairshirt and that speak in the thinnest ascetical whispers about the theological substance of the text. Let us enjoy, instead, the freedom of drawing near to the text, of allowing the demands of perspicuity and fruitfulness to play fully upon our reading. Let us read with an obedient attention born of believing that the words say exactly what we need to hear.

As we turn to this strangely easy and difficult text, I warn the reader that our efforts cannot begin with a helpful thematic overview of 1 John. It is precisely the larger meaning of 1 John that is so difficult to grasp, and to read from whole to part would entail trying to explain the clear—the luminous words and phases of the text—with the obscure. I propose, then, to begin with what is clear. Like a child whose attention is utterly focused upon an insect or leaf, I propose simply to look at the words. And although this approach might give the initial impression of neglecting the larger context of 1 John, or the Johannine literature as a whole, or the mystery of Christ, I think the truth is otherwise. Concentrated attention upon the semantic concreteness of the text draws us into the full sweep of the Christian drama. By looking closely rather than falling into the temptation to abstraction and abbreviation, we can see further and more deeply. In this way the larger context emerges, but in a fresh way, out of the text itself. The words themselves have the power of life, and in order to read 1 John rightly, we should abide in its tensive field of semantic forces.

Is this approach at all surprising? Consider, for a moment, the Gospel text (John 20:19–31) assigned with 1 John at the beginning of the Easter cycle of readings in the widely used common lectionary. There we read of Thomas, for whom even seeing the risen Lord was not enough. He wished to touch the crucified Jesus in all his disfigurement. Jesus does not mock this human need for sensible, tangible contact. He comes to Thomas and invites him to see and touch and therefore to believe. This, reports the Gospel of John, was one of the many signs, many *semeia*, of the presence of the resurrected Jesus with the disciples. Like Thomas, then, if we wish to believe in the mystery of the risen Lord who is none other than the crucified Jesus, should we not begin by taking up the *semeia*, the words themselves? Should we not allow ourselves to be drawn into the scriptural world of signs? Should we not turn to 1 John and look upon these marks of the nails?

Beginning with Beginning

At the very opening of 1 John we dive into the deep end of the textual world of ease and difficulty. The first verses clearly state what the letter is about and why it is written. The letter, we read, is about the "word of life," and this word is by no means a faint and distant echo, a far and difficult voice, an obscure and secret text. No, the "word of life" is "what we have heard, what we have seen with our eyes, what we have looked at and touched with our hands." This letter, the author assures us, is about familiar stuff; what he is writing about has already been heard and seen and touched by many others, and thus the crucial message about "life" is right out in the open. Indeed not only may we see the matter with our own eyes, but the message is so fully and immediately present before us that we may even take it into our hands.

And these words, minted with sharp blows so that the impressions are firm and true, are written for the purpose of fellowship. The purpose of the vivid words, these memorable images and well-crafted sentences, is not to obscure or hide, not to communicate a teaching or truth that is a special possession of the writer and is to be given only in partial stages or under the cover of a secret code. No, the goal of the letter is to share something in full and to do so in the most straightforward fashion. One can hardly imagine a more direct anticipation by the author of the clarity and directness that constitutes one pole of our engagement of the text.[2]

Yet in these very verses we encounter the other pole—the word or image or formulation that, though perfectly clear and direct and easily taken in hand, seems utterly alive with allusion and suggestion. What is heard and seen and held in fellowship is "that which was from the beginning." Is this a reinforcement of the matter-of-fact quality of the opening? The "word of life" here proclaimed is not only public but also basic to the community; it has been taught from the beginning. Because of this the reader may have fellowship with the writer, for as the author observes in subsequent passages, the subject matter of the letter concerns what "you have had from the beginning" (2:7) and have "heard from the beginning" (3:11). Rest assured, we hear the very opening clause suggesting, this is a letter about the faith once received. The matters discussed are from the very foundation of Christian teaching, and all of us by virtue of our membership in a common community already share this teaching.

But what *is* the "foundation" of Christian teaching? As we ask this question we begin to tumble into a world so dense with possibilities that we cannot but feel blind before what we can so easily hear and see and touch. Can we really rest in a translation of the relative pronoun *what*, which stands as the basis of the author's testimony and the reader's fellowship in that testimony into "teaching"? Should we not allow the emphasis on the visible, tangible form of "what was from the beginning" to ring more fully? And in the special attention drawn to "our hands," should we not consider the possibility that the beginning or "foundation" of the testimony of the letter is the bread and wine that the readers have had since their beginning in baptism?

This twist is by no means unanticipated by the author of 1 John, for as the letter draws to a close, the testimony that has spilled forth from the "the beginning," the words that this particular man has written at this particular time, is subordinated to the greater testimony of God, a testimony woven into the witnesses of "the water and the blood" (5:8).

So this "beginning," which stands as the basis of the fellowship that 1 John both presupposes and seeks to make more complete, is a power of life. It is not just the "word of life," or perhaps more accurately, it is a "word of life" that is not just a teaching but also a set of practices, liturgical acts centered on the water of baptism and the body and blood that give life. In short, "the beginning" cannot be restricted to "word or speech," as 1 John 3:18 reminds us, but must spill out into "truth and action."

This opening verse does not stop with the double possibility of a "beginning" that is either a teaching—a form of speech—or a ritual act—the doing of a deed that marks the Christian life. The entire notion of "beginning" also suggests a cosmological frame of reference. So we might rightly consider that the "beginning" or *arche* that the author of 1 John saw and touched and wishes to pass on to his readers is not just the common dogmatic and liturgical inheritance of every Christian community but more, much more. Is it the "word of life" that was in the beginning with God and was God and through whom all things were made (John 1:1)? Is this the *arche* that is the basis of the testimony of 1 John? Far more than a stylized appeal to basic communal teaching or a suggestive allusion to ritual practice, is the "beginning" that sets the letter in motion the *logos*, the Word that is more certain and evident and tangible than the very cosmos itself?

Here we should guard against any thought that the cosmological scope of the Eternal Word either excludes or supersedes the rather more plain, sociopersonal sense of "what was from the beginning." A merging of these frames of reference is precisely the effect of the allusive density of 1 John's characteristic words and formulations, and of the Johannine literature as a whole. Thus, as we read in John's Apocalypse, not only do we begin in the Christian life through the teaching and fellowship of the apostles but also "from the foundation of the world" when our names are written "in the book of life" (Rev. 13:8). The cosmological frame of reference blurs into the sociopersonal frame. It is as if one were to reach into the limpid semantic pool of the Johannine language only to find that one has entirely misjudged the depth. One cannot simply reach in and touch bottom. One must jump in and begin to dive.

And the diving does not touch bottom. Is the *arche* that sets 1 John in motion an evocation of the power of witness that belongs to those who were with Christ "from the beginning" (John 15:27), a promise that follows closely on the heels of Jesus' commandment "that you love one another as I have loved you" (John 15:12), and the point at which all discipleship and witness to Jesus must begin and the message that the author of 1 John assumes his readers "have heard from the beginning" (3:11)? The effectiveness and importance of being with Christ "from the beginning" is reinforced by the common lectionary. There the opening verses of 1 John are matched with Acts 4:5–12, where Peter witnesses before the high-priestly family to the power of Christ in a particularly direct fashion, showing a fulfillment of Christ's promise in John 15:27. Peter was with Jesus "from the beginning," and now, before the high-priestly family, he is filled with the Spirit who proceeds from the Father, and in that power Peter proclaims the name of Jesus Christ of Nazareth.

However, the lectionary matching does not settle the question. Or rather, the very testimony of Peter to "the name of Jesus Christ of Nazareth" (Acts 4:10), the power of which is very much on the mind of the author of 1 John (see 2:22; 3:23; 4:2; 5:1), is an invitation for us to seek rather than rest, for Peter proclaims this "name" as the power of salvation. He with whom Peter was from the beginning sets in motion decisive events and transformations. Similarly, in 1 John "the name of the Son of God" contains the effective promise of eternal life. To be with Christ "from the beginning" means allowing Christ to be the "cornerstone"—the foundation or *arche* of everything that follows in one's life. "This man is standing before you in good health," proclaims Peter of the lame man who now walks, "by the name of Jesus Christ of Nazareth" (Acts 4:10). The opening verses of 1 John establish just such a *solus Christus* sequence: "what was from the beginning" is the power of fellowship—fellowship among the believers and fellowship with the Father and the Son (1 John 1:3). This *arche*—and here we may allow all the previous senses of *arche* (foundational apostolic teaching, basic practices of baptism and Eucharist, the Eternal Word, the man Jesus with whom Peter was from the beginning)—is the key to a joy that may be complete (1 John 1:4). The *arche* is the very power and joy of our *telos*.

Not only does the depth of this opening verse of 1 John suggest multiple senses of "beginning," but the semantic field of allusion also reinforces the particular way in which the *arche* and *telos*, the *alpha* and *omega*, come into the tightest interrelationship in the singular figure of Christ. This semantic field is not only evident in the patterns of the opening verses. If we allow ourselves to follow the purely verbal suggestions of *arche*, to stretch from *arche* to *arche* within the canon, then the same patterns recur in the most surprising places. Consider, for example, the *arche* that launches 1 John—a word, as we have seen, that is full of possible senses. It is itself the *arche ton semeion* (first of the signs), the first semantically dense word in a letter full of such signs. Guided by this verbal suggestion—the first of the signs—might our attention not focus on the first of Jesus' signs, the wedding at Cana (see John 2:1–11)?

This guidance bears good fruit. In the wedding story we read of a gathering in which the source of joyous celebration has been exhausted. "They have no wine" is a report sufficient to end this party. However, by Jesus' direction the festival continues. He orders the servants to fill stone jars set aside for the waters of ritual purification, and from these jars the steward of the feast tastes a fine wine, exclaiming at the odd reversal of the convention of serving the best wine first and saving the poor wine for last. With the steward's discovery of the good wine, which had been water just moments before, not only are the conditions established for the continuation of the party, but in a sense the feast begins afresh, for this new wine is not a poor wine that signals the dulled senses of the revelers and the inevitable end of the party but is rather the good wine of "beginning."

This, then, is the pattern of the *arche ton semeion* toward which the first use of *arche* in 1 John points: a continuation that is a new beginning. And this pattern invites layer upon layer of christological themes. The marriage feast of God and Israel is neither broken nor continued in Christ. Rather, the joy of Sinai is renewed by the full presence of the *arche* of the festal celebration. And how does this wine of "beginning" come to the lips of the steward? He tastes that which has been poured into the stone jars set aside for the waters of purification, and *this* wine from *those* jars is the good wine of "beginning." In 1 John, purification is also the crucial hinge on which turns the hope for complete joy, the joy of fellowship, the joy of abiding in God and in each other, the joy the marriage feast celebrates. The cleansing blood of Jesus, the Son of God, allows us to "walk in the light" and to "have fellowship with one another" (1 John 1:7).

Now, in the semantic depths of 1 John, waters deep enough to invite a reading of the miracle at Cana as part of the meaning of the very opening verse of the letter, we come upon yet another sense of *arche.* "What was from the beginning" is "the blood of Jesus" (1:1, 7). Yet this is a "beginning" that, as the steward of the feast recognizes with surprise, comes at the "end." What the steward of the feast exclaims in wonderment the author of 1 John writes with utter simplicity and directness. God is love, and our perfection *(telos)* is to abide in God, and in him to abide in love. That which is God and in which we are to abide is none other than the love of him who laid down his life for us (3:16). The blood of Jesus that cleanses us of sin is the love that is God and in which we find our perfection. The "beginning" of our fellowship with God is also our perfection, our "ending."[3]

The pattern of "beginning" and "ending" in the story of the wedding at Cana, a pattern brought before us by the purely verbal suggestion of the position of *arche* as the first semantically dense word in 1 John, would seem, then, to have more than a merely verbal relationship to the text. Indeed, with the pattern fully in view, we can journey quite far from the verbal cues of *arche* and *telos.* For example, the author of 1 John gives a similar twist to the "old" and "new" commandment of love that is God's "word." "Beloved," we read in a verse that echoes the opening of the letter, "I am writing you no new commandment, but an old commandment that you have had from the beginning" (2:7). Not only does this verse echo the "from the beginning" formulation that opens the letter, but the sentence also concludes with an allusion to the "seen, heard, and touched" formulation—"the old commandment is the word that you have heard." Yet like the "ending" wine that is in fact the wine of "beginning," so the "old" commandment that is from the beginning is the "new" commandment that has secured the triumph of the perpetual feast of marriage celebration. The love that was "from the beginning" and is as old as the time when God walked with Adam and Eve in the garden (see the equation of abiding with God and walking with him in 1 John 2:6) is a love that has the power to achieve its *telos.* Just as the wine of "beginning" is the key to the renewed celebration at Cana, so also the "old commandment," a commandment "from the beginning," is the key to the "new" commandment "that is true in him" (2:8) and that secures the triumph of the light over the darkness.

If we allow ourselves to follow the use of *arche* in 1 John, then we enter more fully into one of the christological patterns that run throughout Scripture. It is a pattern announced by John the Baptist at the very beginning of the Gospel of John: "He who comes after me ranks ahead of me because he was before me" (John 1:15, repeated in 1:30). The love that is God and that is made manifest in the death of his Son (1 John

4:9) is the Alpha and Omega. The cross is the *arche* and *telos*, the expiation of our sins (1 John 4:10) which makes fellowship with God possible, the perfection of love that casts out fear (1 John 4:18), and the form of our abiding in God.

Easter Fullness

The point of reading 1 John is not to argue that these particular allusive trajectories are necessary in order to grasp the meaning of the text. The leap from the first verse of 1 John into the *arche ton semeion* of the Gospel of John and then back again into the "old" and "new" commandments urged by the author of 1 John, and from there into the fathomless depths of the cross, may strike some readers as implausible. Perhaps this train of suggestive reading, keyed not only to the remarkable verbal echoes of *arche* but also to patterns of thematic relationship, stretches 1 John to the point of breaking. This may be so, but what is important is that we recognize the way 1 John so clearly and vigorously demands interpretive adventure. Words such as *arche*, patterns of beginnings that are endings and endings that are beginnings: these features of 1 John burst with possibilities.

To try to read 1 John without giving concentrated attention to such features of the text is to try to avoid what is on the page. For example, we read, "If we say that we have fellowship with him while we are walking in darkness, we lie and do not do what is true" (1:6). Here the utter simplicity of the *logic* draws even more attention to the difficulty of *sense*. First John is full of such inferences, and the constant pressure they put upon the reader is by no means analytical. We are not grappling with the extended and complex logic of a Pauline argument. Instead in this use of logic, as in every other aspect of 1 John, the challenge to the reader is highly focused. The words and their reference are the problem.

Taking 1 John seriously, then, entails allowing oneself to be pulled through the plenitude of sense evoked by the particular semantic intensity of the razor-sharp formulations that give the letter its distinctive character. We must take each possibility seriously, hearing, seeing, and touching each suggestive train in turn. For the reader, and for those commissioned to preach on what they have read, this is a demand both easy and heavy. The demands are light because more than any other New Testament text, 1 John creates an atmosphere of remarkable interpretive freedom. Precisely because the text shimmers with phrases and formulations cut like diamonds, the interpreter does not need to carefully measure his or her reading by the constraints of the letter as a whole or even by the context of particular passages. If something catches our eye in

1 John, then its power of suggestion is so strong that we need to work very little at the technical aspect of interpretation. For example, when we come upon the most famous formulation in 1 John—"God is love"—not only is the grammar simple and the particular context in which the formulation occurs clear (e.g., "whoever does not love does not know God, for God is love"), but the larger questions of the overall argumentative purpose of the letter or the paranetical situation addressed are so inconclusive and peripheral that they drop out as exegetically significant. And so we are left with the luminosity of the words. One reads or listens with the assumption that precisely *these* words, written in *these* sentences, as part of *this* text, are saying what needs to be heard.

Yet what could be more difficult than words such as these: "We love because he first loved us" (4:19)? Here the difficulty is not that one has nothing to say; rather, the challenge rests in knowing where to start and when to finish. Is this verse not a simple and profound statement of both the Augsburg Confession's trust in the prevenient grace of Christ ("he first") and the Council of Trent's confidence in the real efficacy of that grace ("we love")? And will not a fruitful and full reading of this passage require a close examination of the Reformation debates and, even more, the courage to bring those debates to the judgment of the text? Or, to take a different angle, is this verse not an open invitation to consider how "he first loved us"—in the creation of a cosmos fit for human inhabitance, in Sarah's fruitfulness, in the career of Israel, in the life and death of that first-century Palestinian Jew Jesus of Nazareth—and by this invitation does not the word *love* become an icon for the whole sweep of the biblical narrative, so that to fully interpret the meaning of *love* in 1 John eventually requires interpreting the whole of the Bible? Or, starting again from this verse, do we not hear liturgical echoes of the eucharistic feast, in which our sharing in Christ is made possible by his self-offering to us, and in these echoes should not the reading of this verse and the whole of the text of 1 John be keyed to the rhythms and relations of the eucharistic liturgy? Truly, this easy verse is so translucent to the central mysteries of the faith that the difficulties of saying what it is *all about* are endless.

Other passages illustrate this same interpretive challenge. The *telos* of perfection in love (see 4:18) suggests a recapitulation of the possibilities of *arche*, now in the higher key of fellowship achieved rather than sought. The emphasis of 1 John on the *name* of the Son of God (5:13; also 4:15 and 5:5) invites a meditation of the power of invoking God's name in the Old Testament, a power that Jesus affirms in John 17:11–12 (the text paired by the common lectionary with 1 John 5:13) and that is invoked in Christian baptism—but also the cosmic scope of the name sets the stage for a retelling of Jesus' death against the background of God's eternal triune identity—"The Father has sent his Son as the Savior of the world" (1 John 4:14). The affirmation that God has given us a love that takes away sins (3:5) not only leads to a meditation on the way the blood of Christ is a love that cleanses (clearly linked to the witnesses of the water and the blood; see 5:8) but also directs our attention to the ways God's love in Christ is an effective form of holiness in the life of the church (drawing attention to the witness of the Spirit, which agrees with the witnesses of the water and the blood; see again 5:8). This effective form of holiness, fully and genuinely present in the life of the church, is a perfection that is part of what we have had from the beginning. It is matter of great emphasis in 1 John—"no one who abides in him sins" (3:6)—and our reading must draw the many forms of holiness into the semantic field of 1 John. Observations about baptism and Eucharist, about church unity and continuity, about the reliability of Scripture (no one who abides in his word speaks falsely?), about prayer and the moral life all tumble out of the move from *arche* to *telos*.

Again, the point is not the necessity of any of the snarled strands of allusion I have abbreviated here. What is crucial about reading 1 John is our disposition of openness to the extraordinarily fertile power of its language. *Precisely because* the letter says what it says, we need to say much more. If we are to receive the gift of the Holy Scriptures as they have been given—as directing us toward what was from the beginning— we cannot but journey into the depths of the signs. Here 1 John epitomizes the effect of the canon as a whole. Because this is the Word of the Lord, it is a text that gathers everything up into its particular expressions. The signs have depth because all things fall within the range of their semantic power.

Reading 1 John is, then, an invitation to follow the allusive gravitational pull of the text. Hans Urs von Balthasar, without a doubt one of the twentieth century's most penetrating readers of the Johannine literature, observes that when we allow 1 John to speak to us with the full power of its language, "the aesthetic experience is the union of the greatest possible concreteness of the individual form and the greatest possible universality of meaning."[4] Formulations such as "God is love" and "Jesus is the Son of God" do not constitute a use of words that suggests something more important. The text of 1 John shimmers with what has been seen, heard, and touched. The text speaks plainly, directly, and clearly, and what is said is a proclamation that has the power of fellowship: our fellowship with each other, our fellowship with God, and the fellowship of the Father with his Son. Like the name of God that the psalmist invokes as the very power of salvation, a power of invocation that the author of 1 John echoes when he explains, "I write these things to you who believe in the name of the Son of God, that you may know that you have eternal life" (5:13), so does the particular linguistic structure of 1 John contain the power to draw us into the fullest possible destiny in God's love.

In this way, then, 1 John is the paradigmatic Easter text. The resurrection is the lightning bolt that imparts the most intense electrical charge to the life and death of that first-century Palestinian Jew Jesus of Nazareth. The marks in his hands are not the marks of the triumph of death over life but are the marks that save. These marks bring a doubting Thomas to faith, for in the wounds he sees the risen Lord as none other than the crucified Jesus. Thomas abides in the depths of the concrete form of that man and his death, and in this way he abides in the glory of his triumph. In no sense, then, do the empty tomb and the triumph of the risen Lord point beyond the particular fate of the man Jesus. To see the marks of the nails, as does Thomas, is to fall into the bottomless depths of the cross.

In precisely the same way the language of 1 John has a semantic reach that draws us into the light but never points beyond itself. The words themselves are the *arche* and *telos*. The text says what it says in its succinct, well-crafted sentences. These words are the indispensable concrete form of our fellowship with each other, with God, and in God. They are the marks, the *semeia*, of the nails, and we must never turn away from them. To enter into the bottomless depths of seeing and saying what is entailed in our fellowship with God, we must allow the signs of Scripture, the marks of the nails, to speak to us in all their irreducible particularity. We must abide in the *semeia* so that we might abide in the One who bears the marks.

If we are to so abide, we must turn with Nehemiah toward the ruined church. But let our reading of 1 John encourage hope among the fallen walls. Let us remember that just as our Lord was ruined by sin and death, the present wounds of his body—wounds we see in the many failures of Christianity in the West—are real assaults for which we ought to weep. "The sacred stones lie scattered at the head of every street" (Lamentations 4:1). Yet, at the same time, they are the marks upon his body by which we shall come to believe in him and dwell in him as the one who, crucified, has risen. For however desolate might be our condition, it is written:

> For behold, darkness shall cover the earth,
> and a thick darkness the peoples;
> but the Lord will arise upon you,
> and his glory will be seen upon you.
> and nations shall come to your light,
> and kings to the brightness of your rising.
>
> Isaiah 60:2–3 RSV

Notes

Chapter 1: Introduction

1. Reinhard Hütter, *Suffering Divine Things: Theology as Church Practice* (Grand Rapids: Eerdmans, 2000). I am indebted to Hütter. His account of the central role of the *vita passiva* for theology has reassured me that the positive program of this book is materially correct if inadequately expressed.

2. John Nelson Darby, *Collected Writings*, ed. William Kelly (Sunbury: Believers Bookshelf, 1971–2), 1:143. I owe Ephraim Radner many debts, as the reader will see, one of which is the observation that Darby repeatedly spoke of the church in ruins.

3. It is not accidental that Darby's profound awareness of the ruination of the church emerged after the legalization of Roman Catholic worship in Great Britain. No longer could the divisions of the church be hidden by the threats of secular power.

4. Darby, *Collected Writings*, 1:141.

5. Ibid., 1:146.

6. Ibid., 1:144.

7. For a provocative assessment of the modern desire to escape from the past, see Pierre Manent's evocation of the "sense of distance and even antipathy" that a seminal figure such as Montesquieu establishes between the present and the past: *The City of Man*, trans. Marc A. LePain (Princeton: Princeton University Press, 1998), p. 24. Very quickly, as Manent suggests, the discipline of "critical" history becomes a key instrument for breaking the charms of immediacy that gives the past its authority over the present. Manent also charts the ways in which emergent modern sociology pulled apart elements of social existence for analysis, thus ushering in the "age of separation" (p. 82). Manent's striking insights, however, are limited by his focus on the canonical literature of modern political theory. Both the "sense of distance" and the "age of separation" are much more fully visible in the post-Reformation ecclesiastical cultures that antedate Montesquieu and his successors.

8. René Descartes, *Discourse on the Method of Rightly Conducting the Reason and Seeking the Truth in the Sciences* (1637). I follow the translation of John Veitch, found in the collection *The Rationalists* (New York: Anchor Books, 1974), p. 46.

9. Ibid., pt. 2 (Veitch, p. 48).

10. Ibid., pt. 2 (Veitch, p. 48).

11. Darby, *Collected Writings*, 1:154–55.

12. Ibid., 1:153.

13. I count myself an Augustinian, the more radical the better. However, as I have attempted to suggest here, the dominant grace/free-will axis of Western theology, especially after the Reformation, no longer picks out decisive theological differences. What unifies a crass Pelagian and a harsh predestinarian is a common commitment to separation and distance from the ruined church.

14. Ephraim Radner, *The End of the Church: A Pneumatology of Christian Division in the West* (Grand Rapids: Eerdmans, 1998). Radner also wrote an essay that employs the figural interpretation of Nehemiah that I draw upon here, "The Cost of Communion: A Meditation on Israel and the Divided Church," in *Inhabiting Unity,* ed. Ephraim Radner and R. R. Reno (Grand Rapids: Eerdmans, 1995), pp. 134–52. However, when I first read that essay I did not understand the real meaning of the figure, because I did not see the present "type" for ruined Jerusalem in the church. Only after reading *The End of the Church* did I grasp the significance of Radner's use of Nehemiah. For a fuller development of the figure, see my reflections on theological exegesis in chap. 10. Also, I must thank Bruce D. Marshall for clarifying the logical structure of Radner's analysis and for driving home the consequence of this analysis for our theological vocations. See his fine review essay "The Divided Church and Its Theology," *Modern Theology* 16, no. 3 (July 2000): 377–96.

15. For a rigorous display of this contradiction and its consequences, see Bruce D. Marshall, "The Unity and Disunity of the Church and the Credibility of the Gospel," *Theology Today* 50 (April 1993): 78–89.

Chapter 2: Postmodern Irony and Petronian Humanism

1. All these quotations are from Ralph Waldo Emerson's essay "Self-Reliance," in *Essays: First and Second Series* (Cambridge: Riverside, 1929), pp. 46–53.

2. John Locke, *An Essay Concerning Human Understanding,* ed. Peter H. Nidditch (Oxford: Oxford University Press, 1975), p. 541.

3. For a classic statement of this cautious humanism, see Bertrand Russell's peroration on behalf of critical philosophy at the end of *The Problems of Philosophy*. For Russell, philosophy makes us sensible of the limitations of our knowledge, and thus "it removes the somewhat arrogant dogmatism of those who have never travelled into the region of liberating doubt" (reprint Oxford: Oxford University Press, 1959, p. 157). An impartial philosophical view allows us to transcend the "prison" and "strife" of merely private interest and personal prejudice. This openness permits the "free intellect" to attain higher and more universal knowledge.

4. For an autobiographical account of the benefits for faith of the putatively atheistic approach of logical atomism, see Donald MacKinnon's essay "Philosophy and Christology," found in *Borderlands of Theology* (New York: J. B. Lippincott, 1968), pp. 55–81. MacKinnon reports that engagement with philosophers such as Bertrand Russell brought him to see that knowing is a finding, not a fashioning, and that truth depends on particularity, not an idea of the whole.

5. See my analysis in R. R. Reno, *Redemptive Change: Atonement and the Christian Cure of the Soul* (Harrisburg, Penn.: Trinity Press International, 2002).

6. For a compelling account of the cultural sensibilities that form the defensive posture of postmodern humanism, see Philip Rieff, *The Triumph of the Therapeutic: Uses of Faith After Freud* (New York: Harper & Row, 1966). For Rieff, the therapeutic imperative has many facets, but it is unified in the overriding end sought: freedom from demand and interdiction, freedom from assent and commitment.

7. Recall, for example, the hue and cry surrounding the Vatican statement concerning interreligious and ecumenical dialogue, *Dominus Jesus*. The mere fact that the Congregation for the Doctrine of the Faith reiterated rather conventional Christian propositions about the uniqueness and necessity of Jesus Christ for salvation was sufficient to touch raw nerves. In the end, the offense is not what the Vatican teaches but that it undertakes to state, with clarity, what is true and what is false.

8. An English translation may be found in Jacques Derrida, *Margins of Philosophy*, trans. Alan Bass (Chicago: Unversity of Chicago Press, 1982), pp. 1–27. The quotations later in this paragraph are from p. 22.

9. See Derrida's ironic comments about the "general strategy of deconstruction" and its status as a "science" in Jacques Derrida, *Positions*, trans. Alan Bass (Chicago: University of Chicago Press, 1981), pp. 35–36, 41–42.

10. Derrida, *Margins*, p. 27.

11. Augustine, *Confessions* 8.7.

Chapter 3: *Pro Nobis*

1. See Bruce Marshall's devastating criticisms in *Trinity and Truth* (Cambridge: Cambridge University Press, 2000). See also my review of Marshall in *First Things*, no. 106 (October 2000): 53–57.

2. From Søren Kierkegaard, *Journal*, quoted in *Works of Love*, trans. Howard and Edna Hong (New York: Harper & Row, 1962), translator's introduction, p. 11.

3. In what follows I use the Rex Warner translation, Augustine, *Confessions* (New York: New American Library, 1963).

4. David Hume, *Essays Moral, Political, and Literary*, ed. Eugene F. Miller (Indianapolis: Liberty Fund, 1985), pp. 73–79.

5. Ibid., p. 73.

6. Ibid., p. 74

7. Ibid., p. 78.

8. Ibid., p. 77.

Chapter 4: The Radical Orthodoxy Project

1. John Milbank, *Theology and Social Theory: Beyond Secular* Reason (Oxford: Blackwell, 1993).

2. John Milbank, *The Word Made Strange* (Oxford: Blackwell, 1997), p. 2.

3. Catherine Pickstock, *After Writing: On the Liturgical Consummation of Theology* (Oxford: Blackwell, 1998).

4. Graham Ward, *Barth, Derrida, and the Language of Theology* (Cambridge: Cambridge University Press, 1995).

5. John Milbank, Catherine Pickstock, and Graham Ward, *Radical Orthodoxy: A New Theology* (London: Routledge, 1999).

6. Pickstock, *After Writing*, p. xiii.

7. Milbank, Pickstock, and Ward, *Radical Orthodoxy*, p. 4.

8. Milbank, *Word Made Strange*, p. 113.

9. Milbank, *Theology and Social Theory*, pp. 422–23.

10. Milbank, *Word Made Strange*, p. 64.

11. Milbank, *Theology and Social Theory*, pp. 305–6.

12. Milbank, *Word Made Strange*, p. 153.

13. All quotations from Milbank, *Theology and Social Theory*, p. 397.

14. Milbank, *Word Made Strange*, pp. 145–46.

15. Ibid., pp. 156–57.

16. Graham Ward, "The Displaced Body of Jesus Christ," *Radical Orthodoxy*, p. 172.

17. Editor's introduction, *Radical Orthodoxy*, p. 3.

Chapter 5: The Theological Vocation in the Episcopal Church

1. See John Keble's remarkable and prescient observations about the connections between patristic doctrine and patristic exegetical practice, "On the Mysticism Attributed to the Early Fathers of the Church," *Tracts for the Times*, no. 89 (1840–1). For Keble, spiritual/ecclesiastical discipline, exegetical sensibility, and the effective perspicuity of doctrine are bound together. The fathers, Keble writes, "were natives, and could speak the language idiomatically, without stopping to recollect the rules of grammar" (*Tracts for the Times* [reprint New York: AMS Press, 1969], vol. 6, p. 40). To reject the habituating forms of patristic ascetical discipline and spiritual exegesis paves the way for rejecting doctrine, or rendering the creed an ancient artifact honored but irrelevant to the speech and practice of the modern church.

2. See Philip Turner, "Episcopal Oversight and Ecclesiastical Discipline," *Pro Ecclesia* 2, no. 4 (fall 1994): 436–54.

3. See Michael Ramsey, *The Gospel and the Catholic Church* (London: Longmans, Green, 1936).

4. There are reasons not to trust such assessments. See Urban T. Holmes's cynical report of the need to deceive in order to revise, "Education for Liturgy: An Unfinished Symphony in Four Movements," in *Worship Points the Way*, ed. Malcolm C. Burson (New York: Seabury, 1981), pp. 116–41. When, one must wonder, can one trust the deceiver to speak truthfully?

5. A cursory skim of the sixteenth- and seventeenth-century literature yields the impression that the Anglican Reformers typically treated profession of true doctrine as the primary form of public demarcation between the church and the world (and between true and false church). See, for example, Richard Field, *Of the Church* 1.10: "It cannot be but that they that are of the true Church must by profession of the truth make themselves know in such sort, that by their profession and practice they may be discerned from other men" See, however, George Hickes, *The Case for Infant Baptism*, for a figural assimilation of circumcision to baptism, emphasizing how both incorporate the person into a nation or society set apart by God. For the same social and public significance of baptism, see tract 41 of *Tracts for the Times*. There baptism is described as the "material part of piety," which is "separation from the enemies of God."

6. For some suggestive observations about the important role of ordained ministry in the establishment and maintenance of a distinct and visible church, see Richard Hooker, *Laws* 5.77.2: "Ministerial power is a mark of separation, because it severeth them that have it from other men, and maketh them a special order consecrated unto the service of the Most High in things wherewith others may not meddle."

7. See a description of this sensibility in Linda Moeller, "Baptism: Rite of Inclusion or Exclusion?" in *Leaps and Boundaries: The Prayer Book in the Twenty-first Century*, ed. Paul V. Marshall and Lesley A. Northup (Harrisburg, Penn.: Morehouse, 1997), pp. 81–92.

8. See, for example, Pheobe Pittingell, introduction to *Enriching Our Worship: Supplemental Materials Prepared by the Standing Liturgical Commission*, 1997 (New York: Church Publishing, 1998), pp. 7–12.

9. This in contrast to the prevailing contemporary and jejune interpretation of the *via media* as a habit of balancing, a sensibility of prudent compromise. For a modern restatement of the way *via media* serves as a path toward truth, not as a goal in itself, see E. L. Mascall, *Via Media: An Essay in Theological Synthesis* (London: Longmans, Green, 1956).

For a trenchant account of the breakdown of the classical view and the baleful consequences, see S. W. Sykes, *The Integrity of Anglicanism* (New York: Seabury, 1978). Sykes is sometimes unfairly critical of modern Anglican figures such as F. D. Maurice, but he is certainly accurate in his account of how their ideas and rhetoric have been misused by subsequent church leaders.

10. See, for example, Ramsey's perceptive and less than sanguine account of the relationship between the apostolic practice of Anglicanism ("the facts of its existence") and Anglican self-understanding that is sometimes less than edifying ("the opinions of English divines"), *Gospel and the Catholic Church*, pp. 205–6. This leads Ramsey to conclude that the role of Anglicanism is not to exemplify a particularly winsome version of Christianity but to witness to the enduring power of the gospel in spite of its failures in faith, theology, and ecclesiastical discipline. "It is sent not to commend itself as 'the best type of Christianity,' but by its very brokenness to point to the universal church wherein all have died" (p. 220). By my reading, Anglicanism is able "to point" toward the original and everlasting dependence of the church on the given particularity of apostolic language and practice, and does so by having little else to offer the present age ("its very brokenness").

11. One seminal history is Hans Frei, *The Eclipse of Biblical Narrative* (New Haven, Conn.: Yale University Press, 1974). Frei's work is integrated into a more comprehensive and ambitious etiology of modern alienation from Scripture in Ephraim Radner, *The End of the Church* (Grand Rapids: Eerdmans, 1998).

12. John Henry Newman makes the following observation about the relationship between the health of the church and the role of Scripture: "As to proof of the authority of scripture. This has hitherto rested on the testimony borne to it by the existing Church" (*Oxford University Sermons* [Notre Dame, Ind.: University of Notre Dame Press, 1997], pp. 69–70). Precisely because the Calvin-influenced traditions adopt a distinction between "visible" and "invisible" church, these traditions have been forced to develop extrinsic theories of biblical infallibility in order to protect the plain sense of Scripture from the logic of their ecclesiologies.

13. Thus Robert Lowth's lectures on the *Sacred Poetry of the Hebrews* (1753) are much more telling than Schleiermacher's speeches. That Lowth should find it necessary to defend the spiritual integrity of the psalms—the liturgical center of Western Christian formation for more than a millennium—is much more important than the speculative anxieties of Schleiermacher's cultured despisers.

14. On the point, Brevard Childs has been one of the most consistent voices urging the recovery of exegetical traditions that treat Christ as the unifying *skopos* of Scripture. See *Biblical Theology of the Old and New Testaments* (Philadelpia: Fortress, 1992). See also George Lindbeck's attempts to retrieve the patristic figural identification of the church with the Old Testament's Israel, "The Story-Shaped Church: Critical Exegesis and Theological Interpretation," in Garrett Green, ed., *Scriptural Authority and Narrative Interpretation* (Philadelphia: Fortress, 1987), and "The Church" in Geoffrey Wainwright, ed., *Keeping the Faith: Essays to Mark the Centenary of Lux Mundi* (London: SPCK, 1989).

15. See Philip Turner's two-part essay on marriage canons and divorce, "The Marriage Canons of the Episcopal Church," *Anglican Theological Review* 65, no. 4 (October 1983): 371–93; 66, no. 1 (January 1984): 1–22.

16. This is not unique to the United States. The hoary "three-branch theory" has been popular among Anglicans as a rationalization for schism. See William Palmer, *Treatise on the Christian Church* (1838). On the logic of the ecclesial self-falsification, see Bruce D. Marshall, "The Disunity of the Church and the Credibility of the Gospel," *Theology Today* 50 (April 1993): 377–96.

17. For a similar assessment, see Robert Louis Wilken's observation that "it is a particular temptation in our day to make the liturgy an instrument for something else, e.g.,

catechesis or evangelism" ("With Angels and Archangels," *Pro Ecclesia* 10, no. 4 [fall 2001], p. 465).

18. See the Majority Opinion of the Ecclesiastical Court in the trial of Bishop Walter Righter, and R. R. Reno, "An Analysis of the Righter Decision," *Pro Ecclesia* 5, no. 4 (fall 1997): 392–96.

19. Richard Hooker, *Law of Ecclesiastical Polity* 4.14.6.

Chapter 6: The Drive Toward Change

1. For an analysis of feminist theology and its revisionist project, see my essay, "Feminist Theology as Modern Project," *Pro Ecclesia* 5, no. 4 (fall 1996), pp. 405–26.

2. See, for example, the introductory rationale for the report of the Liturgical Commission of the General Synod of the Church of England, *Patterns of Worship* (London: Church House Publishing, 1989). The commission notes that the idea of supplemental and variable schemes for public worship betokens a "new era of flexibility in the Church of England worship," and in this set of proposed additions the Commission seeks to address the needs of "Urban Priority Areas" (a code for areas of non-English-speaking, non-Anglo-Saxon residents) and so-called family services that employ more accessible forms of worship.

3. Both quotes from Pheobe Pittingell, introduction to *Enriching Our Worship: Supplemental Liturgical Materials Prepared by the Standing Liturgical Commission*, 1997 (New York: Church Publishing, 1998), pp. 8–9.

4. Urban T. Holmes, "Education for Liturgy," in *Worship Points the Way*, ed. Malcolm C. Burson (New York: Seabury, 1981), p. 131.

5. For proof that I am not making up these platitudes, see Mark Harris, *The Challenge of Change: The Anglican Communion in the Post-modern Era* (New York: Church Publishing, 1998).

6. Both quotes from Lynn N. Rhodes, "Leadership from a Feminist Perspective," *Word and World* 13, no. 1 (winter 1993): 14–15.

7. Letty Russell, *Growth in Partnership* (Philadelphia: Westminster Press, 1981), p. 33.

8. See F. D. Maurice's analysis of the debilitating logic of these assumptions: *The Kingdom of Christ*, vol. 2, chap. 4, sec. 3, "Forms of Worship."

9. For a trenchant affirmation of the dogma of inevitable change, see Clayton L. Morris, "Prayer Book Revision or Liturgical Renewal? The Future of Liturgical Text," in *Leaps and Boundaries: The Prayer Book in the Twenty-first Century*, ed. Paul V. Marshall and Lesley A. Northup (Harrisburg, Penn.: Morehouse, 1997).

10. Holmes, "Education for Liturgy," p. 138.

11. Ellen K. Wondra, "O for a Thousand Tongues to Sing . . ." in *Leaps and Boundaries: The Prayer Book in the Twenty-first Century*, ed. Paul V. Marshall and Lesley A. Northup (Harrisburg, Penn.: Morehouse, 1997), p. 223.

12. See Richard Hooker, *Of the Laws of Ecclesiastical Polity*, bk. 5, chaps. 15–16.

Chapter 7: Sex in the Episcopal Church

1. David Brooks, *Bobos in Paradise: The New Upper Class and How They Got There* (New York: Simon & Schuster, 2000).

2. L. William Countryman, *Dirt, Greed, and Sex: Sexual Ethics in the New Testament and Their Implications for Today* (Philadelphia: Fortress, 1988), pp. 66–77 for a discussion of Acts 10, and pp. 243–47 for applications to contemporary sexual morality.

3. John Henry Newman, *Oxford University Sermons* (Notre Dame, Ind.: University of Notre Dame Press, 1997), p. 27.

Chapter 8: Toward a Postliberal Ecclesial Spirituality

1. For a sociological approach, consult Robert Wuthnow, *After Heaven: Spirituality in America Since the 1950s*, (Berkeley: University of California Press, 1998). Wuthnow identifies many facets of the now widespread perception that one needs to "work on" spirituality in order to nurture a satisfactory religious life. He draws a helpful distinction between traditional spiritualities of "dwelling" and contemporary spiritualities of "seeking." Nonetheless, his use of the word *spirituality* is varied and confusing. Sometimes spirituality means the inner motivation for religious observance. In other places spirituality indicates intentional religious practices. Spirituality can also serve as a synonym for *religious experience*. The one feature that unifies these divergent senses of spirituality is an emphasis on intensity and potency. Something is "spiritual" if it exerts strong influence over the person. In this chapter I hope to provide a definition of spirituality that brings this common feature to the fore.

2. William Temple, *Religious Experience and Other Essays and Addresses* (London: James Clarke, 1958), pp. 57–63.

3. Ibid., p. 58.

4. Ibid.

5. William Temple's great work of apologetics, *Nature, Man and God* (London: Macmillan, 1951), was motivated by his pressing sense of the urgency of recognizing that "personality" is the underlying power of all things. For Temple, not only is such a perspective necessary for properly inhabiting the Christian inheritance, it is also necessary for a cogent account of the natural world and human endeavor. In all things, "personality" is the source of life.

6. Temple, *Religious Experience*, p. 63.

7. The history of modern theology is best understood as the intellectual justification for and refinement of modern spirituality. Friedrich Schleiermacher is not just seminal in this regard, he is exemplary. The pastoral basis for his great work of theology, *The Christian Faith*, is explicit and systematic. The phenomenology of the feeling of absolute dependence allows him to analyze first-order Christian language and practice in terms of the potency of Jesus' God-consciousness. Schleiermacher defines the feeling of absolute dependence as "the highest grade of human self-consciousness" (par. 5), and thus Jesus is the power of life because he is the perfection of that highest grade. In other words, Jesus perfectly manifests the power of "personality" we all seek in our lives. His God-consciousness is the object of our common spiritual ambition. Once we recognize this perfection in Jesus, we can see the life-giving features of traditional Christian teaching.

8. See, for example, John Shelby Spong, *Why Christianity Must Change or Die: A Bishop Speaks to Believers in Exile* (San Francisco: HarperSanFrancisco, 1998).

9. See my *reductio ad absurdum*, R. R. Reno, "The Sin of Faith," in *Can a Bishop Be Wrong?* ed. Peter C. Moore (Harrisburg, Penn.: Morehouse, 1998), pp. 74–92.

10. See, for example, William Temple's *Readings in St. John's Gospel, First and Second Series* (London: Macmillan, 1955).

11. See Linda Moeller, "Baptism: Rite of Inclusion or Exclusion?" in *Leaps and Boundaries: The Prayer Book in the Twenty-first Century*, ed. Paul V. Marshall and Lesley A. Northup (Harrisburg, Penn.: Morehouse, 1997), pp. 81–92.

12. A. G. Hebert, *Liturgy and Society* (London: Faber & Faber, 1935), p. 12.

13. I follow the translation of Origen's *On First Principles* by G. W. Butterworth (Gloucester, Mass.: Peter Smith, 1973). The citations are given by the traditional divisions of book, chapter, and paragraph.

14. Origen's affirmation of the sole sufficiency of Scripture is echoed by Hans Urs von Balthasar. The ascent of the soul to vision of the divine consummates the inner longings of the human heart. However, this ascent never transcends the first-order language and

practice of the church. Speaking of the central role of Scripture, Balthasar writes, "Contemplation's ladder, reaching up to heaven, begins with the word of scripture, and whatever rung we are on, we are never beyond this hearing of the word. In contemplation, just as we can never leave the Lord's humanity behind, neither can we get 'beyond' the word in its human form" (*Prayer* [San Francisco: Ignatius, 1986], p. 9).

15. For a rich and detailed account of the diverse functions of allegorical reading that formed the background of Origen's exegetical practice, see David Dawson, *Allegorical Readers and Cultural Revision in Ancient Alexandria* (Berkeley: University of California Press, 1992).

16. For a very important explanation of the divine strategy of "hardening" and "veiling," see Origen, *On First Principles* 3.1.1–24. The theme of this chapter is free will, and across remarkable twists and turns of argument and exegetical digression, Origen comes to the conclusion that the difficulties of faith, placed before us by God ("he covered up the deeper mysteries of the faith in veiled speech," commenting on Mark 4:11–12 in paragraph 17), serve to bring our labors of understanding and self-discipline to the consummating conclusion that the grace of God carries us to his glory. The divine physician gives us the medicine of confusion and difficulty so that we can recognize our dependence on his power.

17. Origen is easily misread as reframing Christianity in terms of Greek antitheses of time and eternity, spirit and matter. He does presuppose these antitheses, but over the course of his explanation of the divine plan of salvation, Origen argues that the weight and burden of time and matter are elements of divine grace. For we must be shaped and formed into new persons. Therefore time is the gift of divine patience, and carnal life trains us for a life proper to his glory. Time and material life, like the carnal difficulties of Scripture, provide a purposeful darkness, a gracious travail.

18. For Radner's compelling account of the "death" of the church in the wake of Christian divisions initiated by the Reformation see Ephraim Radner, *The End of the Church: A Pneumatology of Christian Division in the West* (Grand Rapids: Eerdmans, 1998). For a more accessible outline of his account, see the scriptural meditation by Ephraim Radner, "The Cost of Communion: Israel and the Divided Church," in *Inhabiting Unity*, ed. Ephraim Radner and R. R. Reno (Grand Rapids: Eerdmans, 1995), pp. 134–52.

Chapter 9: The Daily Office

1. For an elegant and appreciative description of this strength of Anglicanism, see David S. Yeago, "Theological Renewal in Communion: What Anglicans and Lutherans Can Learn from One Another," in *Inhabiting Unity: Theological Perspectives on the Proposed Lutheran-Episcopal Concordat*, eds. Ephraim Radner and R. R. Reno (Grand Rapids: Eerdmans, 1995), pp. 206–23.

2. Richard Hooker, *Laws of Ecclesiastical Polity* 4.40.1.

Chapter 10: Reflections in Aid of Theological Exegesis

1. Augustine *De doctrina Christiana* 1.6. I follow the translation by D. W. Robertson Jr. (Indianapolis: Library of Liberal Arts, 1958).

2. Ibid., 1.11.

3. Ibid., 1.34.

4. For two contemporary efforts to do this heavy lifting in metaphysics, see Nicholas Wolterstorff, *Divine Discourse* (Cambridge: Cambridge University Press, 1995), and Jean-Luc Marion, *God Without Being* (Chicago: University of Chicago Press, 1991). These two Christian philosophers draw on radically different philosophical traditions, but both

undertake to "solve" the problem of distance created by the fact that Christianity requires the use of signs.

5. For suggestions about how God gives us "room" in the gift of created time, see Robert W. Jenson, *Systematic Theology* (New York: Oxford University Press, 1997), 1:226. Jenson's metaphysical innovations simply give greater systematic centrality to the blessings of time and body that Origen tries to express with a "developmental" or "pedagogical Platonism." See above, chap. 8, note 17.

6. See Ephraim Radner's essay "The Cost of Communion: A Meditation on Israel and the Divided Church," in *Inhabiting Unity: Theological Perspectives on the Proposed Lutheran-Episcopal Concordat*, eds. Ephraim Radner and R. R. Reno (Grand Rapids: Eerdmans, 1995), pp. 134–52, as well as his extended uses of this figural interpretation throughout *The End of the Church: A Pneumatology of Christian Division in the West* (Grand Rapids: Eerdmans, 1998).

7. See Origen's *Commentary on the Gospel According to John*, bk. 1.

Chapter 11: The Marks of the Nails

1. Luther highlights these terms of interpretation in his lectures on 1 John. "You see," Luther observes at the outset, "the simplicity of John's way of speaking." Yet this simplicity does not speak simply, for "the language is elliptical." The effect is crucial. As Luther notes, the letter "stammers rather than speaks, and the greatest majesty is combined with the greatest simplicity of expression" (*Luther's Works* [American Edition], ed. Jaroslav Pelikan (St. Louis: Concordia Publishing, 1955-86), vol. 30, p. 221). For Luther, then, to read 1 John requires us to listen to its stammering combination of majesty and simplicity rather than trying to force the text into a false clarity that is neither majestic nor simple.

2. Preaching on 1 John 5:8, John Donne gives expression to this literary effect. He emphasizes the way God has taken utterly clear and direct action on our behalf. In reversing the great malediction brought upon us by the fall, Christ "proceeds strongly and effectually; he produces three witnesses from heaven, so powerful, that they will be heare, they will be beleeved; and three witnesses on earth, so neare us, so familiar, so domestique as that they will not be denied, they will not be discredited" (*The Sermons of John Donne*, ed. George R. Potter and Evelyn M. Simpson [Berkeley: University of California Press, 1959], 5:132). For Donne the most important hope in our lives—to be redeemed from sin—is a hope that not only has the majestic witness of heaven but also might be heard, seen, and touched with an intimate familiarity. In just this way the distinctive literary effect of 1 John is to present us with words that are so direct and clear that they easily become familiar and "domestique." They are words so well forged that they may readily be "taken in hand."

3. This same pattern of *arche* and *telos* occurs at the conclusion of the Gospel of Luke, a passage that is part of the lectionary cycle that includes 1 John. Having received the blessing of Jesus in Bethany amid his teaching of the fulfillment of all those things in which the disciples had "begun"—the law of Moses and the prophets and the Psalms (Lk. 24:44)—the followers of Jesus "returned to Jerusalem with great joy; and they were continually in the temple blessing God" (24:52–53). Like the wedding feast that was renewed by the wine of beginning, the "great joy" of worshiping God is renewed by the power of Jesus to "open the minds" of the disciples to see the fullness of that which was from the beginning.

4. Hans Urs von Balthasar, *The Glory of the Lord* (San Francisco: Ignatius, 1982), 1/1:234.

Index